PC LEARNING LABS TEACHES
WINDOWS 3.1

PC LEARNING LABS
TEACHES
WINDOWS 3.1

LOGICAL OPERATIONS

Ziff-Davis Press
Emeryville, California

Curriculum Development	Logical Operations
Writers	Richard P. Scott and Robert Nichols Kulik
Editor	Jan Jue
Technical Reviewer	Dick Hol
Project Coordinator	Ami Knox
Proofreader	Kayla Sussell
Cover Design	Kenneth Roberts
Book Design	Laura Lamar/MAX, San Francisco
Technical Illustration	Cherie Plumlee Computer Graphics & Illustration and Steph Bradshaw
Word Processing	Howard Blechman and Cat Haglund
Page Layout	Tony Jonick and Anna L. Marks
Indexer	Valerie Robbins

This book was produced on a Macintosh IIfx, with the following applications: FrameMaker®, Microsoft® Word, MacLink® *Plus*, Aldus® FreeHand™, Adobe Photoshop™, and Collage Plus™.

Ziff-Davis Press
5903 Christie Avenue
Emeryville, CA 94608

ISBN 1-56276-051-3
Manufactured in the United States of America
♻ The paper used in this book exceeds the EPA requirements for postconsumer recycled paper.
10 9 8 7 6 5 4 3 2 1

CONTENTS AT A GLANCE

TABLE OF CONTENTS

INTRODUCTION

Welcome to *PC Learning Labs Teaches Windows 3.1*, a hands-on instruction book designed to help you attain a high level of Windows competency as quickly as possible. And congratulations on choosing Microsoft Windows 3.1, a powerful and feature-rich operating system that will help you tap into the full power of your IBM or IBM-compatible computer system.

We at PC Learning Labs believe this book to be a unique and welcome addition to the ranks of "how-to" computer publications. Our instructional approach stems directly from a decade of successful teaching in a hands-on classroom environment. Throughout the book, theory is consistently mixed with practice; a topic is explained and then immediately drilled in a hands-on activity. These activities utilize the enclosed Data Disk, which contains over two dozen sample files.

When you're done working your way through this book, you will have a solid foundation of skills in the following areas of Windows functionality:

- *Desktop Management*   Setting up, working with, and customizing your Windows desktop (windows, icons, color schemes, screen savers, and so on)

- *File Management*   Moving, copying, deleting, viewing, and renaming files and directories

- *Program Management*   Running and exiting programs, switching between multiple programs, creating icons for programs

- *Printer Management*   Installing, changing, and customizing your system printers

- *Word Processing*   Creating, editing, saving, and retrieving text documents

- *Graphics Processing*   Creating, editing, saving, and retrieving graphics documents (pictures)

- *Data Exchange*   Sharing data (text or graphics) among different documents and programs

- *Customization*   Tailoring various aspects of Windows (start-up options, color schemes, desktop icons, and so on) to fit your individual working style

- *Accessory Programs*   Using special utility programs (such as Calendar, Cardfile, and Character Map) to increase your power and flexibility in working with Windows

READ THIS BEFORE BEGINNING CHAPTER 1!

We strongly advise you to read through this entire Introduction before beginning Chapter 1. If, however, you are anxious to dive in, you must first work through the section below entitled "Creating Your Work Directory," as it is crucial to your successful completion of the hands-on activities in this book.

WHO THIS BOOK IS FOR

This book was written with the beginner in mind. While experience with word processing and personal computers is certainly helpful, little or none is required. You should know how to turn on your computer, monitor, and printer, how to use your keyboard, and how to move your mouse. Everything beyond that will be explained in the text.

HOW TO USE THIS BOOK

This book is designed to be used as a learning guide, a review tool, and a quick reference.

AS A LEARNING GUIDE

Each chapter covers one broad topic or set of related topics. Chapters are arranged in order of increasing Windows proficiency; skills you acquire in one chapter are used and elaborated on in subsequent chapters. For this reason, you should work through the chapters in strict sequence.

Each chapter is organized into explanatory topics and step-by-step activities. Topics provide the theoretical overview you need to master Windows; activities allow you to immediately apply this understanding to specific, hands-on examples.

 AS A REVIEW TOOL

Any method of instruction is only as effective as the time and effort you are willing to invest in it. For this reason, we encourage you to review the more challenging topics and activities presented in this book.

 AS A QUICK REFERENCE

General procedures (such as printing a document or copying selected text) are presented as a series of bulleted steps; you can find these bullets (•) easily by skimming through the book.

At the end of every chapter, you'll find a quick reference listing the mouse/keyboard actions needed to perform the techniques introduced in that chapter.

WHAT THIS BOOK CONTAINS

The contents of this book are divided into the following 11 chapters:

Chapter 1—The Windows Environment

Chapter 2—Orientation to Word Processing

Chapter 3—Printing, Moving, and Copying Files

Chapter 4—Creating and Importing Text and Graphics: Paintbrush and the Clipboard

Chapter 5—Additional File-Management Techniques

Chapter 6—Customizing Windows, Part I

Chapter 7—Customizing Windows, Part II

Chapter 8—Advanced Windows Topics

Chapter 9—Working with Non-Windows Programs

Chapter 10—Advanced File-Management Techniques

Chapter 11—Windows Accessory Programs

In addition, there are three appendices:

Appendix A—Installing and Configuring Windows

Appendix B—Upgrading from Windows 3.0 to Windows 3.1

Appendix C—Networking and Telecommunications

To attain full Windows 3.1 fluency, you should work through all 11 chapters. The appendices are optional.

The following features of this book are designed to facilitate your learning:

- Carefully sequenced topics that build on the knowledge you've acquired from previous topics

- Frequent hands-on activities, designed to sharpen your Windows skills

- Numerous illustrations that show how your screen should look at key points during these activities

- The Data Disk, which contains all the files you will need to complete the activities

- A quick reference at the end of each chapter, listing in easy-to-read table form the mouse/keyboard actions you need to perform the techniques introduced in the chapter

WHAT YOU NEED

To run Windows 3.1 and complete this book, you need a computer, monitor, keyboard, and mouse. A printer is strongly recommended, but optional.

 A COMPUTER AND MONITOR

You need an IBM or IBM-compatible personal computer and monitor that are capable of running Microsoft Windows 3.1. The minimum computer you need is an 80286 machine with 1 megabyte of RAM memory and 10 megabytes of free hard-disk space. We recommend an 80386 or higher (80486, 80586) computer with 2 or more megabytes of RAM and 10 megabytes of free hard-disk space. For more specific information regarding the minimum computer configuration you need to run Windows 3.1, please refer to your Windows 3.1 reference manual.

 A KEYBOARD

IBM-type computers come with various styles of keyboards; these keyboards function identically, but have different layouts. Figures I.1, I.2, and I.3 show the three main keyboard styles and their key arrangements.

Windows 3.1 uses three main areas of the keyboard:

- The *function keys*, which enable you to access Windows's special features. On the PC-, XT-, and AT-style keyboards, there are ten function keys at the left end of the keyboard; on the PS/2-style Enhanced Keyboard there are 12 at the top of the keyboard.

Figure I.1   **The IBM PC–style keyboard**

Figure I.2   **The XT/AT–style keyboard**

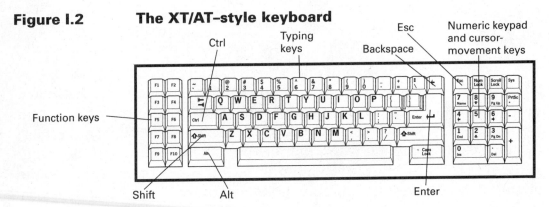

Figure I.3   **The PS/2–style Enhanced Keyboard**

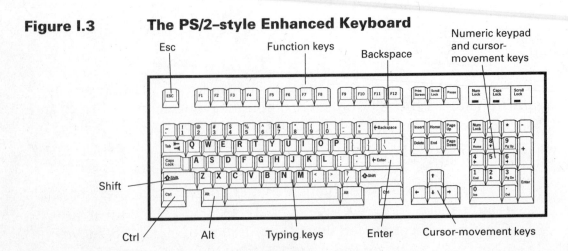

- The *typing keys*, located in the main body of all the keyboards. These include letters, numbers, punctuation marks, and in addition, the Shift, Ctrl, and Alt keys, which you will need to access several of Windows's special features.

- The *numeric keypad*, which groups the numbers (the same ones found across the top row of the typing keys) for convenient entry of numeric data. The numeric keypad also contains the cursor-movement keys: Up, Down, Left, and Right Arrow; Home; End; PgUp (Page Up); and PgDn (Page Down). To enter numeric data using the numeric keypad, Num Lock must be on. (Pressing the Num Lock key will toggle Num Lock on/off.) To use the cursor-movement keys on the keypad, Num Lock must be off. To enter numeric data when Num Lock is off, use the number keys on the top row of the typing area.

The Enhanced Keyboard has an additional cursor-movement keypad to the left of the numeric keypad. This allows you to use the numeric keypad for numeric data entry (that is, to keep Num Lock on) and still have access to cursor-movement keys.

 A MOUSE

You need a mouse to work through the activities in this book. Any of the standard PC mice will do.

 A PRINTER

Although you aren't absolutely required to have a printer to work through the activities, we strongly recommend it. A PostScript-type laser printer is ideal, but a non-PostScript laser or a dot-matrix printer is acceptable.

If you have no printer, simply skip over the steps that involve printing. We do recommend, however, that you read through these steps in order to acquire some familiarity with the printing process.

The printed examples shown in this book were all printed on a Post-Script laser printer. Your printouts may differ somewhat, depending on which printer you are using. Printer choice also affects how text appears on your screen. If you are using a non-PostScript printer, your screen typestyles and sizes may differ from those shown in this book's figures.

CREATING YOUR WORK DIRECTORY

In the course of this book, you will be creating, editing, and saving several files. To keep these files together, you need to create a *work directory* for them on your hard disk. A directory is like a filing cabinet in which a group of related files is stored. Your work directory will also hold the sample files contained on the Data Disk at the back of this book.

Follow these steps to create your work directory:

1. Turn on your computer. After a brief internal self-check, your *operating environment* will automatically load. If you are in Windows, please continue with step 2. If you are in DOS, please continue with step 3. If you are in another—non-Windows, non-DOS—operating environment (for example, OS/2), exit from this environment to DOS and continue with step 3. For help exiting to DOS, see the reference books for your operating environment.

2. Within Windows, use the mouse to move the on-screen pointer to the small box in the upper-left corner of the screen. Double-click on the dash in this box. (Press the left mouse button two times in rapid succession while pointing to the dash.) A box entitled *Exit Windows* will appear in the middle of the screen. Click the mouse pointer once on the **OK** within this box. You have now exited from Windows to DOS. Skip steps 3 through 8, and continue with step 9.

3. You may see this prompt:

```
Current date is Tue 1-01-1980
Enter new date (mm-dd-yy):
```

(Your current date will be different.) If you do not see a date prompt, skip to step 6.

4. If the current date on your screen is wrong, type the correct date. Use a dash (-) to separate the month, day, and year (for example, 3-25-93).

5. Press **Enter**. After you type a command, you must press the Enter key to send this command to the computer.

6. You may see this prompt:

```
Current time is 0:25:32:56
Enter new time:
```

(Your current time will be different.) If you do not see a time prompt, skip to step 9.

7. If the current time on your screen is wrong, type the correct time. Use the format *hh:mm*. Most versions of DOS use a 24-hour clock (for example, 10:30 for 10:30 a.m., and 22:30 for 10:30 p.m.).

8. Press **Enter** to send the time you specified to the computer's internal clock.

9. The DOS prompt will appear:

```
C:\>
```

(Your DOS prompt may differ somewhat from this.)

10. Type **dir** and press **Enter**. The contents of the current directory are displayed, followed by a line reporting the number of free bytes on your hard disk. If you have 1,000,000 or more bytes free, skip to step 11. If you have fewer than 1,000,000 bytes free, you will not be able to create your work directory and perform all of the hands-on file-management tasks in this book. Before you proceed, you'll have to delete enough files from your hard disk to bring the free bytes up to 1,000,000. If you need help doing this, please refer to your DOS reference manual. (Note: Make sure to back up all important files before deleting them.)

11. Insert the enclosed Data Disk (label up) into the appropriately sized disk drive and close the drive doors, if necessary. Determine whether this is drive A or drive B. On a single floppy-disk system, the drive is generally designated as A. On a double floppy-disk system, the upper drive is generally designated as A and the lower as B.

12. Type **a:** if the Data Disk is in drive A, or type **b:** if the Data Disk is in drive B. Press **Enter** to change the current drive to the Data Disk drive.

13. Type **install c: windwork** (making sure to include a space between *install* and *c:* and between *c:* and *windwork*). If you wish to create your work directory on a hard disk that is *not* designated as drive C, substitute your hard-disk drive letter for the *c* in this command—for example, to install onto a drive D hard disk, type *install d: windwork*. WINDWORK is the name of your work directory. Press **Enter** to begin the installation.

14. If all is well, the message *Installation begun.* appears followed by various *Copying files .....* messages. When the procedure is complete, the message *Installation finished!* appears, followed by a line reporting the name of your work directory (c:\windwork).

15. In some cases, however, the following message may appear:

```
Installations aborted! Work directory naming conflict.
```

This message is displayed if a directory with the same name as your proposed working directory (WINDWORK) already exists on your hard disk. If this happens, proceed as follows. Repeat step 13, substituting a new work directory name of your choice for the suggested directory *windwork*. For example, you might type *install c: mywork* or *install c: winfiles*. Your work directory name can be up to 8 letters long. Do not use spaces, periods, or punctuation marks. Do not use the name *windows*, as it is already taken by Windows 3.1.

Note: The hands-on activities in this book refer to your work directory as WINDWORK. If you've chosen another name, please remember to mentally substitute it for the name WINDWORK throughout the book.

CONVENTIONS USED IN THIS BOOK

The conventions used in this book are designed to help you learn Windows easily and efficiently. Each chapter begins with a short introduction and ends with a summary which includes a quick-reference guide to the techniques introduced in the chapter. Main chapter topics and subtopics explain the theory behind Windows features. Hands-on activities allow you to practice these features in realistic work situations.

To help you distinguish between steps presented for your general knowledge and steps you should carry out at your computer as you read, we have adopted the following system:

- A bulleted step, like this, is provided for your information and reference only.

1. A numbered step, like this, indicates one in a series of steps that you should carry out in sequence at your computer.

In these activities, menu choices, keystrokes, and anything you are asked to type are all presented in boldface. Here's an example from Chapter 10:

  1.   Type **budget.abc** and press **Enter** to open the Alphabet file, BUDGET.ABC.

Activities adhere to a *cause-and-effect* approach. Each step tells you what to do (cause) and then what will happen (effect). From the example above,

> Cause: Type **budget.abc** and press **Enter**.
>
> Effect: The Alphabet file BUDGET.ABC is opened.

A plus sign (+) is used with the Shift, Ctrl, and Alt keys to denote a multikey keystroke. For example, *press Shift+F7* means, "Press and hold down the Shift key, then press the function key F7, then release both."

BEFORE YOU START

The activities in each of the following 11 chapters are designed to proceed sequentially. In many cases, you cannot perform an activity until you have performed one or more of the activities directly preceding it. For this reason, we recommend that you allot enough time to work through an entire chapter in one sitting.

You are now ready to begin. Good learning and ... *bon voyage!*

CHAPTER 1:
THE WINDOWS
ENVIRONMENT

Welcome to the world of Windows 3.1! Windows is a *graphical user interface,* which is a fancy way of saying that the program gives your computer's operating system a new face—a graphic one—making it more intuitive and fun to use. Rather than having to learn a computer language and then type long strings of commands at your keyboard, you can give your computer the same instructions by using a mouse (or keyboard) to manipulate graphic symbols on your screen. This will allow you to spend less time telling your computer how you would like it to work and more time using, for example, a word processor.

When you're done working through this chapter, you will know

- How to start Windows

- How the Windows environment functions

- How to run programs

- How to run the File Manager and use the directory window

- How to resize, arrange, activate, and move windows

- How to restore icons to windows

ORIENTATION TO WINDOWS

The Microsoft Windows program is a graphical environment that enables you to manage your files and to run other programs. Here are some of the more important functions that Windows provides:

- It enables you to run more than one program at a time on the same computer.

- It manages your computer's memory and storage, enhancing their performance and extending their capabilities.

- It provides a standard way to communicate with programs. Programs designed to run with Windows have standard commands for tasks such as saving a file and printing. This means that you do not have to learn a different set of commands for each program you use.

- It simulates a familiar environment, in which you work with documents much as you would with papers and file folders. Files are stored in a system that is similar to filing cabinets. Programs such as Calculator, Clock, and Notepad provide you with the computer version of familiar tools for the home and office.

 STARTING WINDOWS

Before you start Windows, it must be installed on your hard disk. If Windows is not already installed, see Appendix A for directions.

Note: The method you use to start Windows may vary. This book assumes that you are not starting Windows through the intervention of a menu or batch file.

Follow these steps to start Windows:

1. Turn on your computer. Momentarily, you will see the system prompt, which will probably appear as C:\>. At this point, the computer is waiting for you to enter a command.

2. Type **win** and press **Enter** to run the Windows program.

3. Examine the screen. An hourglass momentarily appears there indicating that the computer has not yet finished loading the program and processing information. Once Windows is running, the *Desktop* is displayed (see Figure 1.1). This environment is called the Desktop because it enables you to arrange several different tasks in windows on the screen, like arranging a stack of papers on a real desktop. Several small graphic symbols, or *icons*, appear within the *Program Manager* window. Within the Program Manager window there is one open window, the *Main* window. (The position and status of items in your Desktop may vary, depending on what additional programs you may have installed to run under Windows, and on whether you have moved items on your Desktop since installing Windows.)

 USING THE MOUSE

As you move your mouse, the computer responds by moving a *mouse pointer* on the display screen. To move the mouse pointer to the left side of the screen, roll the mouse toward the left side of your desk. To move the mouse pointer to the top of the screen, roll the mouse away from you. Move the mouse in other directions, and the mouse pointer responds accordingly.

Press and release the *mouse button* to communicate with the computer. For the remainder of this book, on a mouse with two or more buttons "mouse button" indicates the left button.

There are four general operations that you will perform with the mouse to accomplish a wide variety of tasks:

- *Pointing:* Positioning the mouse pointer over an item

- *Clicking:* Pressing and releasing the mouse button

- *Double-clicking:* Pressing and releasing the mouse button twice in rapid succession

Figure 1.1   **Windows Desktop**

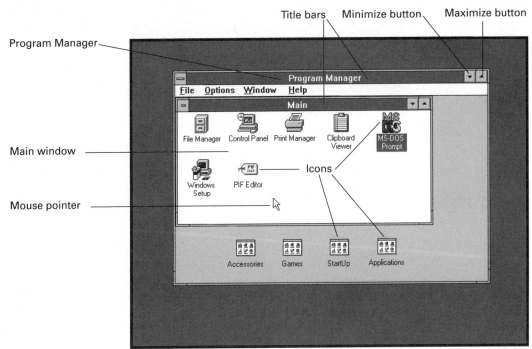

- *Dragging:* Holding down the mouse button while moving the mouse pointer

Windows menu choices that are followed by an *ellipsis* (...) are associated with *dialog boxes,* which you use to supply information about the task you are performing. Dialog boxes can contain *command buttons, option buttons, text boxes, list boxes, drop-down list boxes,* and *check boxes*, which let you select operations, options, and files.

A command button that you will use frequently is the *OK* button. The OK button appears in most Windows dialog boxes. Clicking on OK causes the changes you have made in the dialog box to take effect. A *Cancel* button usually appears with the OK button. The Cancel button allows you to close the dialog box without your changes taking effect.

Let's try using the mouse in different ways, and then explore methods for changing how your mouse moves and reacts to your commands:

1. Examine the arrow on the display screen (see Figure 1.1). You will use this arrow, called the *mouse pointer*, to select commands and other items that appear on the screen.

2. Roll the mouse on the surface next to the keyboard and watch the mouse pointer. Notice that the mouse pointer moves in relation to the movement of the mouse.

3. Position the mouse pointer over the **Accessories** icon. This is called *pointing*.

4. Click the mouse button (press and release the mouse button).

5. Examine the Accessories icon. A list of commands, called a *menu*, appears above the icon, as shown in Figure 1.2.

6. Click on **Restore** by positioning the mouse pointer over the Restore choice and clicking the mouse button.

Figure 1.2   **Accessories menu**

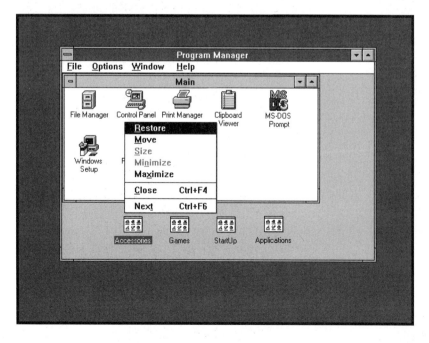

7. Examine the screen. The Accessories icon has become a large rectangle, called a *window.* Compare your screen with Figure 1.3. The Accessories window contains several icons, which represent programs that you can run. Programs are instructions that enable you to perform specific tasks such as typing letters, entering appointments in a calendar, performing mathematical calculations, and creating pictures.

8. In the Accessories window, click on the **Control** menu box (the small box in the upper-left corner of the Accessories window). The Control menu appears (see Figure 1.4).

9. Choose **Close** to reduce the Accessories window to an icon.

Figure 1.3   **Accessories window**

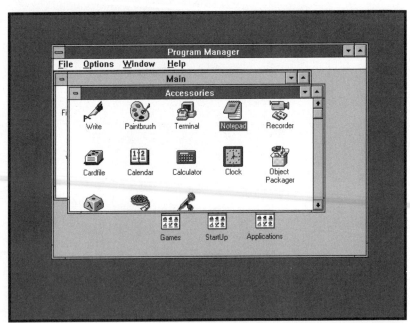

Next, let's open the Control Panel, and then experiment with our mouse settings:

1. In the Main group window, click on the **Control Panel** icon to select it.

Figure 1.4   **Control menu**

Control menu box ⎯

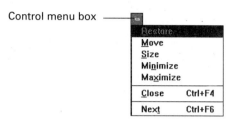

2. Click on **File** in the Program Manager menu to open the File menu, shown in Figure 1.5.

Figure 1.5   **Program Manager File menu**

Program
Manager menu ⎯

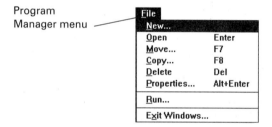

3. In the File menu, click on **Open** to open the Control Panel. The *Control Panel* enables you to change settings such as the color of your Windows screens, the speed at which your mouse responds to movement, the overall look of your Windows Desktop, and the date and time of your computer's clock.

4. In the Control Panel window, click on the **Mouse** icon to select it. At the bottom of the Control Panel window, notice the message stating that you can change your mouse settings (see Figure 1.6).

5. In the Control Panel menu, choose (click on) **Settings** to open the Control Panel Settings menu, shown in Figure 1.7. From this menu, you can open the Control Panel areas represented by its icons.

Figure 1.6   **Selected Mouse icon**

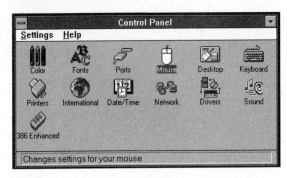

Figure 1.7   **Control Panel Settings menu**

6. In the Settings menu, choose (click on) **Mouse** to open the Mouse dialog box, shown in Figure 1.8. (The dialog box may vary according to the mouse you have installed.)

7. Click on the **left scroll** arrow under the word *Slow* in the Mouse Tracking Speed section of the dialog box, to slow the mouse tracking speed. The slower the tracking speed, the greater the distance you must move the mouse in order to move the mouse pointer a relatively small distance on the screen. Notice that the scroll box (see Figure 1.8) has moved toward Slow. Such scroll boxes serve as relative position indicators.

8. Move your mouse across the desk, and notice how the mouse responds to your movement.

Figure 1.8   **Mouse dialog box**

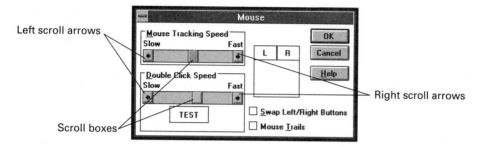

9. Click on the **right scroll** arrow under the word *Fast,* until the scroll box is in its extreme right position. The faster the tracking speed, the shorter the distance you have to move the mouse in order to move the mouse pointer on the screen.

10. Move your mouse across the desk. Notice that less movement is required to move the mouse pointer a similar distance on the screen.

11. Click several times on the **Fast** (right scroll) arrow in the Double Click Speed section of the dialog box.

12. Place your mouse pointer on the **TEST** button, toward the bottom-left corner of the Mouse dialog box, and try to double-click (press and release the left mouse button twice in rapid succession). The TEST button will change color or shade to indicate a successful double-click attempt. Depending on your skills in handling a mouse, you might find it difficult to complete a double-click successfully at the fastest setting.

13. Set the tracking and double-click speeds that are most comfortable for you.

14. Click on **Mouse Trails** to check the Mouse Trails check box. The *X* in the check box shows that the Mouse Trails option is active.

15. Move the mouse around the screen. Notice how the mouse pointer trails around the screen, resulting in a "shooting star" effect. You might find that mouse trails can help you spot and follow the mouse pointer, or you might find the effect annoying.

16. If you prefer to do without the trailing effect, click on **Mouse Trails** to uncheck the Mouse Trails check box. Notice that the *X* has disappeared, indicating that the option is no longer active.

17. Click on **OK** to accept the changes and close the Mouse settings dialog box.

18. Open the Control Panel **Settings** menu, and choose **Exit** to close the Control Panel window and return to the Main group window.

PRACTICE YOUR SKILLS

1. Use the mouse to position the mouse pointer in each of the four corners of your Desktop.

2. Restore the Accessories icon to a window.

3. Close the Accessories window.

RUNNING THE NOTEPAD PROGRAM

To *run* a program or application means to start it. The simplest method of running a program in Windows is to double-click on the desired program icon. For example, to run the Notepad program, first open the Accessories window, if necessary. (Notepad resides in the Accessories group.) Then position the mouse pointer over the Notepad icon and double-click.

The Notepad and Write programs come standard with Windows 3.1. These programs enable you to enter, save, and retrieve text files. As such, they serve as basic word processors. (You'll learn how to use Notepad and Write in Chapter 2.)

Let's run the Notepad program:

1. Position the mouse pointer over the **Accessories** icon, and double-click the mouse button (click twice in rapid succession) to open the Accessories window.

2. Double-click on the **Notepad** icon. The Notepad window is displayed (see Figure 1.9).

Figure 1.9   **Notepad window**

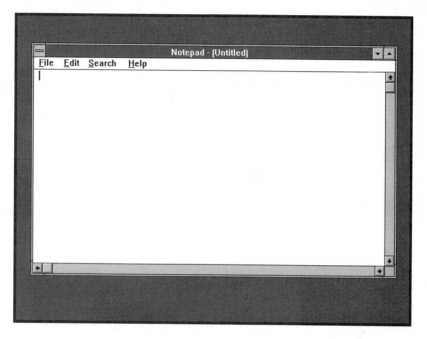

 EXITING A PROGRAM AND CLOSING A WINDOW

To exit a program, choose File, Exit from the program window menu.

Let's exit Notepad, and then close the Accessories window:

1. Choose **File, Exit** to exit the Notepad program and close the Notepad window. (Click on **File** to open the Notepad File menu, and then click on **Exit**.)

2. Examine the screen. The Notepad window has closed, and the Program Manager window is visible once again. Although the Program Manager window was still on the Desktop when you were running Notepad, it was hidden behind the Notepad window.

3. Position the mouse pointer over the Accessories window **Control** menu box (the box containing the horizontal bar in the upper-left corner of the window).

4. Double-click the mouse button to close the window.

USING THE KEYBOARD

Any operation you perform with the mouse can be duplicated by using the keyboard. Using the mouse is generally more efficient; however, at times you might find it more convenient to use the keyboard. Choosing whether to use the mouse or the keyboard for a particular action depends on your preference. Table 1.1 lists some handy Windows keystrokes.

Table 1.1   **Using the Keyboard in Windows**

Desired Result	How to Do It
Select a group icon in Program Manager	Press Ctrl+Tab
Open the window of a selected group	Press Enter
Select an icon in the active window	Press Up, Down, Left, or Right Arrow key
Run the program of the selected icon	Press Enter
Select the menu in the active window	Press Alt
Select another main menu choice	Press Left or Right Arrow key
Open the selected menu	Press Enter, or press Alt and the underlined letter of the desired menu choice
Choose a command within an open menu	Press the underlined letter of the desired choice
Close a menu	Press Esc
Deactivate the window menu	Press Esc

Let's try using the keyboard to perform some of the Windows functions we've learned thus far:

1. In the Main group window, select the **Control Panel** icon.

2. Press the **arrow keys** (Left, Right, Up, and Down) to change which icon is selected in the active window.

3. Press **Ctrl+Tab** several times to select group icons within Program Manager.

4. Continue pressing **Ctrl+Tab** until the Main window is once again selected.

5. Select **Control Panel** by using the keyboard (arrow keys).

6. Press **Enter** to open the Control Panel.

7. Press **Alt** to highlight the Settings choice. This menu is now active, meaning that its menu choices can now be accessed via the keyboard.

8. Press **Right Arrow** to highlight the Help menu choice.

9. Press **Left Arrow** to highlight the Settings menu choice.

10. Press **Enter** to open the Settings menu.

11. Press the **Esc** key to close the Settings menu. Notice that the Settings choice is still highlighted, indicating that the menu is active.

12. Press **Esc** to deactivate the menu.

13. Examine the Control Panel menu. In the Settings menu choice, the letter *S* is underlined.

14. Press **Alt+s** to open the Settings menu. This is an alternate way of opening a Windows menu by using the keyboard. Notice that it is necessary to press the Alt key. Pressing *s* alone will not open the menu.

15. Examine the Exit choice in the Settings menu. Notice that the letter *x* is underlined.

16. Type **x** to exit from Control Panel and close its window.

ORIENTATION TO THE FILE MANAGER

In an office filing system, you store files in labeled folders that you keep in a file cabinet. If your filing system is well organized, then it is easy to find files when you need them.

In a way, computer disks are like the drawers of a file cabinet. Like the file drawers, such disks might contain labeled folders to keep your files organized. Because folders on a computer disk direct you to your files, they are called *file directories* (see Figure 1.10). If you create and use file directories, then it will be easy to find your computer files when you need them.

Figure 1.10   **File directories are like file folders**

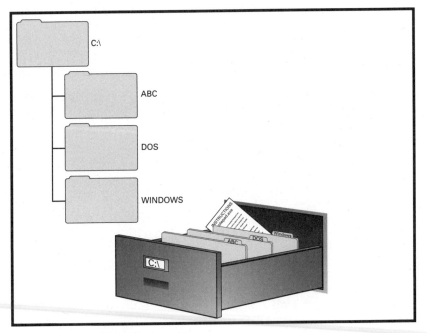

In an office filing system, a single file drawer might contain many folders, each of which might contain files. Furthermore, these folders might contain other folders, which, in turn, might contain files or more folders. Similarly, a disk might contain several directories, and directories might contain *subdirectories*.

RUNNING FILE MANAGER AND EXAMINING THE DIRECTORY TREE

The Windows *File Manager* enables you to view and manage your computer's filing system. To open the File Manager, double-click on the File Manager icon in the Main window. Once opened, the File

Manager window fills the entire Desktop, obscuring the Program Manager and its contents, although they are still available to you.

The contents of a disk appear in a *directory window,* the smaller window within File Manager (see Figure 1.11). (By default, Windows opens your computer's hard-disk directory when you run File Manager.) The directory window is usually divided into two sections. One section shows you the directories and subdirectories on a disk and uses lines to show you the relationship between them. Because this view of your file directories resembles a tree, this part of the directory window is called a *directory tree*. The other section of the directory window shows you the files and directories within a selected directory. This part of the directory window is called the *contents list*.

Figure 1.11   **File Manager window**

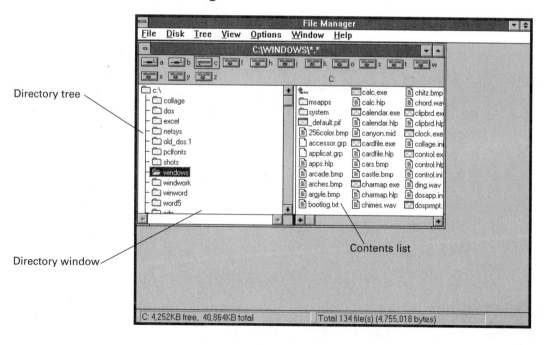

Table 1.2 lists some important File Manager procedures and describes how to perform them.

Table 1.2   **Using File Manager**

Desired Result	How to Do It
Display a directory window	Click on the desired drive and/or directory
Expand a tree for a single directory	Double-click on that directory's icon, and choose Tree, Indicate Expandable Branches to see which directories contain subdirectories
Expand an entire directory tree	Choose Tree, Expand All
View all files in a directory	Click on the directory name
Open a file	Double-click on the file name, or click on the file name and press Enter

Let's run the File Manager and examine our hard disk's directory tree:

1. Verify that the Main window is open within the Program Manager window.

2. Double-click on the **File Manager** program icon (in the Main window) to run the program.

3. Examine the File Manager window, shown in Figure 1.11. Notice the smaller directory window within the larger File Manager window. The title bar of the directory window tells you that it is currently displaying information for the WINDOWS directory. Immediately below the title bar you can see icons that represent any disk drives currently attached to your computer. Notice that the hard-disk drive, drive C, is currently selected. Directories are represented as folders in the left portion of the directory window. The WINDOWS directory folder is currently open, and the folder and directory name are highlighted.

4. From the File Manager menu, choose **Tree, Indicate Expandable Branches** to display plus signs (+) in folder icons that have more directories nested "beneath" them. A minus sign (-) indicates that all of the directories within a directory are currently visible.

5. Choose **Tree** once again, and observe the menu. Indicate Expandable Branches has a check mark in front of it, meaning that this menu option is currently active (see Figure 1.12).

Figure 1.12   **Checked Tree menu option**

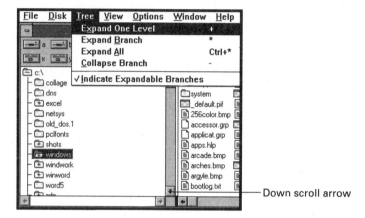

Down scroll arrow

6. Click on **Tree** to close the Tree menu.

7. Click on the **windwork** directory to show a listing of its subdirectories. (If the directory is not visible, scroll it into view by clicking on the appropriate scroll arrows, and then click on the directory.)

8. Click several times on the **down scroll** arrow to the right of the directory tree to place the WINDWORK directory near the top of the directory window.

9. Examine the directory tree. Notice that two of the subdirectory folders, ACCOUNTS and ALPHA, contain plus signs, indicating that these directories can be expanded further.

10. Choose **Tree, Expand All** to fully expand the directories. If necessary, scroll to view WINDWORK and its nested subdirectories. Compare your screen with Figure 1.13.

11. Click on the **accounts** folder icon in the directory tree. The *contents list,* the right portion of the directory window, displays the contents of the ACCOUNTS directory.

Figure 1.13   **Fully expanded directory tree**

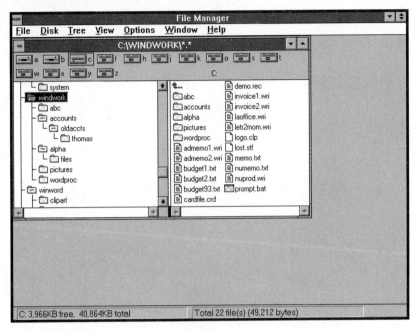

12. Double-click on the **accounts** folder to collapse the tree display of that directory. Notice that OLDACCTS is no longer displayed beneath ACCOUNTS, and the ACCOUNTS folder once again contains a plus sign, indicating that its contents are not currently displayed.

13. Double-click on the **accounts** folder to expand the tree display of that directory. You can control how many levels of the directory display are visible for each directory.

RUNNING A PROGRAM FROM FILE MANAGER

You already know how to run a program when the icon is visible in its group window. However, you can also run a program while you are in File Manager. The benefit of this is that if you happen to be in File Manager and want to open a document already created in, say, Notepad, you need not exit the File Manager to do so.

To run a program from File Manager:

- Double-click on the program file name.

or

- Click on the file name and press *Enter*.

Earlier you learned how to exit a program or close a window through the Control menu. Another way to exit a program is to double-click on the Control menu box.

Let's attempt to open two files from File Manager:

1. Click on the **windwork** folder.

2. Examine the contents list. It shows all of the directories and files contained in the WINDWORK directory.

3. Examine the PICTURES folder. In both the directory tree and the contents list, folder icons are used to represent directories.

4. Examine the BUDGET1.TXT file. Its icon is a dog-eared page with lines of text on it, which represents a document file.

5. Double-click on **budget1.txt** to open the document. Windows uses the file-name extension to determine the program used to open a document. Notice that, because the file has the .TXT extension in its name, Windows has automatically linked it to the Notepad program. Compare your screen with Figure 1.14.

6. Double-click on the **Control** menu box to close the Notepad window.

7. Examine the LOST.STF file. Its icon is like the icon for BUD-GET1.TXT, but it does not have lines on it. The absence of lines means that this document is not associated with a program.

8. Double-click on **lost.stf**. A message box is displayed:

   ```
   No application is associated with this file.
   Choose Associate from the File menu to
   create an association.
   ```

   This means that before you can open this file, you must run a program.

9. Click on **OK**.

Figure 1.14   **Text file opened in File Manager**

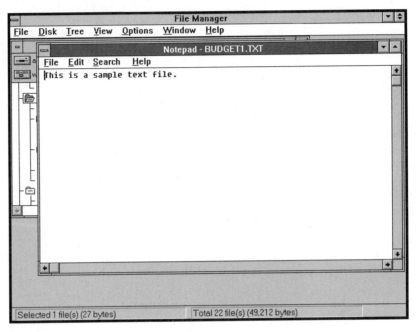

 MAXIMIZING A WINDOW

Maximizing a window usually means to enlarge it so that it fills the entire Windows Desktop. Exceptions to this are windows contained within other programs, which set aside portions of the screen for program-specific features, and therefore allow windows inside them to be maximized to fill most, but not all, of the Desktop.

To maximize a window, click on the window's *Maximize* button, the up arrow in the upper-right corner of the window. To restore a maximized window, click on the window's *Restore* button, the two-headed, vertical arrow in the upper-right corner of the window.

Let's open a different directory, and then maximize the directory window:

1. Click on the **windows** folder. If the windows directory icon is not visible, scroll it into view by clicking on the appropriate scroll arrow.

2. Examine the contents of the WINDOWS directory. There are many files stored in this directory. This is where the instructions for running the Windows program are stored.

3. Click on the **Maximize** button in the directory window to enlarge the window to its maximum size. Compare your screen with Figure 1.15.

Figure 1.15   **Maximized directory window**

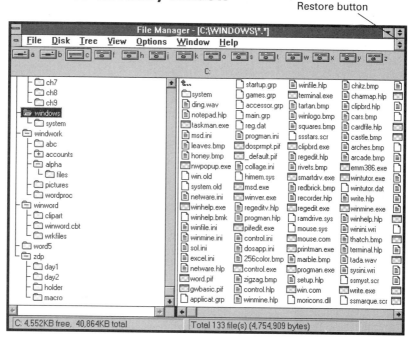

4. Examine the directory window. The title bar shows the titles of both open windows. The Maximize button has been replaced by a Restore button.

5. Click on the **Restore** button. The directory window reverts to its earlier size.

6. Click on the **Maximize** button once again to enlarge the window to full size.

 USING HELP

Microsoft Windows provides a powerful, easy-to-use *on-line Help* system. Help is available whenever you see a Help command button or a Help menu choice. You can access Help by using the mouse to choose Help or by pressing the F1 function key on the keyboard. Within the Help window, certain words and phrases appear underlined and in a different shade. By clicking on these Help *hotspots,* you can view additional Help information that is related to the current Help screen, or *topic*. Hotspots with solid underlines lead to additional Help topics; hotspots with dotted underlines represent *glossary* entries that contain definitions of Windows terms.

Let's use the Help system to find information about icons:

1. Choose **Help** to open the Help menu (see Figure 1.16).

Figure 1.16   **Help menu**

2. Choose **Contents** to open the Help window.

3. Point at the phrase **What Is File Manager?** Notice that the mouse pointer changes to a hand. This is a Help hotspot.

4. Click the mouse button to see a Help topic on icon types.

5. Point at the word **icon** and click the mouse button to see a glossary definition of *icon* (see Figure 1.17). Click the mouse button anywhere to close the glossary definition.

6. From the File Manager Help window menu, choose **File, Exit** to return to the File Manager.

7. Examine the NOTEPAD.EXE file. (Files are arranged alphabetically. If this file is not visible, scroll it into view.) This icon represents the file that stores the instructions, or *program*, that enables Windows to run Notepad. An icon for a program file looks like a miniature window with a title bar.

Figure 1.17   **Help glossary definition**

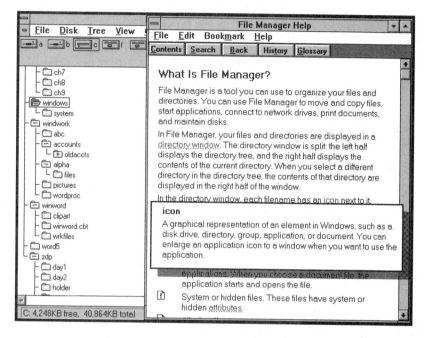

8. Double-click on the **notepad.exe** icon. This is another way to run a program.

9. Examine the screen. The Notepad program is running. A new untitled document is loaded.

10. Double-click on the **Control** menu box to close the Notepad window.

11. Examine the program files in the contents list (the right portion of the directory window). Notice the miniature window icons. Program files might have file-name extensions such as .EXE, .COM, .BAT, or .PIF.

12. Observe the SYSTEM ICON, shaped like a folder. This icon is used to represent a directory.

13. Observe the BOXES.BMP icon, a dog-eared page with lines in it. As you learned earlier, this icon represents a document file. This file happens to be associated with a program, so if you were to double-click on it, the document would open through the associated program.

14. Observe the ACCESSOR.GRP icon, a dog-eared page with no lines. This file cannot be opened by double-clicking on it.

15. Observe the CLOCK.EXE icon, shaped like a miniature window. This, like NOTEPAD.EXE, is a program file. If you were to double-click on this file, it would run the Windows Clock program. (You'll learn about the Clock later in this chapter.)

16. Click on the **Restore** button to restore the directory window to its earlier size and position, before you maximized it.

17. Choose **File, Exit** to close the File Manager.

18. Close the Main window.

ORIENTATION TO PROGRAMS IN THE ACCESSORIES GROUP

Windows provides a group of programs called *Accessories* that enable you to perform many tasks without having to acquire additional programs. For example, you've already briefly seen Notepad, which enables you to create and edit unformatted text documents.

In this section, you'll use a few of these programs. Here's a brief description of the remaining programs in the Accessories group:

- *Write* is a word processor. In addition to creating and editing text, you can work with margin settings, tabs, paragraph alignment, character styles, and other formatting options. (You'll learn more about Write and Notepad in Chapter 2.)

- *Paintbrush* is a graphics program that you can use to create geometric and freehand illustrations (in color if your hardware supports color).

- *Terminal* is a communications program. You can use Terminal to connect with information services and to transfer files between your computer and another computer.

- *Calendar* is an appointment calendar, which you can use to help you keep track of meetings and other appointments. Calendar even has an alarm feature to warn you of impending appointments.

- *Cardfile* provides you with on-screen file cards, on which you can store names, addresses, phone numbers, notes, and other information. Once you've created cards, you can tell the program to search for specific information.

- *Recorder* records sequences of mouse and keyboard activity for later playback. This can be useful for performing repetitive tasks. With one command you can activate a complex sequence that you previously recorded.

- *Object Packager* provides you with a way to combine information from several applications into a single document.

- *Character Map* shows you all of the available characters in a particular font.

- *Media Player* can play multimedia files and run multimedia devices such as videodiscs.

- *Sound Recorder* enables you to play, record, and edit sound files.

In the next two sections, we'll examine the Calculator and Clock programs in greater detail.

USING THE CALCULATOR

Calculator is the Windows version of a desktop calculator. By using a menu option, you can change it from a simple calculator to a multifunction scientific calculator.

Let's try the Calculator:

1. Restore the Accessories icon to a window (double-click on the **Accessories** group icon).

2. Run the Calculator program (double-click on the **Calculator** icon).

3. Examine the Calculator window. It looks like a pocket calculator.

4. Click on the Calculator buttons or type on the keyboard to add **482+7700**.

5. Click on the = button or press **Enter** to add the two numbers. The sum *8182* appears in the Calculator's display.

6. In the Calculator menu, choose **View, Scientific** to add scientific functions to the calculator. Compare your screen with Figure 1.18.

PRACTICE YOUR SKILLS

1. Experiment with the Calculator's functions.

2. Change the Calculator view to **Standard**.

Figure 1.18 **Calculator in Scientific view**

Minimize button

MINIMIZING THE CALCULATOR AND RUNNING THE CLOCK PROGRAM

The Windows *Clock* provides an on-screen clock to help you keep time. You can set the clock to display in a simulated analog mode or in digital mode.

Windows enables you to have many programs running at once. A program runs in its own window. However, you can temporarily "set aside" a program that you are using by reducing its window to an icon, or *minimizing* it. Minimizing windows can help keep your Windows Desktop uncluttered.

Before you examine the clock in the following exercise, you will minimize the Calculator. To minimize a window, click on the window's Minimize button, the down arrow in the upper-right corner of the window. To restore a minimized window, double-click on its icon.

Let's minimize the Calculator window, and then run the Clock program:

1. Click on the **Minimize** button for the Calculator window.

2. Examine the screen. The Calculator window has been minimized to an icon that appears in the lower portion of the screen. It's important to note that the Calculator is still running. This is like setting a real calculator aside on your desk without turning off the power, thereby saving any number still in the calculator.

3. Run the Clock program by double-clicking on the **Clock** icon located in the Program Manager Accessories group.

4. Examine the clock. It displays the time of day and the date (see Figure 1.19).

Figure 1.19   **Windows Clock**

5. From the Clock menu, choose **Settings, Analog** to change to an analog display.

6. Choose **Settings, Digital** to return to a digital display.

7. Choose **Settings, Seconds** to turn off the display of seconds.

PRACTICE YOUR SKILLS

1. Experiment with the available clock settings. If you choose Settings, No Title, you will need to press the Esc key to redisplay the clock menu and title bar.

2. Minimize the Clock window.

3. Minimize the Program Manager window. Compare your screen with Figure 1.20.

Figure 1.20   **Desktop with all running windows and programs minimized**

ORGANIZING THE DESKTOP

You've seen how minimizing open windows can keep your screen less cluttered. You can further organize the elements of your Desktop by adjusting the size and position of open windows.

 ### SIZING WINDOWS

To change the size of a window, position the mouse pointer over any border or corner of the window. At the top and bottom borders, the mouse pointer becomes a vertical, two-headed arrow; at the left and right borders, it becomes a horizontal one; at the four corners of a window, it becomes a diagonal one. When the two-headed arrow is vertical or horizontal, you can drag the border's outline to increase or decrease the window's size in one dimension, in the direction in which you drag the border's outline. When the two-headed arrow is diagonal, you can drag the outline to increase or decrease the window's size proportionately in two dimensions, in the direction in which you drag the outline. When you release the mouse button, the window adjusts to the new size.

Let's restore the icons to windows, and then size them:

1. Double-click on the **Clock** icon to restore it to a window.

2. Position the mouse pointer on the left border of the Clock window. When the mouse pointer is in the correct position, it will become a horizontal, two-headed arrow.

3. Press and hold the mouse button. Do *not* release it.

4. Move the mouse pointer to the right. An outline of the window border follows the mouse pointer.

5. Drag the outline (move the mouse) until it is in the middle of the window.

6. Release the mouse button. The window has adjusted its size.

7. Position the mouse pointer on the bottom border of the Clock window, until it becomes a vertical, two-headed arrow.

8. Drag (press and hold the mouse button, then move the mouse) the border outline upward until it is in the middle of the window.

9. Release the mouse button, and compare your screen with Figure 1.21.

 USING THE TASK LIST TO ACTIVATE WINDOWS

There are two ways to tell if a window is active:

- The title bar of an active window is a more prominent color or shade than the title bar of an inactive window.

- If windows overlap, then the active window is the one on top.

If you wish to work with a program that is running in an inactive window, then you must first activate its window. The simplest and fastest way to activate a visible window is by clicking on its title bar. Another way to activate a window or minimized icon, whether it is visible or not, is by accessing the *Task List*. The Task List lists all the programs that are currently running, even if their windows or icons are obscured by other windows. To display the Task List, press Ctrl+Esc, choose Switch To from any application's Control menu, or double-click on a blank area of the Desktop.

Figure 1.21   **Resized Clock window**

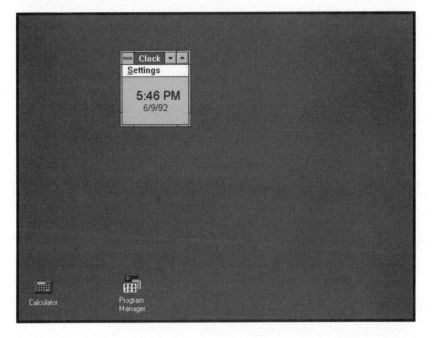

Note: Double-clicking on a blank area of the Desktop would seem to be the easiest and fastest way to display the Task List. However, there will be times when the Desktop is completely obscured by open windows, or even a single maximized window. For this reason, we recommend committing Ctrl+Esc to memory.

Let's use the Task List to activate windows:

1. Press **Ctrl+Esc** to display the Task List.

2. Select **Calculator** (see Figure 1.22).

3. Click on **Switch To**.

4. Examine the Desktop. The program windows overlap. The Calculator window is now active.

5. Type **45**. The number appears in the Calculator's display.

6. Click on the name **Clock** in the Clock window to activate it. (Do *not* click on the Maximize button, the Minimize button, or

the Control menu box.) It is now the top window. Notice, too, the color or shade of its title bar compared with that of an inactive window.

7. Double-click on the blank area of the Desktop. Because the Desktop is visible, you can use the mouse to display the Task List. The Clock is currently highlighted because it was the active application at the time you displayed the Task List.

8. Click on **Cancel** to close the Task List. The Clock window once again becomes active.

Figure 1.22   **Selecting a program in the Task List**

MOVING WINDOWS

Besides changing the size of a window, you can also move a window. To move a window, position the mouse pointer over the title bar and drag to its new location. Remember, though, that a window can only be dragged by its title bar.

Let's practice moving our open windows:

1. Point at the title bar of the Clock window.

2. Drag the window to the lower-right portion of the screen (press and hold the mouse button as you move the mouse), as shown in Figure 1.23. While you drag, an outline of the window appears.

3. Release the mouse button. The window is now in its new position.

Figure 1.23   **Repositioned Clock window**

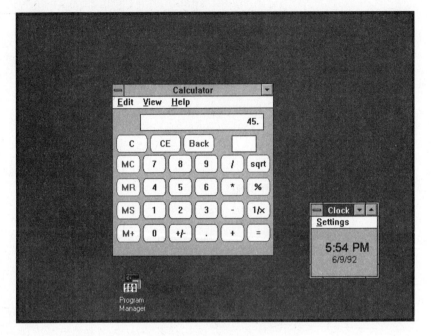

PRACTICE YOUR SKILLS

Drag the Calculator window to the upper-left corner of the Desktop.

USING THE TASK LIST TO EXIT PROGRAMS

To exit programs (this is the same as "closing windows") by using the Task List:

• Display the Task List.

• Select the name of the program you wish to exit.

• Click on *End Task*.

Let's close the Calculator and Clock windows:

1. Press **Ctrl+Esc** to view the Task List.

2. In the Task List, select **Calculator**, if necessary.

3. Click on **End Task** to close the Calculator.

4. In the Clock window, double-click on the **Control** menu box to exit the Clock program.

EXITING WINDOWS

When you have finished using your computer, you should get into the habit of exiting Windows before turning off the power to your computer. This enables the Windows program to perform some important housekeeping activities, such as saving window size and location information, and deleting temporary files from your hard disk. (Windows routinely creates such temporary files during the course of a session.)

To exit Windows:

- Exit all programs except for the Program Manager.

- Choose *File, Exit Windows* from the Program Manager menu or double-click on the *Control* menu box.

- Click on *OK*.

To preserve a particular arrangement of group windows, group icons, and program icons within Program Manager, choose *Options, Save Settings on Exit* in the Program Manager menu before you exit Windows. However, if you want to retain these same settings each time you start Windows, restart Windows, and once again choose *Options, Save Settings on Exit,* so that this option is turned off when you next exit Windows.

Let's restore the Program Manager window, and then exit Windows:

1. Restore the Program Manager icon to a window (double-click on the **Program Manager** icon).

2. Examine the Program Manager window. Its contents, including the location of icons and the Accessories window, are arranged exactly as they were when you minimized the window.

3. Close the Accessories window (double-click on the Accessories window **Control** menu box, or click on the **Minimize** button).

4. Choose **Options** in the Program Manager menu. Notice the check mark before *Save Settings on Exit*.

5. Choose **Save Settings on Exit** to uncheck it.

6. Choose **Options** again. Verify that there is no check mark next to *Save Settings on Exit* (see Figure 1.24).

Figure 1.24   **Options menu**

7. Choose **File, Exit Windows**. The Exit Windows dialog box displays the message

    `This will end your Windows session.`

8. Click on **OK** to exit the Windows program and return to the system prompt.

SUMMARY

Congratulations! You have just completed a whirlwind tour of the Windows environment. In this chapter, you learned how to start and exit Windows, how to use the mouse and keyboard in Windows, and how to run programs. You also examined directory trees in the File Manager, learned how to use the Help feature, and how to exit the File Manager. You learned about the programs in the Accessories group, including how to run the Notepad, Calculator, and Clock programs. Finally, you learned several important techniques for organizing your Desktop, such as maximizing and minimizing windows, sizing and moving windows, and using the Task List to activate or close windows.

Here is a quick reference guide to the Windows features introduced in this chapter:

Desired Result	How to Do It
Start Windows	At the system prompt, type **win** and press **Enter**
Using the Mouse	
Open a program-group window	Click on the program group icon, and choose **Restore** from the menu; or double-click on the program group icon
Close a group window	Click on the group window **Control** menu box, and choose **Close** from the menu; or double-click on the **Control** menu box
Run a program	Click on the desired program to select it, and choose **File, Open** from the Program Manager menu; or double-click on the program icon
Scroll when the contents of a window or selections in a dialog box are not visible	Click on the **up, down, left**, or **right scroll** arrow to move in the desired direction
Accept changes made in a dialog box	Click on **OK**
Cancel changes made in a dialog box	Click on **Cancel**
Exit a program	Choose **File, Exit** from the program window menu if the menu contains a File choice; click on the program window **Control** menu box and choose **Close**; or double-click on the **Control** menu box. To exit from Control Panel, you can choose **Settings, Exit**

Desired Result	How to Do It
Using the Keyboard	
Select a group icon in Program Manager	Press **Ctrl+Tab**
Open the window of a selected group	Press **Enter**
Select an icon in the active window	Press **Up**, **Down**, **Left**, or **Right Arrow** key
Run the program of the selected icon	Press **Enter**
Select the menu in the active window	Press **Alt**
Select another main menu choice	Press **Left** or **Right Arrow** key
Open the selected menu	Press **Enter**, or press **Alt** and the underlined letter of the desired menu choice
Choose a command within an open menu	Press the underlined letter of the desired choice
Close a menu	Press **Esc**
Deactivate the window menu	Press **Esc**
In File Manager	
Display a directory window	Click on the desired drive and/or directory
Expand a tree for a single directory	Double-click on that directory's icon, and choose **Tree, Indicate Expandable Branches** to see which directories contain subdirectories
Expand an entire directory tree	Choose **Tree, Expand All**

Desired Result	How to Do It
View all files in a directory	Click on the directory name
Open a file	Double-click on the file name, or click on the file name and press **Enter**
Maximize a window	Click on the **Maximize** button
Restore a maximized window to its former size	Click on the **Restore** button
Access the Help system	Choose **Help** or press **F1**, select the type of help you desire to open the Help window, and click on Help **hotspots** for information on specific topics
Change the type of calculator displayed	From the Calculator menu, choose **View, Scientific** or **Standard**
Minimize a window	Click on the **Minimize** button
Restore a minimized window	Click on the icon, and choose **Restore** from the menu, or double-click on the icon
Change the Clock display	From the Clock menu, choose **Settings, Analog** or **Digital**
Turn on/off the display of seconds	From the Clock menu, choose **Settings, Seconds**
Size a window	Drag a border of the window in the desired direction to increase or decrease its size
Display the Task List	Press **Ctrl+Esc**, or double-click on a blank area of the Desktop
Activate a visible window	Click on the window's title bar
Activate an invisible window	Press **Ctrl+Esc**, select the name of the desired window, and click on **Switch To**
Close the Task List	Click on **Cancel**

Desired Result	How to Do It
Exit a program or close a window from the Task List	Select the name of the desired window, and click on **End Task**
Turn on/off the option of saving the current window arrangement upon exiting Windows	From the Program Manager menu, choose **Options, Save Settings on Exit**
Exit Windows	From the Program Manager menu, choose **File, Exit Windows**, or double-click on the Program Manager **Control** menu box; and click on **OK**

In the next chapter, you'll learn about Windows's two word processing programs: Notepad, which you've already seen, and Write, which is the more powerful program. You'll also learn how to create documents in these programs.

If you need to break off here, please exit Windows. If you want to proceed directly to the next chapter, please do so now.

CHAPTER 2: ORIENTATION TO WORD PROCESSING

Creating a
Notepad
Document

Creating a
Document by Using
the Write Program

Saving the
Document

Creating a New
Document and
Applying Text
Styles

Exiting the Write
Program

If you've ever used a typewriter to create a memo, a letter, or any other type of document, you know that it's easy to make mistakes. Because letters are committed to paper as you compose the text, even simple typing changes like erasing a character can become difficult. More extensive corrections generally require that you retype the entire document.

Windows comes with two programs for creating text and reading text documents—the Notepad program, which you ran briefly in Chapter 1, and the Write program. These programs are both located in the Accessories group.

In a general sense, Notepad and Write are *word processors,* programs that provide you with a much more efficient way of creating, revising, and saving a document, because you can edit it without having to retype the entire document. In addition, the Write program enables you to make major adjustments, such as changing margins, in a simple series of steps.

When you're done working through this chapter, you will know

- How to create and save a document by using the Notepad program

- How to create and save a document by using the Write program

- How to apply bold and italic styles to a Write document

CREATING A NOTEPAD DOCUMENT

Notepad is particularly useful for writing memos or jotting down notes. When you run the Notepad program, a flashing bar, called the *insertion point,* appears at the top of the document window (see Figure 2.1). When you type, the text is entered at the position of the insertion point.

Figure 2.1   **Notepad window**

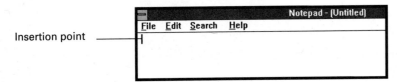

Insertion point

Let's run the Notepad program and create a document:

1. Position the mouse pointer over the **Accessories** icon, and double-click the mouse button (click twice in rapid succession) to open the Accessories window.

2. Double-click on the **Notepad** icon. The Notepad window is displayed.

3. Maximize the Notepad window (click on the **Maximize** button).

4. Examine the Notepad window. The insertion point shows where text will appear when you begin typing (see Figure 2.1).

5. Observe the mouse pointer. When placed in the document window, it becomes an *I-beam.*

6. Type **This is my first document**. Notice that the insertion point advances as you type. If you type a wrong character, you can use one of several methods to correct your mistake: Press the

Backspace key to erase the character immediately to the left of the insertion point, or use the arrow keys or position the I-beam and click to place the insertion point to the left of the letter you wish to delete and press the Del key to erase it. Compare your screen with Figure 2.2.

Figure 2.2   **Creating a Notepad document**

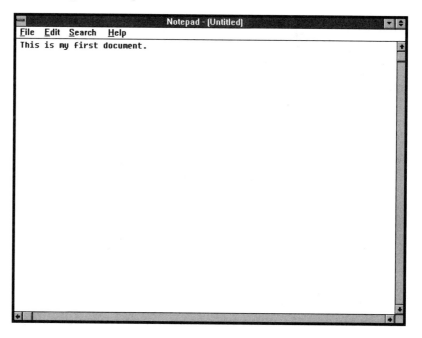

 SAVING A NEW DOCUMENT

The text you just typed is currently stored in computer memory, which is only a temporary storage location. If you were to turn off your computer or exit Notepad, your document would be lost. When the power to your computer is turned off, its memory empties; all your active files are erased. To preserve a document after the computer is turned off, you must save the document to a file on disk (either your hard disk or a removable 3½-inch or 5¼-inch disk) in much the same way you would save a paper document in a file drawer (see Figure 2.3). Likewise, if you change a document that has been saved in a file, then those changes exist only in computer memory until you update the file.

Figure 2.3   **Storing a document in a file**

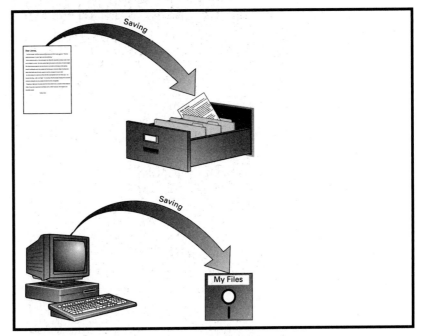

To save a document for the first time:

- Choose *File* to open the File menu.

- From the File menu, choose *Save As.*

- Type a file name in the File Name text box.

- In the Directories list box, double-click on the directory to which you want to save the file.

- Click on *OK.*

 NAMING THE FILE

If you are saving a document for the first time, you must name it. Later, you will use this name to retrieve the document.

To name a document, it is a good idea to follow these conventions:

- File names may contain up to eight characters.

- File names may include all letters or numbers, or a combination of both. Case (upper-case or lower-case letters) is not significant.

- File names may not contain spaces or punctuation marks (except -, _, and .).

- File names should be descriptive, so that a name reflects a file's contents.

- No two file names may be the same.

- An *extension* of one to three characters can be added to the file name, if you wish. Giving similar types of files the same extension can help you keep track of your documents. If you add an extension, you must separate it from the file name with a period (for example, LETTER.TXT).

In many programs, when you name a file you need only specify the characters that precede the period. For example, when you name a document in Notepad, you could type LETTER without adding the extension. Because no extension was specified, Notepad would automatically add the extension .TXT to tell the program that LETTER.TXT. is a text file.

Note: In the following exercise, you'll be saving your Notepad document to a file in the WINDWORK directory. If you have not yet created this directory, please refer to the section "Creating Your Work Directory" in the Introduction.

Let's save the document we created in Notepad:

1. Examine the title bar of the Notepad window. It reads

   ```
   Notepad - [Untitled]
   ```

   because the document has not yet been saved to a file.

2. Choose **File** (click on **File** in the Notepad window) to open the menu, shown in Figure 2.4.

3. Choose **Save As** in the File menu.

4. Examine the screen. The Save As dialog box is displayed (see Figure 2.5).

5. Observe the File Name text box. Its contents are selected, prompting you to specify what file name to give the file.

Figure 2.4   **Notepad File menu**

Figure 2.5   **Save As dialog box**

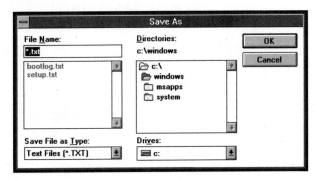

6. Type **myfirst** to name the file. Do *not* press any other keys. Notice that *myfirst* has replaced the previous contents of the text box.

7. Examine the Directories line:

   `c:\windows`

   This indicates the directory to which the file currently would be saved. If you do not specify a different storage location, this file will be saved to the WINDOWS directory on your hard disk. (If you think of drive C as a drawer in a filing cabinet, then the WINDOWS directory is like a folder within the cabinet.)

8. In the Directories list box, double-click on **c:** to display all the directories that branch off the root directory of your computer's hard disk.

9. Double-click on the **windwork** directory. (If the directory name is not visible, click on the **down scroll** arrow of the Directories list box until it is displayed, and then double-click on it.) Notice that the Files list box lists the names of all files currently contained in the WINDWORK directory that have the extension .TXT. Compare your screen with Figure 2.6.

Figure 2.6 **Completed Save As dialog box settings**

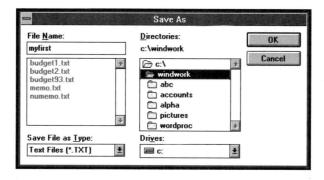

10. Click on **OK** to save the document.

11. Examine the title bar of the Notepad window. The file name appears in the title bar as *MYFIRST.TXT* (see Figure 2.7).

Figure 2.7 **Completed MYFIRST.TXT document**

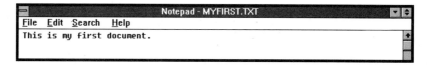

12. Double-click on the **Control** menu box to exit Notepad.

CREATING A DOCUMENT BY USING THE WRITE PROGRAM

In Notepad you can create only documents that contain plain text, which means that you cannot apply styles such as bold or italics. The Write program, on the other hand, does allow you to apply these styles to text. You can also control page formatting features, such as margins, in a Write document. When you have revised the document to your satisfaction, you can obtain a paper copy by printing the document.

In Write, unlike in Notepad, you need not press Enter when you approach the end of a line. The Write program detects that you are running out of line space and automatically continues the flow of text to the next line. This feature is called *word wrap.*

Note: Notepad does contain a Word Wrap feature (in the Edit menu), which can be turned on and off. However, it does not wrap text according to a fixed line length, but does so according to the current width of the Notepad window. So, as you increase or decrease the width of the window, the wrapping changes to accommodate the new width.

Let's run the Write program, and then create a document:

1. In the Accessories window, double-click on the **Write** program icon, which is shown selected in Figure 2.8.

Figure 2.8   **Write program icon selected**

2. Maximize the Write window (click on the **Maximize** button).

3. Examine the Write window menu bar, shown in Figure 2.9. Notice that it offers more menu choices than the Notepad program.

Figure 2.9   **Write window menu bar**

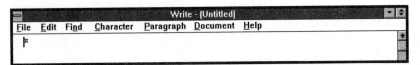

4. Type today's date. The text appears at the flashing insertion point.

5. Press **Enter** three times to end the current line and leave two blank lines.

6. Type **Alice:** and press **Enter** twice.

7. Press **Tab** to indent the first paragraph.

8. Type **Ms. Shapiro ordered one bow window and a dozen storm windows. Please send her a new invoice as soon as possible.** Do *not* press any other keys. Notice that as text approaches the right margin, it automatically wraps down onto the next line.

9. Press **Enter** three times to end the line and create two blank lines.

10. Type your name, and press **Enter** to finish the letter and move down one line. Compare your screen with Figure 2.10.

Figure 2.10   **Completed letter**

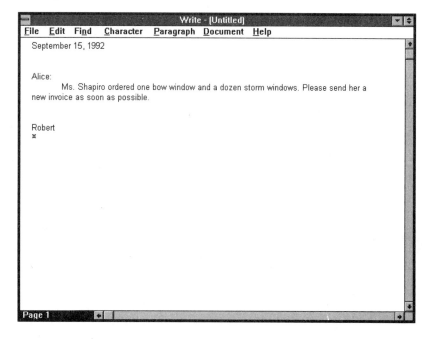

SAVING THE DOCUMENT

Many of the commands available in the File menu are universal within the Windows environment. Save As is one such command. Therefore, whenever you wish to save a new Write document to a file, use File, Save As, just as you would in Notepad. In Write, unless you specify an extension when you name a file, the program will automatically add the extension .WRI to identify documents created with the program.

WINDOWS OPTIONS AND BUTTONS

Sometimes a particular Windows menu option or command button is unavailable. Such an option or button is dimmed; it appears as gray or in a different shade than the available options. For example, the Write program's Find menu enables you to perform tasks such as searching for specific text in a document and moving to another page. However, none of the Find menu options is available in a blank document. (There would be little point in searching for specific text in a document that contained no text.) If you were to open a blank Write document, then choose Find, all of the choices in the menu would be gray.

When a command button appears with a darkened border, it is the default button. A *default* is a setting that is in effect when you run the program. There are certain dialog boxes that enable you to change many of the default settings in specific programs or in Windows in general. You can press **Enter** as a keyboard alternative to clicking on the default button.

Let's use the Save As command to save our Write document:

1. Examine the title bar. As was the case with our untitled Notepad document, this document is also *Untitled* because it has not yet been saved.

2. Choose **File, Save As...** to open the Save As dialog box.

3. Examine the Directories line located above the Directories list box. The current directory is C:\WINDOWS.

4. In the Directories list box, double-click on **c:**.

5. Scroll to view the WINDWORK directory, and double-click on **windwork**.

6. Double-click on the **wordproc** subdirectory. The Directories line should now read

    ```
    c:\windwork\wordproc
    ```

7. Observe the OK button. It is dimmed, indicating that this option is currently unavailable. The program does not allow you to click on OK until you have specified a file name.

8. Click in the **File Name** text box to place an insertion point. You can now enter a file name.

9. Type **myletter** and compare your screen with Figure 2.11.

Figure 2.11   **Completed Save As dialog box settings**

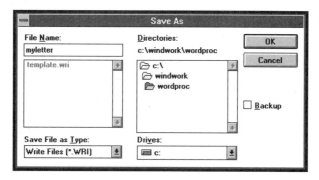

10. Observe the OK button. Notice the dark border around the button. When a button is enclosed by a dark border, you can press Enter as an alternative to clicking on that particular button.

11. Press **Enter** to save the document. The file name is now displayed in the title bar (see Figure 2.12).

EDITING A DOCUMENT AND UPDATING THE FILE

In Write you use the same basic editing techniques available in Notepad. Another important editing technique is *selecting* (or highlighting) text. Selecting text allows you to manipulate it in a number of ways. For example, once you have selected text, you can delete it by pressing the Del key, you can replace it simply by typing the replacement text, or you can move or copy it. (You'll learn more about copying and moving in Chapter 4.) Table 2.1 gives a brief summary of editing procedures.

Figure 2.12   **Completed MYLETTER.WRI document**

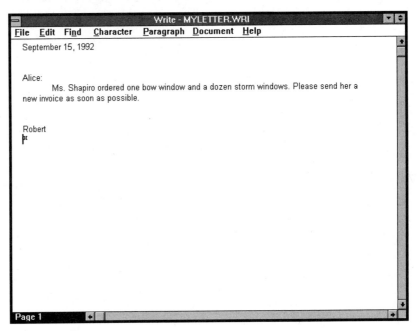

Table 2.1   **Editing Procedures**

Desired Result	How to Do It
Insert text	Click the mouse button to place an insertion point where you want the new text to appear, and then type the text
Select text	Drag across the text
Select a single word	Double-click on the word
Replace selected text	Select the text and type the new text
Delete selected text	Select the text and press Del or Backspace

Once a document has been saved to a file, you no longer need to use Save As to save it. To update a file, choose File, Save.

Let's edit our document, and then update the file so that our changes are saved:

1. Position the I-beam to the left of the *A* in *Alice* and click the mouse button. You will insert text at this point.

2. Type **Dear** and the existing text is pushed to the right of the new text.

3. Press **Spacebar** to add a space after *Dear.*

4. Point to the word *bow* and double-click the mouse button to select the word for editing.

5. Type **bay** to change *bow* to *bay,* and press **Spacebar** to insert a space after the word.

6. Position the I-beam to the left of the word *a* (between *and* and *dozen*), and drag across the words **a dozen** to select the text. Compare your screen with Figure 2.13.

Figure 2.13   **Selected text**

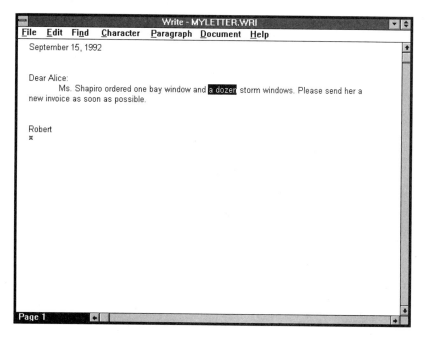

7. Press **Del** to delete the selection. The insertion point appears where you deleted the text.

8. Type **12** to insert the number at the insertion point.

9. Press **Backspace** twice to delete *12*. Pressing Backspace deletes text to the left of the insertion point.

10. Type **twelve**

11. Examine the title bar. You saved the original version of this document under the file name MYLETTER.WRI.

12. Choose **File, Save** to update the file. Figure 2.14 shows the updated document.

Figure 2.14   **Edited and updated MYLETTER.WRI document**

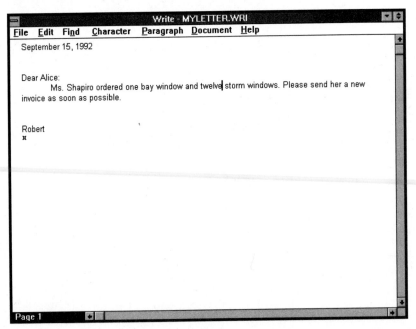

CREATING A NEW DOCUMENT AND APPLYING TEXT STYLES

To open a new Write document, choose File, New from the menu.

Text styles such as bold, italics, and underlining can be applied through the *Character* menu (see Figure 2.15).

Let's open a new document, and then apply the bold and italics styles:

1. Choose **File, New** to open a new *Untitled* document.

2. Type **This is a** and press **Spacebar**.

3. Click on **Character** to open the Character menu (see Figure 2.15).

4. Choose **Bold**. Any text that you now type will have the bold style applied to it.

5. Type **word processor**. The text has the bold style applied to it.

6. Click on **Character** again. Notice that the Bold choice is preceded by a check mark.

7. Choose **Bold** to turn off the bold style.

PRACTICE YOUR SKILLS

1. Press **Enter** twice.

2. Choose **Character, Italic**.

Figure 2.15   **Character menu**

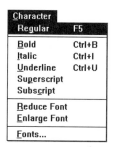

3. Type **Word processors can format text**. Compare your screen with Figure 2.16.

Figure 2.16   **Text with applied styles**

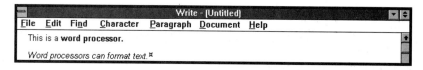

EXITING THE WRITE PROGRAM

To exit Write, double-click on the Control menu box (or use another one of the standard Windows techniques). If you have made any changes to your document since you last saved it, the Write dialog box will appear, prompting you to save the changes. Click on

- *Yes* to update the file with your changes

- *No* if you don't wish to save them

- *Cancel* if you've changed your mind about exiting

Let's exit the Write program:

1. Double-click on the **Control** menu box. The Write dialog box is displayed, asking if you wish to save your changes.

2. Click on **No** to exit Write without saving your changes.

SUMMARY

In this chapter, you learned how to create and save documents in the Notepad and Write programs. You also learned how to edit and update a Write document.

Here is a quick reference guide to the Windows features introduced in this chapter:

Desired Result	How to Do It
Enter or insert text in a document	Point and click to place the insertion point where you wish to enter text, and then begin typing
Save a new document	Choose **File, Save As**, type a file name in the *File Name* text box; in the *Directories* list box, double-click on the directory to which you want to save the file; click on **OK**
Run the Write program	Double-click on the **Write** program icon in the Accessories window
End a line of text	Press **Enter**
Select text	Drag across the text

Desired Result	How to Do It
Select a single word	Double-click on the word
Replace selected text	Select the text and type the new text
Delete selected text	Select the text and press **Del** or **Backspace**
Indent a line	Press the **Tab** key
Update a file	Choose **File, Save**
Create a new document	Choose **File, New**
In the Write Program	
Make text bold	Choose **Character, Bold**, type the text you want to make bold, and choose **Character, Bold**; or select the text you want to make bold, and choose **Character, Bold**
Italicize text	Choose **Character, Italic**, type the text you want to italicize, and choose **Character, Italic**; or select the text you want to italicize, and choose **Character, Italic**
Exit the Write program	Double-click on the **Control** menu box

In the next chapter, you will learn how to scroll in a document, how to print a document, and how to copy and move files.

If you need to break off here, please exit Windows. If you want to proceed directly to the next chapter, please do so now.

CHAPTER 3: PRINTING, MOVING, AND COPYING FILES

Scrolling a Document

Examining Print Options and Printing a Document

Application and Secondary Windows

Copying and Moving Files

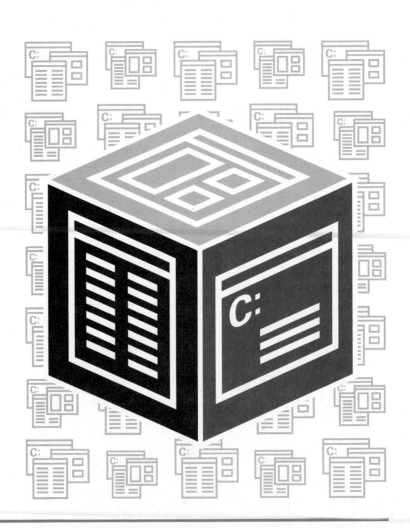

The method of printing a file in Windows is common to almost all Windows programs, so once you've learned to print in Write, for example, you'll also be able to print from virtually any other program that runs in the Windows environment.

There will also be times when you will want to copy or move a file from, say, one directory to another. For this purpose, Windows provides you with two indispensable commands: *Copy* and *Move*.

When you're done working through this chapter, you will know

- How to move around in a document by using the scroll bar
- How to print documents from Windows programs
- How to use the File Manager to copy or move a file
- How to copy an entire file directory

SCROLLING A DOCUMENT

For a lengthy document, it is obviously impossible to display all its pages at once on your Desktop. This can even be true for a document that is a single page long, depending on the type size (the size of the individual characters of text), the space between the lines of text, and the number of lines on that single-page document. For this reason, most Windows programs provide *scroll bars,* rectangular areas at the right and/or bottom of a window (see Figure 3.1). You use the scroll bars to move up and down or right and left. If you think of the information in a window as something you view *through* the window, it will be easier to understand the concept of scrolling.

Figure 3.1   **Parts of a scroll bar**

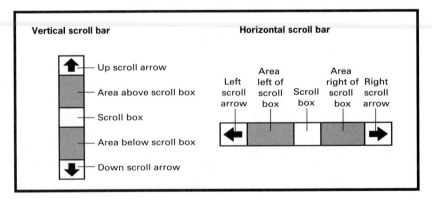

You've already briefly used the scroll arrows to view information not visible in portions of dialog boxes. Table 3.1 lists all the procedures for scrolling.

Table 3.1   **Scrolling Procedures**

Desired Result	How to Do It
Move up one line	Click on the *up scroll* arrow
Scroll up continuously, line by line	Click on the *up scroll* arrow
Move down one line	Click on the *down scroll* arrow
Scroll down continuously, line by line	Click on the *down scroll* arrow
Move up one screen of text	Click on the area *above* the scroll box, or press *PgUp*
Move down one screen of text	Click on the area *below* the scroll box, or press *PgDn*
Move to a specific location in the document	Drag the *scroll box* to a position in the scroll bar representing the relative desired position within the document
Move to the top (beginning) of the document	Drag the *scroll box* to the top of the scroll bar
Move to the bottom (end) of the document	Drag the *scroll box* to the bottom of the scroll bar
Move left	Click on the *left scroll* arrow, click in the area to the *left* of the scroll box, or drag the *scroll box* left
Move right	Click on the *right scroll* arrow, click in the area to the *right* of the scroll box, or drag the *scroll box* right

Let's open a document created using the Write program, and then practice some scrolling methods:

1. Run the Write program (open the **Accessories** window, and double-click on the **Write** program icon).

2. Maximize the Write window.

3. Choose **File, Open** to display the Open dialog box.

4. In the Directories list box, change to the **windwork** directory (double-click on **c:**, and double-click on **windwork**).

5. In the File Name list box, click on **laoffice.wri** to select it, and click on **OK** (or double-click on **laoffice.wri**) to open the document.

6. Examine the document, shown in Figure 3.2. This is a business letter. Notice that part of the document is not visible.

Figure 3.2   **Opened LAOFFICE.WRI document**

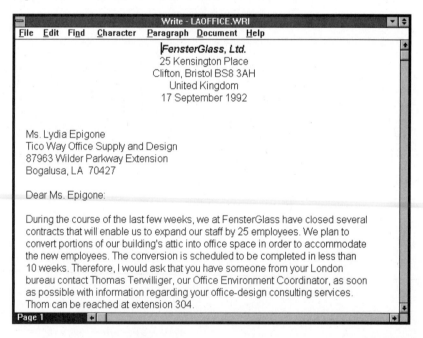

7. Click on the **down scroll** arrow several times to move down in the document one line at a time.

8. Click in the area **below** the scroll box (or press **PgDn**) to move down to the next screen of text.

9. Click on the **up scroll** arrow several times to move up in the document one line at a time.

10. Click in the area **above** the scroll box (or press **PgUp**) to move up to the previous screen of text.

11. Drag the **scroll box** to the middle of the scroll bar to move quickly to the middle of the document. Notice that, because this is only a single-page document, the end of the document is also visible.

PRACTICE YOUR SKILLS

Use any combination of scrolling techniques to return to the beginning of the document.

EXAMINING PRINT OPTIONS AND PRINTING A DOCUMENT

As mentioned earlier, the procedure for printing a document is the same for virtually all Windows-based programs. In addition, some programs provide you with special printer setup options, which allow you to change the configuration of your printer, or even to change printers if there is more than one printer connected to your computer. (See your printer manual for information specific to your printer.)

To print a document:

- Choose *File, Print*.
- In the Print dialog box, change any options as desired (for example, the number of copies you wish to print).
- Click on *OK*.

If you have more than one printer connected to your computer, and wish to switch from one to another,

- Click on the *Setup* button in the Print dialog box to open the *Print Setup* dialog box.
- Select the desired printer in the *Printer* portion of the dialog box.
- Click on *OK* to return to the Print dialog box.

Let's examine some print options, and then print the LAOFFICE.WRI document:

1. Choose **File, Print...** to open the Print dialog box, shown in Figure 3.3.

Figure 3.3   **Print dialog box**

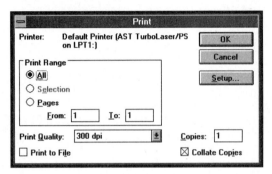

2. Examine the Print dialog box. It shows the type of printer that is connected to your computer and enables you to change several options related to printing. (Your printer selection may vary from the one shown in the following figures.) The *Copies* box, in the lower-right portion of the dialog box, allows you to specify how many copies of the document you wish to print. In the *Print Range* portion of the dialog box, you can specify whether you wish to print all of the pages in a document or a range of pages.

3. Click on **OK** to print the document. Compare your screen with Figure 3.4.

 THE PRINT MANAGER

When you print a document in Windows, the printing is actually handled by a separate program called *Print Manager*. Each time you send something to a printer—for example, a Write document—it becomes what is known as a *print job*. Print Manager runs in the background, feeding print jobs from programs to the printer. When there is a problem with a particular printer or print job, it is sometimes useful to run the Print Manager yourself. (The Print Manager is located in the Main group of the Windows Program Manager.)

Print jobs are listed in a queue displayed in the Print Manager window, in the order in which they were sent to the printer. It's important to note that closing the Print Manager cancels all pending print jobs, so remember to allow your job(s) to print before exiting the program.

Figure 3.4   **Printed LAOFFICE.WRI document**

> *FensterGlass, Ltd.*
> 25 Kensington Place
> Clifton, Bristol BS8 3AH
> United Kingdom
> 17 September 1992
>
> Ms. Lydia Epigone
> Tico Way Office Supply and Design
> 87963 Wilder Parkway Extension
> Bogalusa, LA 70427
>
> Dear Ms. Epigone:
>
> During the course of the last few weeks, we at FensterGlass have closed several contracts that will enable us to expand our staff by 25 employees. We plan to convert portions of our building's attic into office space in order to accommodate the new employees. The conversion is scheduled to be completed in less than 10 weeks. Therefore, I would ask that you have someone from your London bureau contact Thomas Terwilliger, our Office Environment Coordinator, as soon as possible with information regarding your office-design consulting services. Thom can be reached at extension 304.
>
> Thank you in advance for your prompt attention to this matter.
>
> Sincerely,
>
>
> Tad Fenster
> Vice President, International Sales
>
> TF:tef

Let's create a situation that prevents our document from printing, then we'll use the Print Manager to identify and correct the problem:

1. Turn off your printer, or take the printer off line.

2. Choose **File, Print** to open the Print dialog box.

3. Click on **OK**. Momentarily, the Write message box is displayed, stating that the document is now printing. The Cancel button allows you to cancel the printing process at this point. Then the Print Manager message box is displayed, stating that the printer is off line or not selected (see Figure 3.5).

Figure 3.5   **Printer off line or not selected message box**

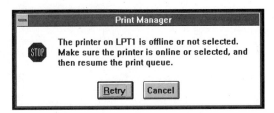

4. Click on **Cancel** to clear the message.

5. Press **Ctrl+Esc** to access the Task List.

6. Select **Print Manager** and click on **Switch To** (or double-click on **Print Manager**) to open the Print Manager. Notice the information in the Print Manager window, which states that the printer is stalled (see Figure 3.6).

Figure 3.6   **Diagnosing a stalled printer**

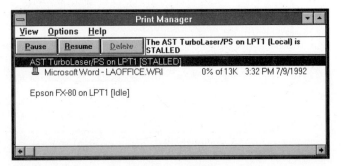

7. Minimize the Print Manager (click on the **Minimize** button) to keep the program running and return to the LAOFFICE.WRI document.

8. Choose **File, Print...** to send another copy of the document to the printer.

9. In the Print dialog box, click on **OK**. Once again, the Print Manager message box is displayed.

10. Click on **Cancel** to clear the message.

11. Display the Task List (press **Ctrl+Esc**).

12. Switch to the Print Manager (select **Print Manager**, if necessary, and click on **Switch To**).

13. Examine the print queue. There are now two print jobs waiting for the stalled printer.

14. Select **2 Write - LAOFFICE.WRI** (see Figure 3.7), and click on **Delete**. As a safeguard against accidentally deleting a print job, the Print Manager message box asks if you want to quit printing the document (see Figure 3.8).

Figure 3.7   **Selecting a print job for deletion**

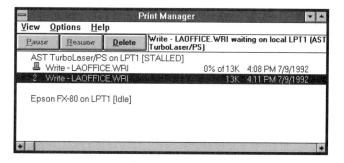

15. Click on **OK** to remove the print job from the print queue.

16. Turn your printer back on, or put the printer back on line.

17. Click on the name of your printer, which is displayed above your print job.

Figure 3.8   **Quit Printing message box**

18. Click on **Resume** to resume printing. The remaining print job is now being sent to the active printer.

19. Exit the Print Manager.

20. Exit the Write program.

APPLICATION AND SECONDARY WINDOWS

The main window that opens when you run a program is called the *application* window. The Program Manager, File Manager, Write, and Control Panel windows are all examples of application windows. In this book, for clarity and consistency, we refer to windows that appear within an application window as *secondary* windows.

There are many types of secondary windows. For example, group windows appear within Program Manager, and directory windows appear within File Manager. (In sophisticated Windows word processing programs and spreadsheet programs, the secondary windows are called document windows and worksheet windows, respectively.) Secondary windows share the application's menu bar. However, each window has its own Control menu.

Note: You should not confuse the term *application window* with the Applications group window. In fact, according to the definitions outlined above, the Applications group window is a secondary window, its related application window being the Program Manager window.

USING THE KEYBOARD TO OPEN AND CLOSE APPLICATION AND SECONDARY WINDOWS

In Chapter 1, you learned how to use the mouse to manipulate a window's Control menu and Control menu box. You can also use the keyboard to control application and secondary windows.

To open an application window's Control menu, press Alt+Space-bar; to close the Control menu, press Alt+F4. To open a secondary window's Control menu, press Alt+-; to close the Control menu, press Ctrl+F4.

To hide the menu, leaving the Control menu box selected, press the Esc key. To deselect the Control menu box, press Esc a second time.

Let's use the keyboard to compare application and secondary windows:

1. Close all group windows except the Main group window (open it, if it is closed).

2. Compare the Control menu boxes in the Main and Program Manager windows (see Figure 3.9). The Control menu box in the Main window contains a shorter bar than the one in the Program Manager window. The long bar represents the Spacebar on the keyboard; the short bar represents the - (hyphen or dash) key on the keyboard. These keys can be used with the Alt key to open the Control menus.

Figure 3.9   **Comparing Control menu boxes**

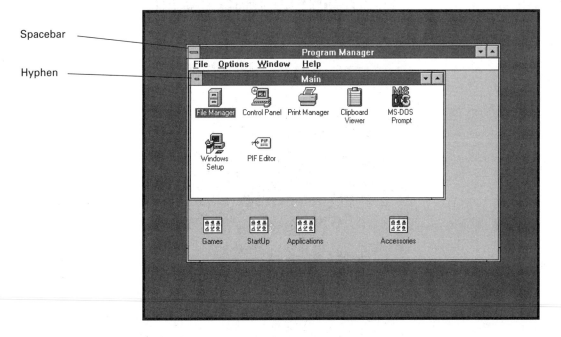

3. Examine the title bars in the Main and Program Manager windows. The Main window (the secondary window) is contained in the Program Manager window (the application window). Therefore, both windows are active.

4. Press **Alt+-** to open the Control menu for the Main window.

5. Examine the menu. Notice that the menu lists the shortcut for closing secondary windows, Ctrl+F4.

6. Press **Esc** to hide the menu options. Notice that the Control menu box appears darker than that of the Program Manager window, which means that the Control menu box is still selected.

7. Press **Esc** to deselect the menu.

8. Press **Ctrl+F4** to close the Main group window.

9. Press **Alt+Spacebar** to open the Control menu for the Program Manager window. Notice that the shortcut key for closing application windows, Alt+F4, is listed.

10. Press **Esc** twice to hide and deselect the Program Manager Control menu.

11. Press **Alt+F4** to close the Program Manager window. The Exit Windows dialog box is displayed.

12. Click on **Cancel** (or press the **Esc** key) to remain in Windows.

COPYING AND MOVING FILES

The Copy and Move procedures are two of the most commonly used procedures in Windows. You can copy one or more files or an entire directory to another directory or disk drive. Both of these procedures are quite similar. However, when you *copy* a file or directory, you create a *duplicate* of the file or directory; when you move a file or directory, you *move* it to its *new location*. So, the main difference between the two is that once you move a file, the file is removed from its original location (see Figure 3.10).

 COPYING A FILE

The File Manager makes it relatively easy to copy or move a file: Simply drag the file icon from one location to another. However, before you do so, you will need to perform a certain amount of setup work. Both the *source*—the location of the item you wish to copy, including the item itself—and the *destination*—the directory to which you wish to copy or move the item—must be visible within the File Manager window. Drive icons, directory icons, or directory windows can all represent the destination directory.

Figure 3.10   **Copy versus Move**

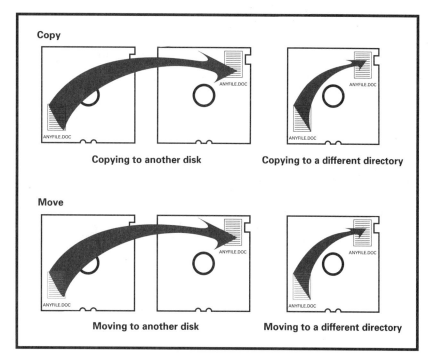

Copying to another disk	Copying to a different directory
Moving to another disk	Moving to a different directory

To create an additional directory window in File Manager, choose *Window, New Window*. To arrange directory windows, choose *Window, Tile*. The Window, Tile command provides a convenient shortcut for arranging multiple directory windows in File Manager. This command arranges all of the directory windows that are open within File Manager so that they are all the same size and entirely visible.

Note: The amount of space apportioned to each directory window depends on the number of open windows and the size of the File

Manager window. Therefore, before you use the Window, Tile command, make sure that the File Manager window is maximized.

To copy a file to a different directory, press and hold the Ctrl key, and drag the file icon from the source directory to the destination directory. To copy a file to another disk drive, drag the file icon from the source drive and directory to the destination drive.

Let's prepare to copy a single file by displaying both the source and destination directory windows, and then copy the file:

1. Open the Main group window.

2. Run File Manager. Drive C is currently selected.

3. Open the **windwork** directory folder (double-click on **windwork**).

4. In the directory window, select the **abc** directory.

5. Examine the contents list. The abc directory is empty. The Up icon represents the parent directory, windwork (see Figure 3.11).

Figure 3.11   **ABC directory window**

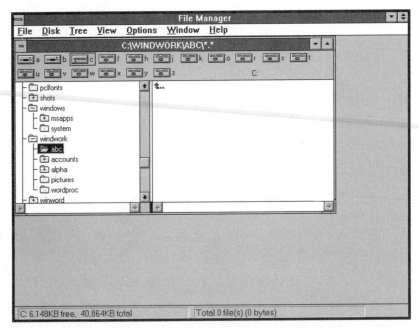

6. Choose **Window** to open the Window menu, shown in Figure 3.12. Notice the check mark next to the name of the current directory window.

7. Choose **New Window** to open a new directory window. There are now two C:\ABC directory windows.

8. In the new active window, open the **windwork** directory folder.

9. Observe the contents list. Notice the file *memo.txt.* Soon, you will copy this file to the ABC directory.

Figure 3.12   **Window menu**

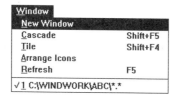

10. Choose **Window**. Notice that both directory windows are now listed at the bottom of the menu, and that the active one is checked (see Figure 3.13).

Figure 3.13   **Open directory windows listed in the Window menu**

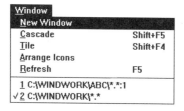

11. Choose **Tile** to display both directory windows at the same time.

12. Observe the two directory windows, shown in Figure 3.14. Notice that each window has its own title bar, Control menu box, and Maximize and Minimize buttons.

Figure 3.14   **Tiled directory windows**

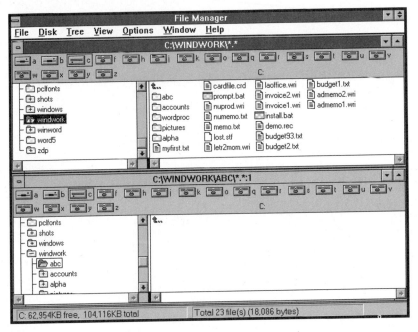

13. If necessary, scroll to verify that the directory names are visible in their respective windows.

14. If necessary, activate the C:\WINDWORK*.* window.

15. Press and hold the **Ctrl** key, and drag the **memo.txt** file icon to the C:\WINDWORK\ABC*.*:1 directory window. Do *not* release the mouse button until the icon is visible in the contents list of the destination directory window. The mouse pointer might change shape or appearance as you drag over different portions of the screen, indicating areas to which you can or cannot copy.

16. First release the mouse button, and then release the Ctrl key. The Confirm Mouse Operation message box is displayed, asking you to confirm the action (see Figure 3.15).

17. Click on **Yes**. The message *Copying...* is momentarily displayed.

18. Examine the directory windows. The memo.txt file has been copied to the C:\WINDWORK\ABC directory.

Figure 3.15   **Confirm copying message box**

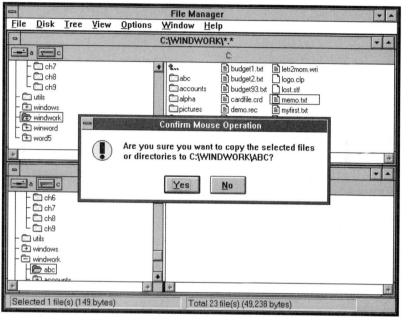

 MOVING A FILE

To move a file to a different directory on the same disk, drag the file icon from the source directory to the destination directory. To move a file to another disk drive, press and hold the Alt key, and drag the file icon from the source directory to the destination directory.

Let's display two new directory windows, and then move a file from one directory to the other:

1. Close the C:\WINDWORK\ABC*.* directory window (double-click on its **Control** menu box).

2. Choose **Window, New Window** to create a second window to view the files in another directory.

3. Select the **accounts** directory (a subdirectory of windwork).

4. Choose **Window, Tile** to tile the windows. Notice that, because the ACCOUNTS directory window was active, it is now positioned above the other window.

5. Examine the ACCOUNTS directory window. It contains a sub-directory folder, but no files.

6. In the C:\WINDWORK*.* directory window, display the sub-directories of windwork, if necessary, and double-click on the **wordproc** directory folder to display its contents. Compare your screen with Figure 3.16.

Figure 3.16   **ACCOUNTS and WORDPROC directory windows**

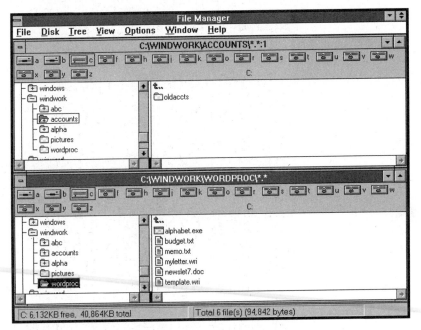

7. Drag the **budget.txt** file icon to the contents list of the ACCOUNTS directory window, and release the mouse button. The Confirm Mouse Operation message box asks for confirmation of the procedure (see Figure 3.17).

8. Click on **Yes**. The message *Moving...* is momentarily displayed.

9. Examine the two directory windows. The budget.txt file has been moved to the ACCOUNTS directory.

PRACTICE YOUR SKILLS

1. Open a third directory window.

2. Show the directory listing for drive C (your computer's hard disk).

3. Open the ABC directory window.

4. Tile the windows.

Figure 3.17   **Confirm moving message box**

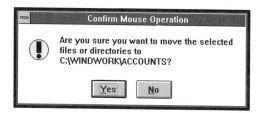

5. Change the ACCOUNTS directory window to display the contents of the WINDWORK directory.

6. Copy the **admemo1.wri** file from the WINDWORK directory to the ABC directory. Compare your screen with Figure 3.18.

7. Close the C:\WINDWORK\WORDPROC*.* directory window.

8. Tile the remaining windows.

COPYING A DIRECTORY

You will often need to copy all the files in a directory. You could accomplish this by copying one file at a time, until all the files were copied. However, if the directory contains more than a few files, this could take some time. The easiest and most efficient way to overcome this problem is by copying the entire directory. When you copy a directory, you copy all of the files *and* subdirectories contained in the directory. To take this to its extreme, if you want to copy the entire contents of a disk, you need only copy the disk's root directory, which can contain files and other directories, and *their* files and subdirectories, and so on.

The method for copying a directory is the same one you used to copy a file: Press and hold the Ctrl key, and drag the directory icon to the desired destination directory. To copy a directory to another disk drive, drag the directory icon from the source drive to the destination drive.

Figure 3.18   **Moved admemo1.wri file**

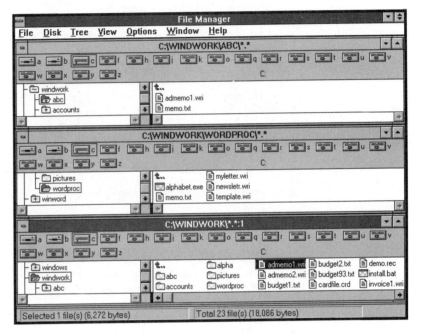

Let's copy the entire FILES directory to the ABC directory:

1. Change the WINDWORK directory window to display the contents of the FILES directory (a subdirectory of alpha).

2. Press and hold the **Ctrl** key, and drag the **files** directory icon from the FILES directory window to an empty space in the contents list of the ABC window.

3. Release the mouse button, and then release the **Ctrl** key. The Confirm Mouse Operation message box asks for confirmation.

4. Click on **Yes**.

5. Compare the contents lists of the two directory windows. The ABC directory now also contains the subdirectory folder named *files*.

6. In the ABC directory window, click on the **files** directory. Notice that the contents lists of the two directory windows are identical (see Figure 3.19).

Figure 3.19   **Copied directory**

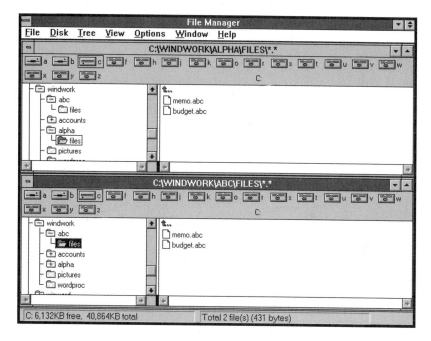

7. Choose **File, Exit** to exit File Manager.

8. Close the Main group window (double-click on the **Control** menu box, or press **Ctrl+F4**).

SUMMARY

In this chapter you learned how to scroll through a Write document. You examined some available printing options, and then printed a document. You learned how to open and close application and secondary windows by using the keyboard. Finally, you learned how to copy and move files, and how to copy a directory.

Here is a quick reference guide to the Windows features introduced in this chapter:

Desired Result	How to Do It
Scrolling	
Move up one line	Click on the **up scroll** arrow
Scroll up continuously, line by line	Click on and hold the **up scroll** arrow
Move down one line	Click on the **down scroll** arrow
Scroll down continuously, line by line	Cilck on and hold the **down scroll** arrow
Move up one screen of text	Click on the area **above** the scroll box, or press **PgUp**
Move down one screen of text	Click on the area **below** the scroll box, or press **PgDn**
Move to a specific location in the document	Drag the **scroll box** to a position in the scroll bar representing the relative desired position within the document
Move to the top (beginning) of the document	Drag the **scroll box** to the top of the scroll bar
Move to the bottom (end) of the document	Drag the **scroll box** to the bottom of the scroll bar
Move left	Click on the **left scroll** arrow, click in the area to the **left** of the scroll box, or drag the **scroll box** left
Move right	Click on the **right scroll** arrow, click in the area to the **right** of the scroll box, or drag the **scroll box** right
Print a document	Choose **File, Print**, change any options in the Print dialog box as desired, and click on **OK**

Desired Result	How to Do It
Open the Print Manager	Press **Ctrl+Esc**, select **Print Manager** from the Task List, and click on **Switch To**, or double-click on **Print Manager**
Delete a print job	In the Print Manager window, click on the print job you want to delete, press the **Del** key, and click on **OK**
Resume printing after the printer has stalled	Make sure the cause of the stall has been corrected, click on the printer name, directly above the print queue in the Print Manager window, and click on the **Resume** button

Control Windows Using the Keyboard

Open an application window's Control menu	Press **Alt+Spacebar**
Close an application window's Control menu	Press **Alt+F4**
Open a secondary window's Control menu	Press **Alt+-**
Close a secondary window's Control menu	Press **Ctrl+F4**
Hide a window's Control menu	Press **Esc**
Deselect the Control menu box	Press **Esc**
Open an additional directory window in File Manager	Choose **Window, New Window**
Tile windows	Choose **Window, Tile**

Desired Result	How to Do It
Copy a file to a different directory	Press and hold the **Ctrl** key, and drag the **file icon** from the source directory to the destination directory
Copy a file to another disk drive	Drag the **file icon** from the source drive and directory to the destination drive
Move a file to a different directory	Drag the **file icon** from the source directory to the destination directory
Move a file to another disk drive	Press and hold the **Alt** key, and drag the **file icon** from the source drive and directory to the destination drive
Copy a directory	Press and hold the **Ctrl** key, and drag the **directory icon** to the desired destination directory
Copy a directory to another disk drive	Drag the **directory icon** from the source drive to the destination drive

In the next chapter, you will learn how to use the Windows Paintbrush and Clipboard programs to create an illustration and then import it into your document.

If you need to break off here, please exit Windows. If you want to proceed directly to the next chapter, please do so now.

CHAPTER 4: CREATING AND IMPORTING TEXT AND GRAPHICS: PAINTBRUSH AND THE CLIPBOARD

Creating a Graphic with Paintbrush

Orientation to the Clipboard

Examining a Word Processing Document with Graphics

You have now learned about several programs that Windows offers: a couple that you can use to create text documents, one that controls aspects of the Windows environment, another that keeps time, and so on. Windows also comes with a program that enables you to create graphic images—for example, freehand or geometric drawings—and even import these images into a word processing program, such as Write.

To import a graphic image or any other kinds of data from one file or program to another, you can use one of Windows's most powerful features, the special area called the *Clipboard*. Windows enables you to copy or move information from one program to another program. When you instruct a program to, say, copy selected text, the copy is placed on the Clipboard. The copied information can then be pasted into another part of the document, to another file in the same program, or to another program.

When you're done working through this chapter, you will know

- How to use the Paintbrush program
- How to create a graphic drawing
- How to enter and format text in Paintbrush
- How to add a graphic border
- How to copy or move data to the Clipboard
- How to paste data from the Clipboard to another file
- How to use the Clipboard to merge different types of information into one document

CREATING A GRAPHIC WITH PAINTBRUSH

You can use Paintbrush to create simple or complex color illustrations. When you "paint" using Paintbrush, the image is actually drawn on screen, in the Paintbrush program window. No painting environment would be complete without painting tools such as a brush, roller, and palette of paints, and Paintbrush provides all the tools necessary to create some quite sophisticated illustrations. The Paintbrush window and its components are shown in Figure 4.1.

The main parts of the Paintbrush window are the *Drawing area,* the *Tool bar,* the *Linesize box,* and the *Palette.* To create and edit an image, simply select a tool from the tool bar, and then use the mouse to click on the place in the drawing area where you want to begin using the tool. Table 4.1 describes in brief what each tool is used for.

Table 4.1　　**Description of the Paintbrush Tools**

Tool	Use
Scissors and Pick	Cutting tools that select a portion of a picture for moving, copying, or formatting; the Scissors can define irregular shapes, and the Pick defines rectangular areas
Airbrush	Sprays paint in dots to create a smudge effect in the foreground color

Figure 4.1   **Paintbrush window**

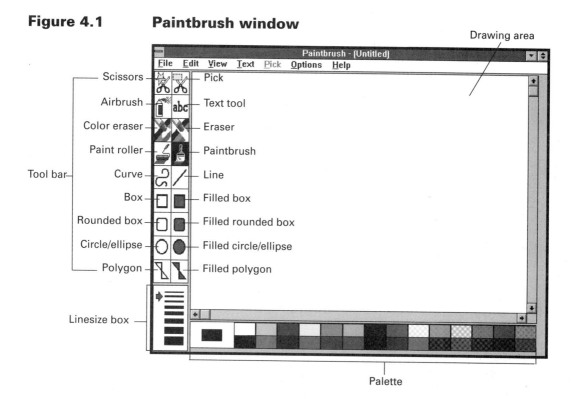

Table 4.1   **(continued)**

Tool	Use
Text tool	Adds text labels or captions to an image
Color eraser and Eraser	Erase a portion of a drawing
Paint roller	Spreads paint over a selected area
Paintbrush	Paints freehand shapes and lines
Curve	Draws curved lines in a specific line width
Line	Draws straight lines
Boxes	Create hollow or filled boxes with square or rounded corners

Table 4.1   **(continued)**

Tool	Use
Circle/ellipse	Create hollow or filled circles and ovals
Polygon tools	Create hollow or filled polygons (geometric shapes with three or more sides)

Let's run the Paintbrush program, and then examine the elements of the Paintbrush window:

1. Open the Accessories group window.

2. Run the **Paintbrush** program (double-click on the **Paintbrush** icon, shown highlighted in Figure 4.2).

Figure 4.2   **Paintbrush program icon**

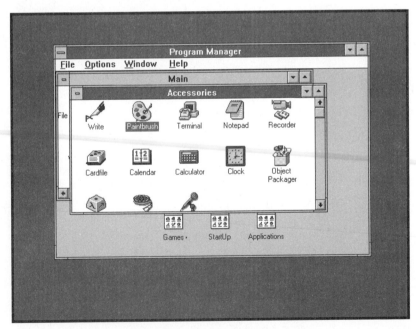

3. Maximize the window, and then compare your screen with Figure 4.1.

4. Examine the Paintbrush program window. Notice that it contains elements common to those of other Windows programs: the Control menu box, the File and Edit menus, scroll bars, the title bar, and the Minimize and Restore buttons.

5. Observe the tool bar along the left border of the window (see Figure 4.1).

6. Click on the **Line** tool to select it. The Line tool icon darkens, indicating that you are in line-drawing mode (see Figure 4.3).

Figure 4.3   **Selected Line tool**

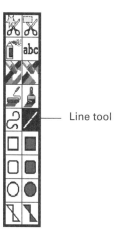 —— Line tool

7. Position the mouse pointer over the drawing area (the large, blank area to the right of the tool bar), and observe the mouse pointer. It is shaped like a cross hair or a large plus sign.

8. Position the mouse pointer near the upper-left corner of the drawing area. Drag to the lower-right corner of the drawing area to paint a bold diagonal line, shown in Figure 4.4.

9. Select the **Paintbrush** tool (see Figure 4.5).

10. Position the mouse pointer over the drawing area, and observe the mouse pointer. It appears as a dot.

11. Position the mouse pointer in the top center portion of the drawing area.

Figure 4.4   **Painting a straight line**

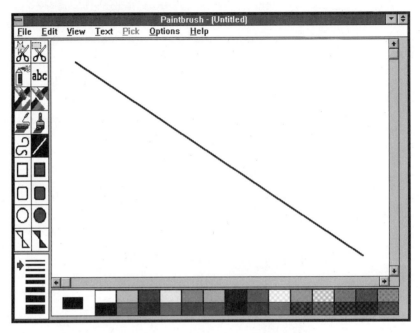

Figure 4.5   **Selected Paintbrush tool**

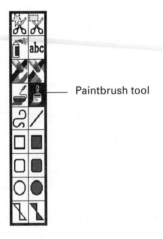

Paintbrush tool

12. Drag the mouse left and right across the drawing area, moving downward to create a wavy or zigzag line. Notice that the line looks as though you were using a paintbrush or felt-tip marker (see Figure 4.6).

Figure 4.6   **Drawing freehand using the Paintbrush tool**

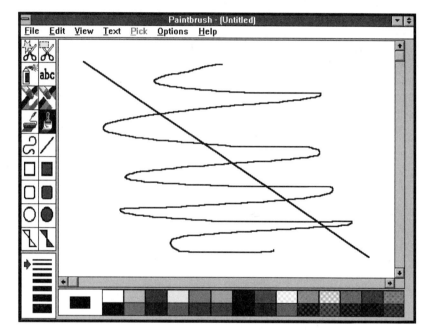

 ENTERING AND CHANGING THE APPEARANCE OF TEXT

In many Windows applications you can specify a font (typeface) and a size for text you have typed. The height of text characters is measured in *points*. There are 72 points in one inch, so text that is 36 points will be about one-half inch tall. Many programs also allow you to specify type *styles* for text. Typical styles include bold, italics, and underlining.

When you add text in Paintbrush, you can change the font, size, and style settings only until you do any of the following:

• Select a tool

• Use a scroll bar

- Open another application
- Move the insertion point by clicking
- Change the window's size

Once you perform any of these actions, the text's paint has "dried," and you can change the area where the paint has been applied only by erasing it and starting over.

Let's enter text in our drawing, and then change its appearance:

1. Select the **Text** tool, which is shown selected in Figure 4.7.

Figure 4.7   **Selected Text tool**

Text tool

2. Position the mouse pointer over the drawing area, and observe the mouse pointer. It is shaped like an I-beam.

3. Click in the lower-left corner of the drawing area to place the insertion point.

4. Type your name. After you have finished typing your name, do *not* move the insertion point. Notice that your name appears in a plain typeface.

5. Choose **Text** to open the Text menu, shown in Figure 4.8. Notice that this menu contains some of the same options as the Write program's Character menu (see Chapter 3).

Figure 4.8   **Text menu**

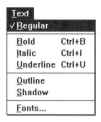

6. Choose **Fonts** to open the Font dialog box, shown in Figure 4.9. The Font box, near the upper-left corner of the dialog box, shows the current font, while the Font list box, directly below it, lists all the available fonts. The Font Style box lists available text styles. The Size box lists available type sizes. The Effects box allows you to add features such as Strikeout, which places a horizontal line through text, and underlining. The Sample box displays a sample of what the text will look like as you change or add features.

Figure 4.9   **Font dialog box**

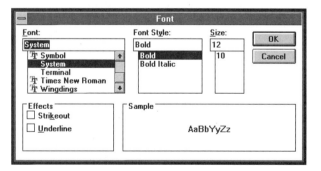

7. Set the Font to **Roman** (scroll in the Font list box and click on **Roman**). Notice that this particular font offers more font styles and sizes.

8. Set the Size to **18**. Note how the text will look in the Sample box. Compare your screen with Figure 4.10.

9. Click on **OK** to exit the dialog box and change the appearance of the text.

Figure 4.10   **Changed settings in the Font dialog box**

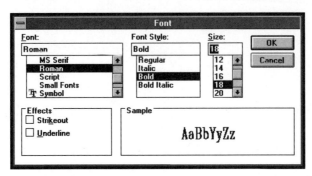

10. Choose **File, New**. Because you can have only one Paintbrush file open at a time, a prompt appears that reminds you to save your work.

11. Click on **No** to open a blank drawing without saving the current one.

PRACTICE YOUR SKILLS

1. Experiment with Paintbrush's tools. Try other tools, such as the Airbrush and the Eraser.

2. Choose **File, New** to erase the screen (do not save the "current image").

 ADDING A BORDER AROUND THE GRAPHIC

You've seen that to insert any graphic object in the drawing area, you must specify where you want the object to appear. You accomplish this by clicking in the location where you wish to begin drawing or typing text. When you use the Box and Circle tools, you also must drag from the object's starting point to its endpoint, as you did when you used the Line tool. When you release the mouse button, the object is "painted" at that location.

Let's enter text, change its appearance, and then add a rectangular border around it:

1. Select the **Text** tool.

2. Place the insertion point near the left border of the drawing area, about halfway down.

3. Type **FensterGlass, Inc.**

4. Examine the text you just typed. The text appears in the font and style you last selected.

5. Choose **Text**, **Fonts** to open the Font dialog box.

6. Choose **Roman**, if necessary, to change the text to the Roman font.

7. Change the Font Style to **Italic**.

8. Change the Size to **48**. (A text height of 48 points is equivalent to two-thirds of an inch.) Compare your screen with Figure 4.11.

Figure 4.11   **Changing text appearance to Roman, Italic, 48 points**

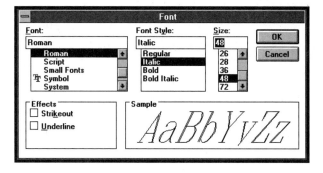

9. Click on **OK** and compare your screen with Figure 4.12.

10. Select the **Box** tool, shown selected in Figure 4.13.

11. Position the mouse pointer below and to the left of the text. This is where you will begin to draw the box, which will enclose the text.

12. Drag upward to just above and to the right of the text, until the outline forms a border around the text.

13. When you are satisfied with the size of the border, release the mouse button, and compare your screen with Figure 4.14.

Figure 4.12   **Text with applied font, style, and size**

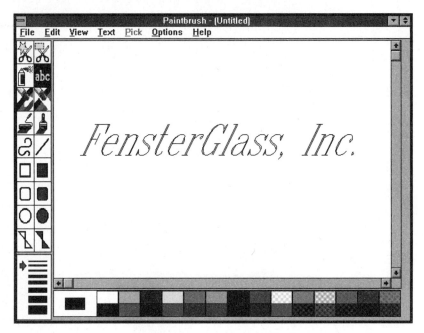

Figure 4.13   **Selected Box tool**

Box tool ———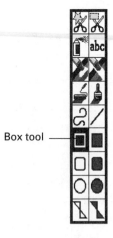

Figure 4.14 **Added graphic border**

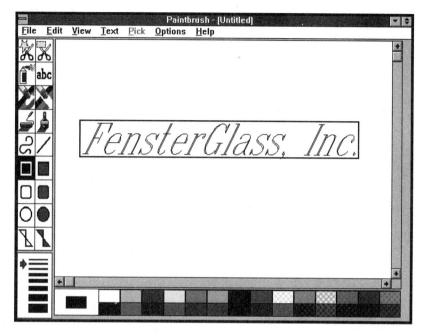

14. Keep this graphic on the screen to be used in the Clipboard exercise that follows.

ORIENTATION TO THE CLIPBOARD

The Clipboard is actually a sophisticated program, though you don't need to run it in the same way you would run a program such as File Manager or Notepad. To send information to the Clipboard, you must first select the data. Then choose Edit to open the menu. The Edit menu is one of the menus common to almost every Windows program. The three most commonly used Edit menu options are *Cut, Copy,* and *Paste.* For example, the Paintbrush Edit menu is shown in Figure 4.15.

Edit, Cut *removes* the selected data from the file you are working in and places it on the Clipboard. Edit, Copy *copies* the selected data to the Clipboard, keeping the original intact. Edit, Paste places a copy of the Clipboard contents at the position of the insertion point.

Figure 4.15   **Paintbrush Edit menu**

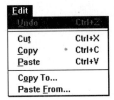

Note: The Clipboard serves as a *temporary* storage area for the information you are copying or moving. Data moved or copied to the Clipboard will remain there only until the next time you use Edit, Cut or Edit, Copy—or until you exit Windows.

 MOVING TEXT OR A GRAPHIC TO THE CLIPBOARD

To move or copy text or a graphic to the Clipboard: Select the text or graphic that you want to move or duplicate, then choose Edit, Cut if you wish to move the selection or Edit, Copy if you wish to duplicate it.

Let's select the FensterGlass, Inc. graphic we worked on earlier (see Figure 4.14) and move it to the Clipboard:

1. Select the **Pick** tool (the right Scissors tool, which appears to be cutting out a rectangle; see Figure 4.16).

Figure 4.16   **Selected Pick tool**

Pick tool

2. Drag from just below and to the left of the rectangle to just above and to the right of the rectangle. The graphic (the FensterGlass logo) is selected, as indicated by the dashed rectangle that encloses it (see Figure 4.17).

Figure 4.17   **Selected graphic**

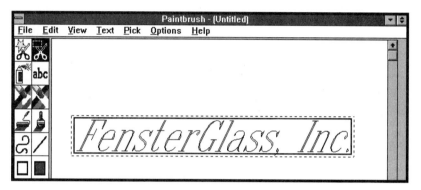

3. Choose **Edit**, **Cut**. The logo is no longer visible; it has been moved to the Clipboard.

 PASTING TEXT OR A GRAPHIC FROM THE CLIPBOARD

Once you have moved or copied data to the Clipboard, you can then paste it to the desired location. To paste the Clipboard contents, first display the desired destination. If the desired destination is another file using the same program, you will need to open that file. If the destination is a file using another program, you will need to run that program, and then open the appropriate file. Next, place the insertion point where you want the Clipboard contents pasted. Then choose Edit, Paste.

Note: When you paste the Clipboard's contents, they are not removed from the Clipboard. Actually, only a copy of the Clipboard contents is pasted to the destination. This means that you can continue pasting copies of these same contents to as many different locations as you desire. However, remember that the Clipboard's contents are lost the next time you choose Edit, Cut or Edit, Copy, or when you exit Windows.

Let's open a graphic file created in Paintbrush, and then we'll paste the contents of the Clipboard to the existing graphic:

1. Choose **File**, **Open**. Because you can have only one Paintbrush file open at a time, a prompt appears as a reminder to save your work.

2. Click on **No**. Since the drawing is currently blank—its contents were moved to the Clipboard—there is no reason to save it.

3. In the Open dialog box, change the Directories line to display **c:\windwork\pictures** (double-click on **c:**, double-click on **windwork**, and double-click on **pictures**). Notice that the directory contains two graphic files, denoted by the .BMP file-name extension (see Figure 4.18). Just as the Write program recognizes its files by the .WRI extension, so too Paintbrush uses the .BMP extension to recognize its files.

Figure 4.18   **Contents of PICTURES directory**

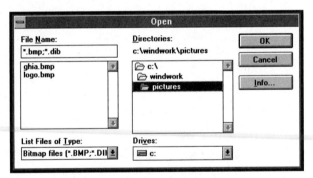

4. Open the **ghia.bmp** file (select the file name, and click on **OK**; or double-click on the file name). The graphic is now displayed in the drawing area.

5. Choose **Edit**, **Paste** to paste the Clipboard's contents into the document. The logo automatically appears at the top of the drawing area. Notice that it is surrounded by a dashed rectangle, indicating that the logo can be dragged to a different location. In this case, however, it won't be necessary to move the logo.

6. Position the mouse pointer on a blank portion of the drawing area, and click to deselect the pasted logo. Compare your screen with Figure 4.19.

Figure 4.19 **Graphic with logo pasted from the Clipboard**

7. Choose **File, Save As** to save the graphic file under a new name.

8. Type **mylogo** to name the file, and click on **OK**. The file will be saved to the PICTURES directory.

9. Examine the title bar. It shows that the graphic is saved under the file name MYLOGO.BMP. Because no file-name extension was specified, Paintbrush automatically added the .BMP extension.

10. Exit the Paintbrush program and close the Accessories window.

EXAMINING THE CONTENTS OF THE CLIPBOARD

There will be times when you will want to examine the contents of the Clipboard. Normally, the contents of the Clipboard are not visible; however, you can view them by running the Clipboard Viewer, a program that resides in the Main group. While the contents of the Clipboard are stored there only temporarily, you can use the Clipboard Viewer to save the contents to a file. (You'll learn more about the Clipboard Viewer in Chapter 8.)

Let's use the Clipboard Viewer to examine the Clipboard contents:

1. Open the **Main** group window, if necessary.

2. Run the Clipboard Viewer program (double-click on the **Clipboard Viewer** icon, shown selected in Figure 4.20).

Figure 4.20   **Selected Clipboard Viewer program icon**

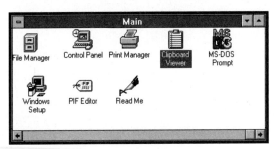

3. Maximize the Clipboard Viewer window.

4. Examine the contents of the window (see Figure 4.21). A copy of the logo remains in the Clipboard. As long as the logo remains on the Clipboard, it can be pasted into another file.

5. Exit the Clipboard Viewer, and close the Main group window.

EXAMINING A WORD PROCESSING DOCUMENT WITH GRAPHICS

Thus far, you've used the Clipboard to transfer data from one file to another within the same program. However, you can also import data from one program to another. This is one of Clipboard's handiest features. For example, you can copy a graphic created in Paintbrush to a word processing document created in Write. Clearly, the benefit of having this ability is that you can use each program to its maximum advantage, and then combine those advantages into one product. (You'll learn more about importing graphics to a word processing document in Chapter 8.)

Figure 4.21   **Logo in Clipboard Viewer window**

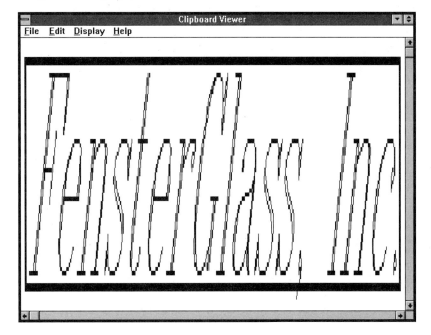

You can also use the Clipboard to copy information from non-Windows programs (programs without the capability to run in the Windows environment). You'll learn about this feature in Chapter 9.

Let's open a document created using the Write program, with graphics created in and imported from Paintbrush:

1. Run the Write program (in the Accessories group), and maximize its window.

2. Choose **File, Open**.

3. In the Open dialog box, change the Directories line to **c:\windwork\wordproc**.

4. Open the **newsletr.wri** file.

5. Scroll in the document to examine the entire company newsletter (use PgDn or the scroll bars). Two graphics have been brought into this document from Paintbrush: the newsletter title, *Clear Perspectives,* and the advertisement to which you added the logo earlier.

6. If your printer has graphics capability, print the document (choose **File**, **Print** and click on **OK**). The printed document is shown in Figure 4.22.

7. Exit the Write program and close the Accessories group window.

SUMMARY

In this chapter you learned how to use the Paintbrush program to create a drawing. You also learned how to insert text in your drawing, and then change its appearance. You learned how to add a border around text in a graphic. You then learned how to move data to the Clipboard, and paste it from the Clipboard to another file. You also saw how the Clipboard can be used to merge different types of information into one document.

Here is a quick reference guide to the Windows features introduced in this chapter:

Desired Result	How to Do It
Run the Paintbrush program	Double-click on the **Paintbrush** program icon
Select a tool from the tool bar	Click on the desired tool
Use a selected tool	Click on the portion of the drawing area where you wish to begin using the tool, click and drag from that point to draw, release the mouse button when desired
Use the Line, Box, or Circle tools	Select the desired tool, click in the drawing area where you wish to begin using the tool, drag until you reach the desired endpoint, release the mouse button
Use the text tool	Click in the drawing area where you wish to begin typing text, begin typing

Figure 4.22   **Printed NEWSLETR.WRI document**

CLEAR
PERSPECTIVES

A publication for the employees of FensterGlass, Incorporated

As fall arrives, it is time to review FensterGlass's progress over the past nine months. As always, there are many changes in the wind. Some of our old friends have left FensterGlass after many years of service. While we miss them, let's offer a warm welcome to all our new employees.

Sales are up from last year. Sales of our traditional line of bay and bow windows in the second quarter of this year were phenomenal. This year's sales represented a 54% increase over last year. Overseas sales accounted for 12% of the total volume; this is up from 6% last year. **Byron Williams,** our new Director of International Markets, has really turned things around. We look to the international market as next year's biggest growth market.

The housing industry grew as forecasted in our yearly outlook. Because of the industry's growth, the demand for our products increased. Our new synthetic-materials window frames will be introduced next month as the *TerraVista* product line. *TerraVista,* our first product line using the new *interLoc* feature, is the brainchild of **Ashweta Thomas,** Director of Research and Development.

The potential for significant new revenues comes from a new market, the automobile industry. Sales to the European automobile industry increased our third-quarter revenue dramatically. Domestic sales will begin next quarter with the introduction of the *Classical Glass* campaign. The ad is pictured below.

Introduces the Classical Glass series of automotive glass...

Our replacement glass is a clear improvement!

Figure 4.22   **(continued)**

Gordon Silverstein, Director of Automotive Markets, predicts huge growth in that market next year, when we become an original equipment manufacturer. Last month, we signed an agreement with Macco Plastics that will make us the nation's largest producer of automotive safety glass.

New accounting methods have been implemented by **Laurie Lopez,** who in February took over the position of Senior Accountant. We now have tighter control over production expenses, and we are better able to track profits and losses. Accounting's computer network will soon be expanded through a satellite connection to include the new Louisiana office. This will further increase the efficiency of our accounting system.

Since the restructuring announced last year, we have streamlined production systems. The manufacturing facility was successfully relocated to Bogalusa under the direction of Production Manager **Mark Lindham.** The California group has cut the defect ratio on all the product lines. At the next Sales Meeting in Cancun, **Larry Neesan** and **Roberta Bondello** will present a report on how they have accomplished these outstanding results. Also at that meeting, **Dom Fantagrossa** will present an interesting demonstration of computer-control systems. His Nashville group has been running a computer-controlled manufacturing line using laser beams to measure warp tolerances.

It has been an impressive year with many changes. You should be proud of what you have done. KEEP UP THE GOOD WORK!

Desired Result	How to Do It
Change the appearance of text	After you have entered text, and without having performed any other operation, choose **Text**, **Fonts**; select the desired Font, Font Style, and Size; click on **OK**
Open a new Paintbrush drawing area	Choose **File**, **New**
Move data to the Clipboard	Select the data that you want to move, choose **Edit**, **Cut**
Copy data to the Clipboard	Select the data that you want to copy, choose **Edit**, **Copy**
Paste data from the Clipboard	Once you have moved or copied the selected data to the Clipboard, open the file that represents the desired destination, if necessary; place the insertion point where you want the Clipboard contents to be pasted; choose **Edit**, **Paste**

In the next chapter, you'll learn some advanced file-management techniques, such as moving, copying, and deleting *groups* of files.

If you need to break off here, please exit Windows. If you want to proceed directly to the next chapter, please do so now.

CHAPTER 5:
ADDITIONAL
FILE-MANAGEMENT
TECHNIQUES

Preparing a Floppy
Disk for Use

Working with
Directories

Moving and
Copying Groups
of Files

Deleting Files

In Chapter 3 you learned the basics of file management using the Windows File Manager program. This chapter reinforces those techniques, while providing you with more powerful procedures for managing your personal computer files.

When you're done working through this chapter, you will know

- How to prepare a floppy disk for use

- How to create directories and organize files on a disk

- How to copy or move more than one file at a time

- How to delete single or multiple files

PREPARING A FLOPPY DISK FOR USE

When you purchase disks, they often are not ready to be used. Different kinds of computers use the same kinds of disks, but they do not all use the same operating system. Your computer's operating system ultimately determines how the computer organizes the information on a disk. You prepare disks for use by a process known as *formatting.*

It's important to note that formatting a disk erases any information that the disk may already contain. Therefore, before you decide to format a previously used disk, make sure that it does not contain information that you want to save.

To format a disk:

- Run the File Manager (located in the Main program group).

- Insert the disk into a disk drive (your computer may have one or more floppy-disk drives).

- Choose *Disk, Format Disk.*

- If you have more than one floppy-disk drive, select the drive that contains the disk (typically drive A or B).

- Select the desired disk capacity.

- Click on *OK.*

 DISK AND DRIVE CAPACITIES

Standard floppy disks come in one of two sizes, 5¼-inch and 3½-inch. Both 5¼-inch and 3½-inch disks are manufactured to hold different maximum amounts of information. The maximum amount of information that a disk can hold is known as the disk's *capacity.* Disk capacity is measured in *bytes,* a unit of measure roughly equal to one character of text. For example, a high-capacity 3½-inch disk has the potential to hold about 1.4 million bytes, or 1.4 *megabytes (Mb),* of information.

The actual capacity of a disk is determined when the disk is formatted. At the point when you specify the disk capacity, Windows will suggest a disk capacity. The program automatically assumes that you want to format the disk to the maximum capacity allowable by your computer's drive. Windows obtains this information by "scanning" the drive.

The type of disk drive you use affects the way you can format disks. Disk drives are manufactured in the same standard sizes and capacities as floppy disks. Low-capacity drives can format only low-capacity disks, but high-capacity drives can format either high- or low-capacity disks. You can use a low-capacity disk in a high-capacity drive, but you cannot use a high-capacity disk in a low-capacity drive.

Note: As a rule, you should always format disks to the capacity indicated by the disk manufacturer.

Let's format a disk:

1. Open the **Main** group window, if necessary.

2. Run the **File Manager** program.

3. If more than one directory window is open, close all but one, and then maximize the remaining window.

4. Insert a new disk in drive A of your computer (or insert a used disk that contains files you no longer need).

5. Click on the **C** drive icon.

6. Choose **Disk, Format Disk** to open the Format Disk dialog box (see Figure 5.1).

7. If you have more than one floppy-disk drive, choose drive A.

8. Click on **OK**. The Confirm Format Disk message box asks for confirmation that you want to format the disk in drive A (see Figure 5.2).

9. Click on **Yes**. The message

   ```
   Now formatting disk
   ```

   is displayed during formatting. After formatting is completed, the Format Complete message box displays the disk capacity and the amount of disk space available, and asks if you'd like to format another disk (see Figure 5.3).

Figure 5.1   **Format Disk dialog box**

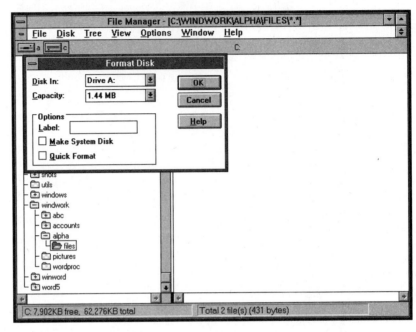

Figure 5.2   **Confirm Format Disk message box**

Figure 5.3   **Format Complete message box**

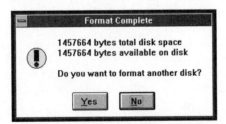

10. Click on **No**.

11. Click on the **A** drive icon to show the contents of the newly for-matted floppy disk. In the directory tree window, only the root directory is displayed, as the disk contains no other directories (see Figure 5.4). The contents list displays the message

   No files found.

Later, we'll use this disk to practice file-management tasks.

Figure 5.4   **Drive A root-directory window**

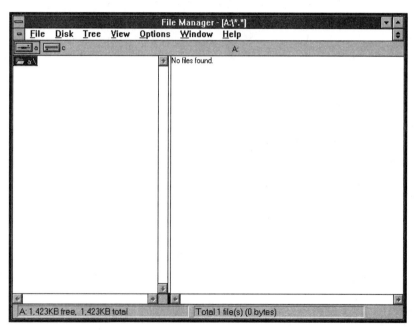

WORKING WITH DIRECTORIES

When you format a disk by using the Disk, Format Disk command, the disk contains only the root directory. You must create any other directories that you want to use.

When you create directories, you might want to create a system similar to one that you would use in a filing cabinet. For example, rather than storing all of your letters in one folder, and all of your contracts in another folder, you might have a folder for each account you work with. Each folder could contain all of the contracts, letters, invoices, and other documents associated with a particular client.

You should consider setting up a similar filing system on your disks by creating a logical directory structure. Using the above example, you might create a directory named ACCOUNTS, and then create subdirectories representing each account. Each subdirectory would then contain information relevant to that account.

CREATING AND NAMING A DIRECTORY

To create a directory in File Manager:

- In the directory tree, select the directory within which you want to create the new directory.

- Choose *File, Create Directory*.

- In the Create Directory dialog box, type the directory name.

- Click on *OK*.

When you name a directory, it is a good idea to follow the same conventions that you use for naming files:

- Directory names may contain up to eight characters.

- Directory names may include letters, numbers, or a combination of both. Case is not significant.

- Directory names may not contain spaces or punctuation marks (except -, _ , and .).

- Directory names should be descriptive, so that their names reflect their contents.

- Directory names should be unique.

Note: It is possible for two or more directories to have the same name, as long as they do not share the same parent directory. However, this can lead to confusion.

Let's create two new directories:

1. Choose **File, Create Directory** to open the Create Directory dialog box.

2. Type **mydir**, and compare your screen with Figure 5.5.

3. Click on **OK**.

Figure 5.5   **Create Directory dialog box**

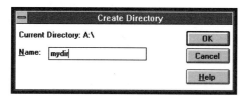

4. Examine the directory tree. Your directory has been added to the tree. Because the root directory is currently selected, the MYDIR directory is listed as its contents (see Figure 5.6).

Figure 5.6   **Newly created MYDIR directory**

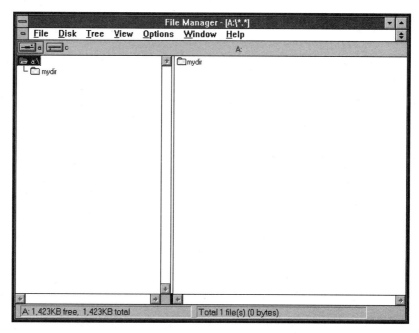

5. Select the **mydir** directory in the directory tree window (click on **mydir**).

6. Choose **File, Create Directory** to open the Create Directory dialog box.

7. Type **mysubdir** to name the directory. Compare your screen with Figure 5.7.

Figure 5.7   **Creating a subdirectory**

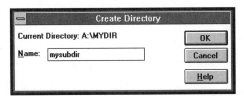

8. Click on **OK**. You can see that the new directory MYSUBDIR is actually a subdirectory of MYDIR. Because MYDIR is currently selected, MYSUBDIR is shown as its contents in the contents list (see Figure 5.8).

Figure 5.8   **Newly created directory and subdirectory**

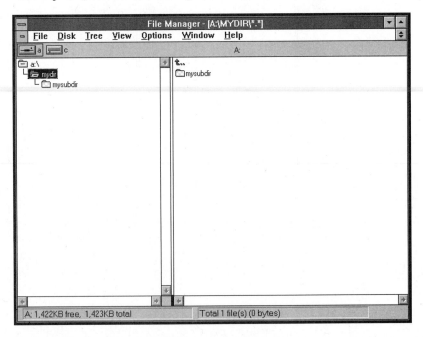

MOVING AND COPYING GROUPS OF FILES

Using File Manager, you can copy or move more than one file at a time by using the same techniques that you use to copy or move a single file (see Chapter 3). The only difference between working with single files or multiple files is the number of files that you select.

When you select files to be copied or moved, you can include directories in the selection. Then the directories will be copied or moved along with the files. Note that all files and subdirectories contained in selected directories will be included in the operation. For this reason, it is important to remember that if you wish to move or copy *only* files, you should not include any directories in your selection.

SELECTING MULTIPLE FILES

To select multiple files in the File Manager directory window:

- Click on one of the files that you want to select.
- Press and hold the Ctrl key, and then click on each of the other files that you want to select.

To select multiple contiguous files:

- Click on the first file—the leftmost and uppermost—of the contiguous group that you want to select.
- Press and hold the *Shift* key, and then click on the last file in the group that you want to select.

MOVING A GROUP OF FILES

To move a selected group of files to a different directory on the *same* disk:

- Display the destination directory window.
- Drag any one of the selected file icons from the source directory to the destination directory.

To move the group of selected files to a *different* disk:

- Display the window of the destination drive and directory.
- Press and hold the *Alt* key, and drag any one of the selected file icons to the destination drive and directory.

COPYING A GROUP OF FILES

To copy a selected group of files to a different directory on the *same* disk:

- Display the destination directory window.

- Press and hold the *Ctrl* key, and drag any one of the selected file icons from the source directory to the destination directory.

To copy the group of selected files to a *different* disk:

- Display the window of the destination drive and directory.

- Drag any one of the selected file icons to the destination drive and directory.

Let's select a group of files. Then we'll copy the group of files from a directory on our hard disk to one of the new directories we just created on our floppy disk:

1. Open a new window (choose **Window, New Window**).

2. Click on the **C** drive icon to display the directory tree of drive C.

3. Click on the **wordproc** directory (a subdirectory of windwork). The contents list shows that the WORDPROC directory contains five files (see Figure 5.9).

4. Click on **myletter.wri** to select it.

5. Press and hold the **Shift** key, and click on **template.wri** to select the three contiguous files, from myletter.wri to template.wri. Notice that the newsletr.wri file is now also selected.

6. Click on **alphabet.exe**. Notice that this file is now selected, but the three files you selected in steps 4 and 5 are no longer selected. When you select a single file by clicking on it, the existing selection is deselected.

7. Click on **myletter.wri** to select it.

8. Press and hold the **Shift** key, and click on **template.wri** to select all of the files from myletter.wri to template.wri.

9. This time, press and hold the **Ctrl** key, and then click on **alphabet.exe**. All four files are now selected.

10. Tile the windows (choose **Window, Tile**), and compare your screen with Figure 5.10.

Figure 5.9   **Contents of WORDPROC directory**

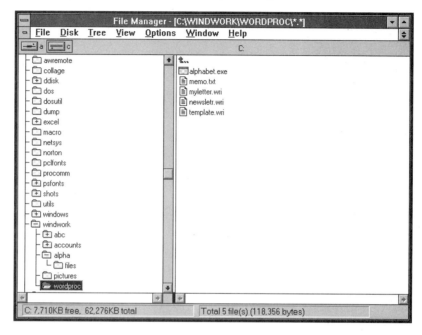

11. Point at any one of the selected files.

12. Drag the selected files to the contents list of the MYDIR directory window. The mouse pointer will change to a stack of papers as you drag. The Confirm Mouse Operation message box asks you to confirm the procedure (see Figure 5.11).

13. Click on **Yes**. The Copying... message box will be momentarily displayed.

14. Examine the contents list of the MYDIR directory window. The files have all been copied.

15. Click on the **a:** folder icon to open the root directory.

16. In the C:\WINDWORK\WORDPROC directory window, drag the **wordproc** folder icon to the a:\ folder icon. You can drag files to a folder icon or to a drive icon.

17. Click on **Yes** to confirm the operation. The C:\WINDWORK\-WORDPROC directory and its contents have been copied to the A:\ directory. Compare your screen with Figure 5.12.

Figure 5.10   **Selected group of files**

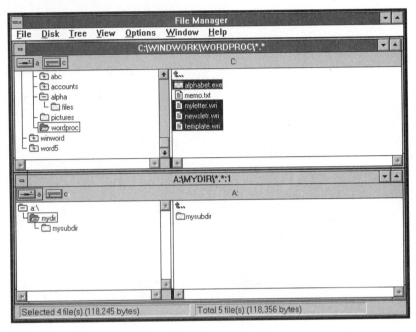

Figure 5.11   **Confirm Mouse Operation message box**

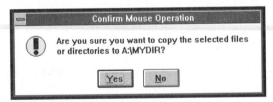

DELETING FILES

Just as it is sometimes necessary to remove old, unneeded, or duplicate files from an office filing system, it is sometimes necessary to delete files from a computer filing system. In Windows's File Manager, you can delete one file at a time, or you can select many files or directories and delete them all at once.

Figure 5.12   **Copied WORDPROC directory**

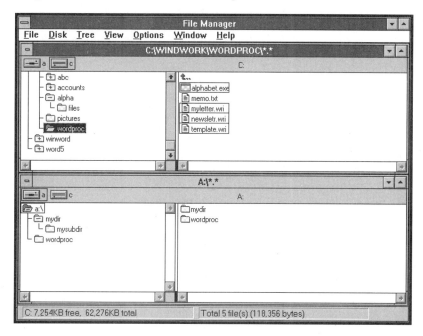

DELETING A SINGLE FILE

To delete a single file:

- Select the file you want to delete.

- Choose *File, Delete* or press the *Delete* key.

- In the Delete message box, click on *OK.*

- When prompted for the second time, click on *Yes.*

Let's delete a file:

1. In the A:\ directory window, select the **wordproc** directory.

2. In the contents list of the A:\WORDPROC directory window, select **alphabet.exe**.

3. Choose **File, Delete**. The Delete message box asks for confirmation (see Figure 5.13).

4. Click on **OK**. For the second time, you are asked to confirm the deletion.

Figure 5.13   **Delete message box**

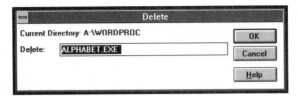

5. Click on **Yes** to delete the file.

6. Examine the A:\WORDPROC directory listing. The alphabet.exe file has been deleted.

PRACTICE YOUR SKILLS

In the A:\WORDPROC directory, delete the **memo.txt** file, and then compare your screen with Figure 5.14.

Figure 5.14   **Remaining contents of the A:\WORDPROC directory**

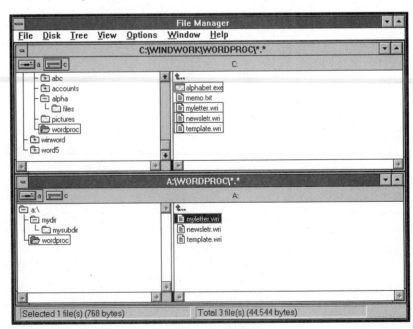

DELETING MULTIPLE FILES

You follow the same procedure for deleting a group of files as you used to delete a single file. The only difference is that you must first select all the files you wish to delete.

To select all the files in a directory:

- Make sure the directory icon is selected in the directory tree window.

- Choose *File, Select Files.*

- Click on *Select.*

- Click on *Close.*

You have seen that when you delete a file, the program twice asks you to confirm that you do indeed want to delete the file. When you want to delete more than one file, the program will prompt you in this manner for each file you want to delete. For example, if you are deleting 20 files, File Manager will prompt you 20 times—once for each file! For this reason, when you plan to delete many files, you might find it convenient to turn off the *Confirmation option,* which tells the program whether to prompt you.

To turn off the Confirmation options, choose *Options, Confirmation.* The first time you open the Confirmation dialog box, all the options will be checked. To turn off an option, uncheck it. For example, to turn off the Confirmation options to delete files and directories, uncheck *File Delete* and *Directory Delete.* Then click on *OK* to save the changes and return to the directory window.

Let's see how the Confirmation option works when we try to delete a group of files, and then we'll turn the option off and try the same procedure:

1. In the contents list of the A:\WORDPROC directory window, select all three files (select **myletter.wri**, press and hold the **Shift** key, and click on **template.wri**).

2. Press **Del**. The Delete message box asks you to confirm the operation.

3. Click on **OK**. The Confirm File Delete message box asks for confirmation for each file separately.

4. Click on **No** three times to abort the procedure (once for each file). (Clicking on Cancel is a way to abort the entire

procedure at once.) Before we continue, we'll turn off the Confirmation options.

5. In the drive A window, select the **mydir** directory.

6. Choose **File, Select Files** to open the Select Files dialog box (see Figure 5.15). The asterisks (*) shown in the dialog box are *wildcard* characters. Wildcard characters are special characters that can substitute for the actual characters in a file name. The *.* in the File(s) box tells the program to select all of the files in the directory, regardless of their file names.

Figure 5.15 **Select Files dialog box**

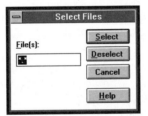

7. Click on **Select**, and click on **Close** to select all the files and subdirectories in the A:\MYDIR directory.

8. Observe that the Up icon is not selected. Because the Up icon represents the parent directory, it should *not* be selected. (Deleting the parent directory would, in this case, result in the deletion of the root directory and all its contents; in other words, the entire disk.)

9. Choose **Options, Confirmation** to open the Confirmation dialog box.

10. In the Confirmation dialog box, uncheck the **File Delete** and the **Directory Delete** options (see Figure 5.16). File Manager will no longer prompt you to confirm the deletion of files and directories.

11. Click on **OK**.

12. Press the **Delete** key. The Delete message box will now be the only message displayed asking for confirmation.

13. Click on **OK**.

Figure 5.16   **Turning off Confirmation options**

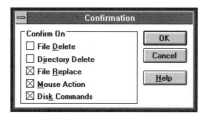

14. Examine the A:\MYDIR directory. The files from the selected directory MYDIR have all been deleted. Compare your screen with Figure 5.17.

Figure 5.17   **MYDIR directory after deleting its contents**

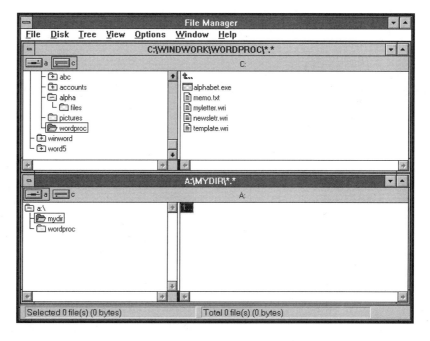

15. Choose **Options, Confirmation** to open the Confirmation dialog box.

16. Click on **File Delete** and **Directory Delete** to check these options. All options should now be checked. Leaving any or all of these options turned off can, for example, result in an accidental deletion.

17. Click on **OK**.

18. Choose **Options** to open the menu. Notice that the Save Settings on Exit choice is currently checked (see Figure 5.18). This choice saves the File Manager window settings, resulting in the same drive and directory windows being opened the next time you run File Manager.

Figure 5.18   **Checked Save Settings on Exit option**

19. Choose **Save Settings on Exit** to uncheck the option.

20. Choose **Options** to open the menu. Notice that Save Settings on Exit is no longer checked (see Figure 5.19).

Figure 5.19   **Unchecked Save Settings on Exit option**

21. Exit File Manager, and close the Main group window.

SUMMARY

In this chapter, you learned some advanced file-management techniques, including formatting a disk, and creating and naming directories. You learned how to move and copy groups of files. You also learned how to delete one or more files and directories.

Here is a quick reference guide to the Windows features introduced in this chapter:

Desired Result	How to Do It
Format a floppy disk	Run the **File Manager**; insert the disk into a disk drive; choose **Disk, Format Disk**; if necessary, select the letter of the drive that contains the disk; if necessary, select the desired disk capacity; click on **OK**
Create a directory	Run **File Manager**; in the directory tree, select the directory within which you want to create the new directory; choose **File, Create Directory**; in the Create Directory dialog box, type the directory name; click on **OK**
Select multiple files in the File Manager directory window	Click on one of the files that you want to select; press and hold the **Ctrl** key; click on each of the other files that you want to select
Select multiple contiguous files	Click on the first file—the leftmost and uppermost—of the contiguous group that you want to select; press and hold the **Shift** key; click on the last file in the group that you want to select
Select all the files in a directory	Select the icon of the directory that contains the files you want to select; choose **File, Select Files**; click on **Select**, click on **Close**
Move a selected group of files to a different directory on the same disk	Display the destination directory window; drag any one of the selected file icons from the source directory to the destination directory

Desired Result	How to Do It
Move a group of selected files to a different disk	Display the window of the destination drive and directory; press and hold the **Alt** key; drag any one of the selected file icons to the destination drive and directory
Copy a selected group of files to a different directory on the same disk	Display the destination directory window; press and hold the **Ctrl** key; drag any one of the selected file icons from the source directory to the destination directory
Copy the group of selected files to a different disk	Display the window of the destination drive and directory; drag any one of the selected file icons to the destination drive and directory
Delete a file or group of files	Select the file or group of files you want to delete; choose **File, Delete** or press the **Delete** key; in the Delete message box, click on **OK**; when prompted for the second time, click on **Yes**
Turn off Confirmation options	Choose **Options, Confirmation**; uncheck the desired option; click on **OK**
Turn on Confirmation options	Choose **Options, Confirmation**, check the desired option; click on **OK**

In the next chapter, you will learn how to customize your Windows environment.

If you need to break off here, please exit Windows. If you want to proceed directly to the next chapter, please do so now.

CHAPTER 6:
CUSTOMIZING
WINDOWS, PART I

Using the Control
Panel to Customize
Your System

Associating Files
with Programs

Working with
Program Manager
Icons

One of Windows's most appealing features is the flexibility of its *user interface*, the method by which it communicates with you, the user. From screen colors to Program Manager icons to desktop management to start-up options: Almost every aspect of Windows's behavior can be modified to suit your needs. Chapters 6 and 7 introduce you to several customization techniques that enable you to tailor Windows to your own operating style and, in doing so, to increase the ease and efficiency with which you work.

When you're done reading through this chapter, you will know

- How to use the Control Panel to customize your system

- How to associate files with programs

- How to work with Program Manager icons

USING THE CONTROL PANEL TO CUSTOMIZE YOUR SYSTEM

The *Control Panel* is a Windows program that enables you to change several of your computer system's hardware and software options. To do this:

- Run *Control Panel* (in the Main group). A window opens, displaying several options.

- Choose (double-click on) the desired Control Panel option and follow its instructions to effect your desired change.

Control Panel options allow you to modify the following settings:

- Screen colors

- Desktop patterns and wallpapers

- Screen and printer fonts

- Mouse operation (speed and button placement)

- Keyboard operation (delay before repeat, repeat rate)

- Available printers

- International formats for date, time, currency, and numbers

- Current date and time

- Communications port settings

 MODIFYING THE DESKTOP

If you are not running Windows, please start it now. Program Manager should be the only open window; if any other windows are open, please close them.

Let's begin by using the Control Panel to modify the appearance of your Desktop:

1. Open the **Main** group, and then run **Control Panel** (see Figure 6.1). Note the many options contained in the Control Panel: Color, Fonts, Ports, Mouse, and so on.

Figure 6.1   **Control Panel**

2. Choose (double-click on) the **Color** option to open the Color dialog box (see Figure 6.2).

3. Click on the **Color Schemes** arrow (the down arrow to the right of the Color Schemes list box) to display the available color schemes.

4. Press **Down Arrow** (on your keyboard) several times, noting the changes in the color scheme that appear in the sample area of the dialog box.

Figure 6.2   **Color dialog box**

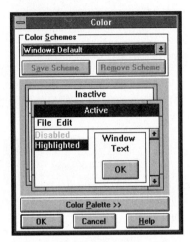

5. Select **Fluorescent**. (You may need to scroll.)

6. Click on the **OK** button at the bottom left of the dialog box. (The other OK button is part of the sample area.) Your screen changes to the Fluorescent color scheme. Every Windows-based program you run from this point on (until you change the color scheme again) will use these colors for its window borders, title bars, OK buttons, menu highlights, and so on.

7. Choose the **Desktop** option to open the Desktop dialog box (see Figure 6.3).

8. Click on the **Wallpaper** arrow to display the available wallpapers. A *wallpaper* is a design that appears on the Desktop behind open windows and icons.

9. Select a wallpaper to your liking, and then click on **Tile** (if it is not already selected). Tile repeats a wallpaper design as many times as necessary to cover the Desktop, much like a tiled floor. *Center,* the other available placement option, positions the wallpaper design in the center of the Desktop without repeating it.

10. Click on **OK** to view your tiled wallpaper.

11. Choose the **Desktop** option again.

12. Click on the **Screen Saver** arrow to display the available screen savers. A *screen saver* is an animated display that

automatically appears on your screen when there is no user activity (keystrokes, mouse movement) for a given time. Screen savers are used to prolong the life of your monitor, by not permitting a static image to remain on-screen very long and potentially "use up" the screen's precious phosphors.

Figure 6.3   **Desktop dialog box**

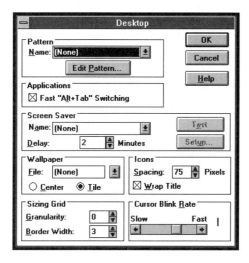

13. Select a screen saver. Click on **Test** to see it.

14. Move your mouse or press any key to exit your screen saver and return to the Control Panel.

PRACTICE YOUR SKILLS

1. Take a few minutes to try out some of the other wallpapers and screen savers.

2. Remove the wallpaper and screen saver. (Hint: Change both to **None**.)

3. Change the color scheme back to **Windows Default**.

4. Close the Control Panel window.

ASSOCIATING FILES WITH PROGRAMS

File Manager allows you to *associate* a file or set of files with a specific program. When you double-click on such a file icon, File Manager starts the associated program and then automatically loads the file into the program's workspace. This feature reduces the two-step process of running a program and then loading a file into a convenient single step.

USING FILE-NAME EXTENSIONS TO ASSOCIATE FILES

Files and programs are associated by file-name extension. For example, by default, all .HLP files are associated with WINHELP.EXE, the Windows Help program, and all .TXT files are associated with NOTEPAD.EXE, the Windows Notepad program. Most files are automatically associated with specific programs. There are times, however, when you may wish to change an association or to create a new association for a previously unassociated file-name extension.

For example, by default, .DOC files are associated with Microsoft Word for Windows. However, many word processing programs use the .DOC extension for their files. If you would like your .DOC files to be associated with a non–Word for Windows word processing program (such as Microsoft Word for DOS), you will have to change your .DOC file/program association.

To associate a file with a program:

- Run *File Manager*.
- Select the file.
- Choose *File, Associate*.
- Select the program in the Associate With list box. If the program does not appear in the list, use Browse to locate and select the program.
- Click on *OK*.

Let's use this procedure to associate a file with the Notepad program:

1. Run **File Manager**.
2. Select your **windwork** directory.

3. Select the file **lost.stf** (click on it once). Note that the LOST.STF icon has no lines in it, indicating that it is not associated with any program.

4. Choose **File, Associate** to open the Associate dialog box (see Figure 6.4).

Figure 6.4   **Associate dialog box**

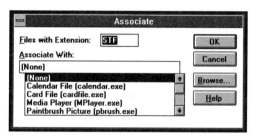

5. In the Associate With list box, select **Text File (notepad.exe)**, and then click on **OK**. Note that the lost.stf icon now has lines in it, indicating that it is associated with a program.

6. Double-click on **lost.stf** to run Notepad and automatically open the LOST.STF file.

7. Exit Notepad to return to File Manager.

PRACTICE YOUR SKILLS

1. Change the association of .STF files to **None**.

2. Verify this. (Hint: Double-click on **lost.stf**.)

3. Exit File Manager.

4. Close the Main group window.

WORKING WITH PROGRAM MANAGER ICONS

Program Manager uses two types of icons:

• *Program-item* icons represent specific programs; for example, the Write and Notepad icons represent, respectively, WRITE.EXE and NOTEPAD.EXE. Program-item icons can also represent specific files that are associated with programs. Double-clicking on a program-item icon runs the program represented by that icon, or runs the program and then opens the associated file.

- *Group* icons are repositories that can hold one or more program-item icons; for example, the Main group holds the program-item icons File Manager, Control Panel, and so on. Group icons cannot hold other group icons. Double-clicking on a group icon restores the icon to a window and, in doing so, displays the program-item icons within.

 CREATING ICONS IN PROGRAM MANAGER

You can create and delete both group icons and program-item icons in Program Manager. When you installed Windows, the Main, Accessories, Games, StartUp, and Applications groups were automatically created, along with a number of program-item icons (File Manager, Control Panel, Notepad, Write, and so on). In time, you will probably want to create additional group icons (to store new program-item icons) and program-item icons (to represent new programs or new file/program associations).

Creating a Group Icon
To create a group icon in Program Manager:

- Choose *File, New* from the Program Manager window.

- Select *Program Group* and click on *OK* to open the Program Group Properties dialog box.

- Type the title of your new group icon in the Description text box.

- Click on *OK*.

Windows automatically creates and maintains a group file for each group icon in Program Manager. These files have the extension .GRP. You'll see an example of such a file in the following activity.

Let's practice creating a program group in Program Manager. If any windows besides Program Manager are open, please close them.

1. Choose **File, New** to open the New Program Object dialog box (see Figure 6.5). Note that Program Group is selected.

Figure 6.5   **New Program Object dialog box**

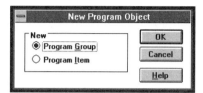

2. Click on **OK** to open the Program Group Properties dialog box. This dialog box allows you to create a new program group in which you can place one or more program-item icons.

3. Type **My Group** in the **Description** text box. This will become the name of your new program group.

4. Click on **OK** and observe your screen (see Figure 6.6). A window named *My Group* has appeared within the Program Manager window. Note that My Group is empty; it contains no program-item icons.

Figure 6.6   **My Group program group, newly created**

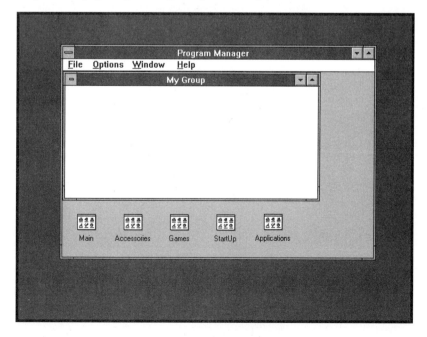

5. Choose **File, Properties** to view the properties for My Group. Note the entry in the Group File text box:

```
C:\WINDOWS\MYGROUP.GRP
```

As mentioned earlier in this section, Windows creates and maintains a .GRP file for each group that you add to Program Manager.

6. Click on **Cancel** to exit the Program Group Properties dialog box.

Creating a Program-Item Icon

To create a program-item icon in a program group:

- Select the group in which you want to place the icon.

- Choose *File, New*.

- Select *Program Item* and click on *OK* to open the Program Item Properties dialog box.

- Type the full path and name of the program—or the file associated with a program—in the Command Line text box; or use Browse to locate and select the program or associated file (you'll use the Browse technique in the following activity).

- Click on *OK*.

Note: Working with a program-item icon does not affect the program or associated file that it represents. You can create, delete, move, copy, and modify program-item icons without actually changing the program or associated file.

Windows assigns a default title and appearance to your new program-item icon. To change an icon's title or appearance:

- Select the program-item icon.

- Choose *File, Properties*.

- Modify the Description text box entry (to change the title).

- Click on *Change Icon* and follow the dialog box instructions to change the icon appearance.

- Click on *OK* to exit the Program Item Properties dialog box.

Let's create a program-item icon that represents an associated file:

1. Choose **File, New** to open the New Program Object dialog box. Note that Program Item is selected. Windows correctly

assumes that you wish to create a program item in your new program group.

2. Click on **OK** to open the Program Item Properties dialog box (see Figure 6.7). This dialog box allows you to create an icon that can run a program or, in the case of this activity, that can run a program *and* open an associated file.

Figure 6.7   **Program Item Properties dialog box**

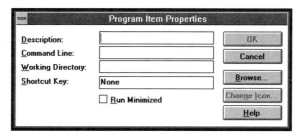

3. Type **My favorite file** in the **Description** text box. This will become the name of your new program-item icon.

4. Click on **Browse** to open the Browse dialog box (see Figure 6.8). Note that this box closely resembles a File Open dialog box.

Figure 6.8   **Browse dialog box**

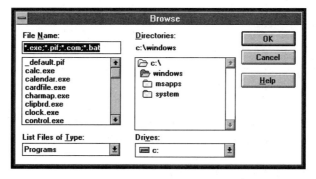

5. Select your **windwork** directory.

6. Double-click in the **File Name** text box to select the current entry. Type ***.txt** and press **Enter**. Examine the File Name list box; only those files that end with *.txt* are displayed.

7. Select **memo.txt**, and then click on **OK**. Examine the Command Line text box; the full path of MEMO.TXT appears:

```
C:\WINDWORK\MEMO.TXT
```

8. Click on **OK** to create the *My favorite file* icon (see Figure 6.9). Note that Windows automatically selects the default Notepad icon, a picture of a half-open notepad.

Figure 6.9 **My favorite file icon, newly created**

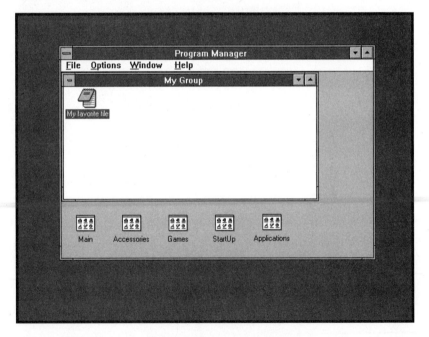

Now let's test our new associated-file program-item icon:

1. Double-click on **My favorite file** to start Notepad and automatically open the file MEMO.TXT. Let's take a moment to examine the logic behind this sequence of events. As mentioned earlier, files that end with .TXT are associated with Notepad. Due to this association, double-clicking on *My favorite file*—which is

equivalent to double-clicking on MEMO.TXT, since this is the file you specified in *My favorite file*'s Command Line text box— causes Notepad to start and then automatically open MEMO.TXT.

2. Exit Notepad.

MOVING AND COPYING A PROGRAM-ITEM ICON

To move a program-item icon to a different group:

- Drag it into the new group.

To copy (rather than move) a program-item:

- Hold the *Ctrl* key as you drag the icon to the new group.

Let's practice moving and copying our *My favorite file* program-item icon:

1. Drag **My favorite file** from the My Group window to the StartUp group icon. The program-item icon is moved; that is, it is deleted from My Group and placed in StartUp. Note that you can move a program-item icon between a group window (My Group) and a group icon (StartUp).

2. Double-click on the **StartUp** group icon to restore it to a window. Verify that it contains *My favorite file* (see Figure 6.10).

3. Press and hold the **Ctrl** key, and then drag **My favorite file** from StartUp to My Group. This time, the program-item icon is copied, not moved.

4. Click on the **StartUp** window to display it and verify that *My favorite file* has not been deleted.

5. Close the **StartUp** window. We'll get back to its copy of *My favorite file* later.

DELETING A GROUP OR PROGRAM-ITEM ICON

To delete a group or program-item icon:

- Select the icon (press *Esc* if you need to close a group-icon Control menu).
- Press *Del.*

Figure 6.10   **StartUp, after moving *My favorite file***

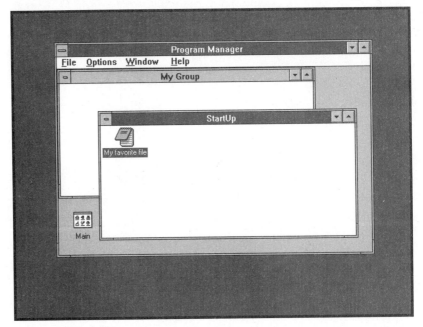

- Click on *Yes* to confirm the deletion.

Note: Deleting a group also deletes all the program-item icons within this group. For this reason, you should be very cautious when performing a group deletion.

Let's delete *My favorite file* from My Group:

1. Select the **My favorite file** icon, if necessary.

2. Press **Del**. Windows prompts

   ```
   Are you sure you want to delete the item 'My
   favorite file'?
   ```

3. Click on **Yes** to delete the *My favorite file* icon. As mentioned earlier, deleting an icon does not delete the program or file associated with this icon. Here you deleted the *My favorite file* icon, but did not delete (or otherwise modify) the associated file MEMO.TXT.

Now let's delete our My Group program group:

1. Close the **My Group** window.

2. Select the **My Group** icon (click once on it). The Control menu appears.

3. Press **Del**. Note that nothing happens.

4. Press **Esc** to remove the Control menu. Windows keyboard shortcuts do not usually work when menus are selected.

5. Press **Del**. Windows prompts

   ```
   Are you sure you want to delete the group
   'My Group'?
   ```

6. Click on **Yes**.

7. Examine the Program Manager window. The My Group icon has been deleted.

 CHANGING GROUP AND PROGRAM-ITEM PROPERTIES

Windows allows you to change the properties of both group and program-item icons. By doing so, you can continually update and refine your Program Manager customization scheme.

Group properties include

- *Description:* The icon title

- *Group File:* The name of the .GRP file

Program-item properties include

- *Description:* The icon title (the default title is the name of the executable file, minus its extension; for example, unless you specify otherwise, *Word* is the title given to an icon representing WORD.EXE)

- *Working Directory:* The directory that the program will use if no path is specified when saving and opening files

- *Shortcut Key:* The key combination that, when pressed, runs the program (pressing an icon's shortcut key is equivalent to double-clicking on the icon)

- *Change Icon:* An option that allows you to change an icon's appearance

- *Run Minimized:* An option that, if checked, runs a program as an icon instead of in a window (for example, many users run the Clock program minimized so that they can see the current time without losing space on their desktops)

To change the properties of a group or program-item icon:

- Select the icon.

- Choose *File, Properties*.

- Specify the new properties.

- Click on *OK*.

Let's use this procedure to change the properties of the *My favorite file* icon we left in the StartUp group:

1. Open the StartUp window and select **My favorite file**, if necessary.

2. Choose **File, Properties** to open the Program Item Properties dialog box (see Figure 6.11).

Figure 6.11   **Changing the Program Item Properties dialog box**

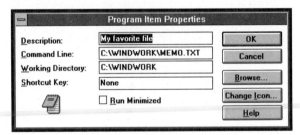

3. In the Description text box, type **Important Memo!** to change the icon title.

4. Select the text in the Working Directory text box, and type **c:\windows** to change the default directory for the associated Notepad program.

5. Click on **Change Icon**. Note that there is only one icon in the NOTEPAD.EXE file.

6. Click on **Browse** to display a list of files that contain icons.

7. Select **moricons.dll**. (You'll have to scroll.) This file contains icons for many popular programs, as well as some general-purpose icons. Click on **OK**.

8. Scroll to examine the available icons and select one. Click on **OK** to return to the Program Item Properties dialog box. Note that your newly selected icon is displayed in the lower-left corner.

9. Click on **OK** to change the icon's properties.

10. Double-click on **Important Memo!** to verify that your modified program-item icon still runs Notepad and opens the file MEMO.TXT.

11. Choose **File, Open**. Note that the default directory is now C:\WINDOWS (you changed it in step 4).

12. Exit **Notepad**.

PRACTICE YOUR SKILLS

1. Delete **Important Memo!** from StartUp. (If you were to keep Important Memo! in the StartUp group, every time you started Windows, Notepad would automatically run and MEMO.TXT would be opened.)

2. Close the StartUp group.

SUMMARY

In this chapter, you explored several powerful Windows customization techniques. You now know how to use the Control Panel to customize the appearance of your Desktop, how to associate files with programs, and how to create, delete, move, and copy Program Manager icons.

Here's a quick reference for the techniques that you learned in this chapter:

Desired Result	How to Do It
Change screen colors	Run **Control Panel**, choose **Color**, select the desired color scheme, click on **OK**
Change wallpaper	Run **Control Panel**, choose **Desktop**, select the desired wallpaper, click on **OK**

Desired Result	How to Do It
Change screen saver	Run **Control Panel**, choose **Desktop**, select the desired screen saver, click on **OK**
Associate a file with a program	Run **File Manager**, select the desired file, choose **File, Associate**, select the program in the Associate With list box (if the program does not appear in the list, use Browse to locate and select it), click on **OK**
Create a group icon in Program Manager	Choose **File, New** from the Program Manager window, select **Program Group** and click on **OK**, type the title of your new group icon in the Description text box, click on **OK**
Create a program-item icon in a program group	Select the group in which you want to place the icon, choose **File, New**, select **Program Item** and click on **OK**, type the full path and file name of the program in the Command Line text box (or, use Browse to locate and select the program file), click on **OK**
Change an icon's title or appearance	Select the program-item icon; choose **File, Properties**, modify the **Description** text box entry (to change the title), click on **Change Icon** and follow the dialog box instructions to change the icon appearance, click on **OK**
Move a program-item icon to a different group	Drag it into the new group
Copy a program-item icon to a different group	Hold the **Ctrl** key as you drag the icon into the new group
Delete a group or program-item icon	Select the icon, press **Del**, click on **Yes** to confirm the deletion
Change the properties of a group or program-item icon	Select the icon, choose **File, Properties**, specify the new properties, click on **OK**

In the next chapter, we'll continue our mini-series on Windows customization by showing you several new ways to tailor Windows to your specific needs. You'll learn how to use different options for starting Windows, how to use the System Configuration Editor to examine your computer system's four major configuration (setup) files, how to manage multiple open programs, and how to customize your Desktop.

If you need to break off here, please exit Windows. If you want to proceed directly to the next chapter, please do so now.

CHAPTER 7:
CUSTOMIZING
WINDOWS, PART II

Options for
Starting Windows

Examining
Configuration Files
with the System
Configuration
Editor
(SYSEDIT.EXE)

Managing Multiple
Open Programs

Customizing Your
Desktop

This is the second in our two-chapter series on Windows customization. We'll begin by stepping back and learning a bit more about how Windows works. After introducing several new ways to start Windows, we'll take you on a brief tour of your computer's all-important *configuration* files: the four main files responsible for configuring (setting up) the operation of Windows and your entire computer system. Next we'll demonstrate some easy-to-use techniques for switching between multiple open programs. We'll end the chapter by showing you some new Desktop customization options.

When you're done working through this chapter, you will know

- How to use different options for starting Windows
- How to use the System Configuration Editor to examine your configuration files
- How to manage multiple open programs
- How to customize your Desktop

OPTIONS FOR STARTING WINDOWS

Up to now, you've always started Windows by entering the command *win* at the system prompt. Here you'll learn how to expand your *WIN command* to start Windows and then automatically run a program, open a file in this program, and control the Windows operational mode.

The full syntax of the WIN command is as follows, with optional information enclosed in square brackets:

```
WIN [program] [file] [/mode]
```

The three command options—[program], [file], and [/mode]—are discussed in the following sections. Afterward, we'll show you a fourth start-up option: using the Program Manager StartUp group to run one or more programs automatically when you start Windows.

 THE [PROGRAM] OPTION

The WIN command [program] option enables you to automatically run a program when you start Windows. To do this:

- Add the program file name to the WIN command line.

For example, to start Windows and then run Write, you would enter

```
win write
```

The Write program is in your WINDOWS directory. If, however, the program you want to run is not in your WINDOWS directory, you need to enter the program's full path in the WIN command line. For example, to start Windows and then run a program named DRAW.EXE, located in the directory C:\DRAWINGS, you would enter

```
win c:\drawings\draw
```

THE [FILE] OPTION

The WIN command [file] option enables you to automatically run a program *and* open a file when you start Windows. To do this, add to the WIN command line:

- The name of the program in which the file is to be opened
- The name of the file

For example, to start Windows, run our hypothetical DRAW.EXE program, and then open the file C:\DRAWINGS\ARTWORK7.DRW, you would enter

```
win c:\drawings\draw c:\drawings\artwork7.drw
```

If the file is *associated* with the program in which it is to be opened (see Chapter 6 for a review of file/program association), you can omit the program name from the WIN command. For example, to start Windows, run Notepad, and then open the file C:\WIND-WORK\MYFILE.TXT, you would enter

```
win c:\windwork\myfile.txt
```

This command works because .TXT files are associated with the Notepad program.

For this first activity, the system prompt should be on your screen. If you are running Windows, please exit.

Let's enter a WIN command that will start Windows and then automatically run the Write program:

1. Type **win write** and press **Enter**. After a few moments, a blank Write window appears. As discussed earlier in this section, adding a program file name to your WIN command line starts Windows and then runs the program.

2. Exit **Write**. Note that Program Manager is running minimized; that is, it appears as an icon at the bottom of the screen. When you enter a WIN command to start Windows and automatically run a program (as you did in step 1), Program Manager always runs minimized.

3. Click on the **Program Manager** icon to open its Control menu.

4. Click on **Close**, and then click on **OK** to exit Windows.

Now let's enter a WIN command that will start Windows, run Write, and then open a specific Write file:

1. Type **win write c:\windwork\nuprod.wri** and press **Enter**. The Write window appears, and the file NUPROD.WRI is automatically opened (see Figure 7.1).

Figure 7.1   **Automatically opening a Write file upon Windows start-up**

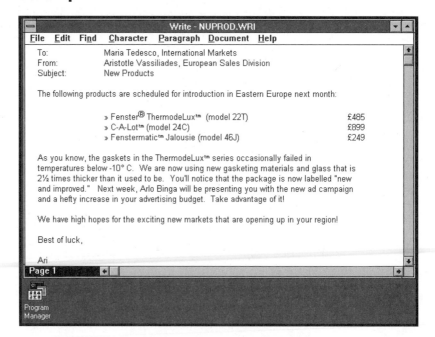

2. Exit Write.

3. Restore the **Program Manager** icon to a window by double-clicking on the icon.

THE [/MODE] OPTION

Windows can run in one of two operational modes: *Standard* or *386 Enhanced*. When you start Windows by typing *win* at the system prompt (or a longer WIN command, such as *win write c:\windwork\nuprod.wri*), Windows examines your computer hardware and automatically runs in the more appropriate of the two modes.

Standard mode is the basic operating mode for Windows. If your computer has an 80286 microprocessor and at least 1Mb of memory, Windows will run in Standard mode. Standard mode uses *extended memory* and allows you to switch between multiple open programs. (Extended memory is RAM memory that lies beyond the first megabyte of your total system RAM. If, for example, your system has 4Mb of RAM memory, the top 3Mb are extended memory.)

If your computer has an 80386 microprocessor or higher (80486, 80586, and so on) and at least 2Mb of memory, Windows will run in 386 Enhanced mode. In addition to using extended memory, 386 Enhanced mode enables your computer to access *virtual memory* by using a portion of your hard disk to simulate memory.

To find out what mode Windows is running in:

- Choose *Help, About Program Manager* from the Program Manager menu.

- Observe the current operational mode (displayed toward the bottom of the About Program Manager window).

At times, you might want to specify the Windows operational mode yourself, rather than let Windows select the default mode for your system at start-up. For example, you might want to specify Standard mode, because Windows tends to run somewhat faster in this mode and may also work better with certain programs or hardware components. Or, you might want to specify 386 Enhanced mode, because Windows can use more memory and run more programs simultaneously in this mode.

To run Windows in Standard mode:

- Add an */s* switch to the end of your WIN command line (for example, *win /s* or *win write /s*).

To run Windows in 386 Enhanced mode:

- Add a */3* switch to the end of your WIN command line (for example, *win /3* or *win c:\windword\myfile.txt /3*).

Note: You can run in Standard mode on any computer capable of running Windows. You can run in 386 Enhanced mode, however, only on a computer with an 80386 microprocessor or higher.

Let's take a moment to examine your computer's memory and system resources:

1. Choose **Help, About Program Manager** to open the About Program Manager window. The About choice on any Help menu displays information about the currently active program.

2. Observe the operational mode, which is displayed in the lower portion of the window. By analyzing your computer hardware, Windows determines whether to run in Standard or 386 Enhanced mode.

3. Observe the *Memory* listing. The amount of free memory reported here depends on your computer hardware. (Note: You may recall that *KB* stands for kilobytes, where one kilobyte equals approximately 1,000 bytes of memory. *13,753 KB free* would mean that there are approximately 13,753,000 available bytes of memory.) If Windows is running in 386 Enhanced mode, the free memory is often larger than your computer's total RAM, because Windows can make use of your hard disk to provide virtual memory (as mentioned in the previous section).

4. Observe the *System Resources* listing. Windows allots a fixed portion of memory to system resources. It uses this memory to track and maintain open windows, open dialog boxes, and other screen elements.

5. Click on **OK** to remove the About Program Manager window.

Now let's try running Windows in Standard mode. (If you are already running in Standard mode, please skip this activity and continue with the section entitled "The StartUp Group.")

1. Exit Windows.

2. Type **win /s** and press **Enter**. The /s switch causes Windows to run in Standard mode.

3. Choose **Help, About Program Manager**. Note that Windows is now running in Standard mode.

4. Observe the amount of free memory. Chances are it is significantly less than in the previous activity, when you ran Windows in 386 Enhanced mode. Why? Because in Standard mode, Windows is limited to the actual amount of available RAM and cannot use virtual memory.

5. Click on **OK** to remove the About Program Manager window.

THE STARTUP GROUP

When you install Windows on your computer, an empty group called *StartUp* is created. The StartUp group has a very special function: Any program-item icon contained in this group will automatically run whenever you start Windows. This feature is very useful when you always want a certain program (or programs) to run at Windows start-up.

For example, let's say you like to run the Clock program whenever you use Windows, so that you can see the time on-screen. Rather than hunting for the Clock icon and then double-clicking on it every time you start Windows, you could copy the Clock icon to the StartUp group and let Windows run Clock for you automatically at start-up.

Programs in the StartUp group run in the order in which their icons appear, left to right. If there are two or more rows of icons, the rows will run left to right and then top to bottom.

Let's use the StartUp group to automatically run Write at Windows start-up:

1. Open the **Accessories** group.

2. Press and hold **Ctrl**, and then drag the **Write** program-item icon into the StartUp group icon. The Write icon is copied to StartUp. Remember that when you copy, move, or delete a program-item icon, you do not affect the program file itself, only the icon that represents it.

3. Open the **StartUp** group to verify that the Write icon was successfully copied.

4. Exit **Windows**.

5. Type **win** and press **Enter**. Windows starts and then automatically runs Write.

6. Exit **Write**. Note that Program Manager appears as a window, not an icon. As demonstrated in the first activity, when you use an extended WIN command to start Windows and automatically run a program (by entering *win write*, for example), Program Manager runs as an icon. However, when you use the StartUp group to automatically run a program, Program Manager runs as a window.

PRACTICE YOUR SKILLS

Let's delete the Write icon we copied to StartUp, so that Write will not automatically run every time you start Windows:

1. Verify that the original **Write** icon is still in the **Accessories** group. When deleting, it's better to be safe than sorry.

2. Open the **StartUp** group and delete the **Write** icon.

3. Close the **StartUp** group.

4. If necessary, close the **Accessories** group.

EXAMINING CONFIGURATION FILES WITH THE SYSTEM CONFIGURATION EDITOR (SYSEDIT.EXE)

SYSEDIT.EXE, commonly referred to as the *System Configuration Editor*, is a program that enables you to view and edit the four main files used to configure (set up) your computer system for optimum operation. These files, AUTOEXEC.BAT, CONFIG.SYS, WIN.INI, and SYSTEM.INI, are all text files and can be opened and edited in any standard text-editing program. The System Configuration Editor opens them in Notepad and groups them together on the screen for your convenience.

Let's use the System Configuration Editor to examine these four files:

1. Open the **Main** group and run **File Manager**.

2. Open the **c:\windows** directory.

3. Open the **system** subdirectory.

4. Run **sysedit.exe**. (Double-click on the **sysedit.exe** file icon in the contents list; you may need to scroll.)

5. Maximize the **System Configuration Editor** window. (Make sure to click on the Maximize/Restore button in the *System Configuration Editor* title bar. When the screen gets cluttered with open windows, it's all too easy to mistakenly click on the wrong window's buttons!) The System Configuration Editor finds and opens the four main configuration files for your computer system.

6. Choose **Window, Tile** to arrange these files on-screen (see Figure 7.2). The contents of the files are discussed in the following sections.

Figure 7.2   **Windows's four major configuration files**

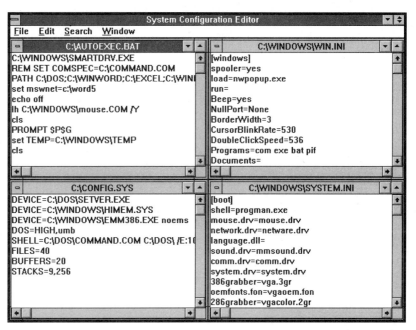

 THE DOS OPERATING SYSTEM

To understand how the system configuration files affect the operation of your computer, you must first step back for a moment and learn some elementary computer theory. When you turn on (or reset) your computer, it automatically runs a program called *DOS*, which stands for *Disk Operating System*. An *operating system* is a program that enables and oversees the primary functions of a computer: displaying text and graphics on the monitor, interpreting keyboard or mouse input, submitting a document to a printer, reading a file from a hard or floppy disk, and so on. Without DOS (or some other operating system), your computer would sit there with a frozen screen, unable to function.

As you learned in Chapter 1, Windows is a graphical user interface (GUI); it is *not* an operating system. DOS must already be running on your computer for you to successfully start Windows. Whenever you see the system prompt on your screen, you are in DOS. Windows—though it seems to be an independent, stand-alone program—is, in fact, completely dependent on DOS and is said to run *on top of* DOS.

Figure 7.3 should help to clarify things. It depicts the hierarchy of control among three programs: DOS, Windows, and Windows's File Manager. As you can see, DOS is the foundation. Windows runs on top of DOS, and File Manager runs on top of Windows.

Figure 7.3   **Hierarchy of program control**

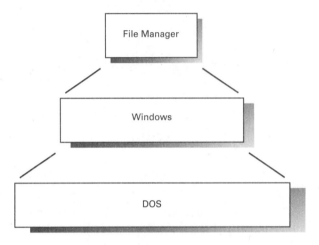

 AUTOEXEC.BAT AND CONFIG.SYS

When you turn on your computer, it automatically runs DOS, and then DOS runs the files AUTOEXEC.BAT and CONFIG.SYS. The information in these files affects the way DOS operates—how it handles memory, how it goes about locating program files, how it displays the system prompt, how it manages your system's hardware devices, and so on. Therefore, these files affect every program run from DOS, including Windows.

- AUTOEXEC.BAT contains DOS commands that run automatically when you boot. One of the most important of these is the *PATH* command, which specifies the DOS *search path*. If DOS cannot find a program file in the current directory, it searches through all the directories specified in this path. Windows also uses the DOS search path to find its programs.

- CONFIG.SYS contains information that customizes DOS for your computer system. *Device drivers*, files that tell DOS how to manage the various hardware devices connected to your system (monitor, printer, video cards, sound cards, and so on), are specified in CONFIG.SYS.

Let's take a closer look at your AUTOEXEC.BAT file:

1. Maximize the **AUTOEXEC.BAT** window. (See Figure 7.4; your AUTOEXEC.BAT file may be significantly different from the one depicted here.)

Figure 7.4   **AUTOEXEC.BAT file**

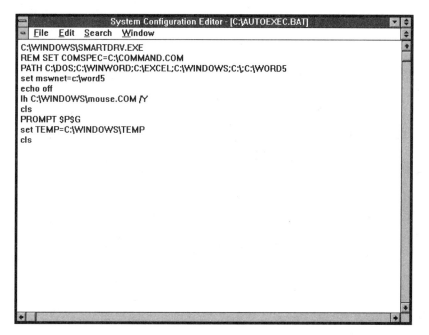

```
System Configuration Editor - [C:\AUTOEXEC.BAT]
 File   Edit   Search   Window

C:\WINDOWS\SMARTDRV.EXE
REM SET COMSPEC=C:\COMMAND.COM
PATH C:\DOS;C:\WINWORD;C:\EXCEL;C:\WINDOWS;C:\;C:\WORD5
set mswnet=c:\word5
echo off
lh C:\WINDOWS\mouse.COM /Y
cls
PROMPT $P$G
set TEMP=C:\WINDOWS\TEMP
cls
```

2. Examine the PATH command. As mentioned earlier in this section, PATH tells DOS and Windows where to search for program files that are not located in the current directory. In Figure 7.4, PATH tells DOS and Windows to search the directories C:\DOS, C:\WINWORD, C:\EXCEL, C:\WINDOWS, C:\, and C:\WORDS.

3. Examine the PROMPT command, which—in this case—causes DOS to display the following system prompt:

   C:\

4. Restore the **AUTOEXEC.BAT** window. (Click on the *lower* of the two **Restore** buttons; the upper button restores the System Configuration Editor window.)

WIN.INI AND SYSTEM.INI

WIN.INI and SYSTEM.INI are *initialization files* that automatically run every time you start Windows. (The terms *configuration file* and *initialization file* are synonymous.) The information in these files affects the operation of Windows and all programs run under Windows.

- WIN.INI contains a variety of settings that customize the Windows environment according to your preferences.

- SYSTEM.INI contains instructions informing Windows how to make the best use of your computer hardware.

There are other Windows initialization files. For example, PROGMAN.INI contains Program Manager settings and CONTROL.INI contains Control Panel settings. These files change automatically to reflect the choices you make while working in Windows.

Let's take a look at your WIN.INI file:

1. Maximize the **WIN.INI** window. (See Figure 7.5; your WIN.INI file may be significantly different from the one depicted here.)

2. Examine the load= line. Program file names that appear on this line will automatically run as icons when you start Windows. In Figure 7.5, the only entry on the *load=* line is NWPOPUP.EXE, a program used to manage *pop-up* programs—a class of non-Windows programs that "pop up" on the screen when you press a certain key combination; Borland SideKick is an example.

3. Examine the run= line. Program file names that appear on this line will automatically run in windows (rather than as icons) when you start Windows. In Figure 7.5, the *run=* line is empty; no programs have been set to automatically run in windows at start-up.

4. Examine the Programs= line (about halfway down the screen). This line enables Windows to recognize program files by their file extension. In Figure 7.5, these extensions include .COM, .EXE, .BAT, and .PIF.

Figure 7.5   **WIN.INI file**

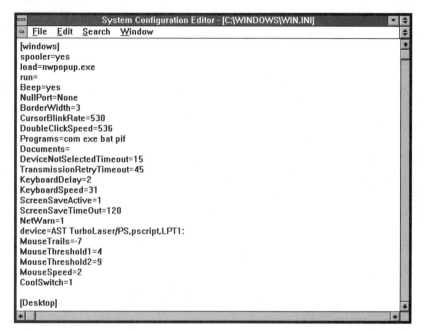

5. Scroll down to examine the [Extensions] section. This section tells Windows which files are associated with which programs.

PRACTICE YOUR SKILLS

1. Scroll through the rest of the **WIN.INI** file and examine its contents.

2. Restore the **WIN.INI** window. (Click on the *lower* **Restore** button; the upper button restores the System Configuration Editor window.)

MANAGING MULTIPLE OPEN PROGRAMS

Because Windows can run several programs at once, you may, at times, find your Desktop filled to overflowing with open windows. Such a screen display can look daunting to a novice Windows user. But, never fear! Windows provides a number of easy-to-use techniques to manage a Desktop packed with open programs.

SWITCHING TO AN OPEN PROGRAM

Use any of these techniques to switch to an open program:

- If the program's window is visible, click on its title bar.

- Press *Ctrl+Esc* or double-click anywhere on the Desktop (that is, not inside an open window) to display the Task List. (Recall that the Task List reports all open programs, even if their windows or icons are not currently visible.) Double-click on the desired open program. You can also use the Task List to

  - Exit a program (by selecting the program and then clicking on *End Task*).

  - Arrange all open program windows so that you can see their title bars (by clicking on *Cascade*).

  - Arrange all open windows so that they do not overlap (by clicking on *Tile*).

  Note: Programs running as icons do not cascade or tile.

- Press *Alt+Esc* to switch back to the most recently used program. Or, press and hold *Alt* and then press *Esc* repeatedly to cycle through all open programs.

- *Alt+Tab* works the same way as Alt+Esc. However, it is faster because it does not redraw the screen until you release the Alt key.

Let's use these last two techniques, Alt+Esc and Alt+Tab, to switch between your currently open (running) programs:

1. Observe the Desktop. Hiding behind the maximized System Configuration Editor window are the Program Manager and File Manager windows. Program Manager was opened automatically the last time you started Windows. You opened File Manager yourself in a previous activity to locate SYSEDIT.EXE and run the System Configuration Editor.

2. Press **Alt+Esc** to switch to the next open program, File Manager.

3. Press and hold **Alt**, and then press **Esc** several times (without releasing Alt) to cycle through all open programs. Release **Alt** when the System Configuration Editor is displayed to switch to the System Configuration Editor.

4. Press and hold **Alt**, and then press **Tab** several times (without releasing **Alt**) to cycle once again through all open programs. This time, the program names are shown in a box (see Figure 7.6), but the actual program windows are not shown. Release **Alt** when *Program Manager* is displayed, to switch to Program Manager. Because the individual program windows are not drawn on-screen, Alt+Tab is a faster method than Alt+Esc for switching between open programs.

Figure 7.6   **Using Alt+Tab to switch between tasks**

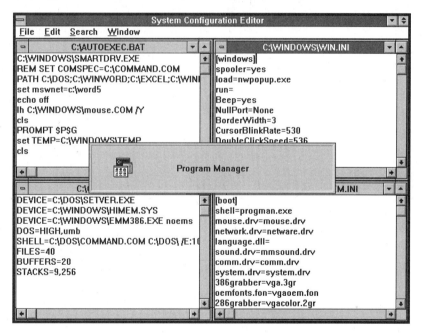

 ARRANGING THE DESKTOP

Let's use the Task List to control the desktop arrangement of your open program windows:

1. Press **Ctrl+Esc** to display the Task List (see Figure 7.7). Note that your three open programs are listed, Program Manager, System Configuration Editor, and File Manager.

2. Click on **Cascade**. The title bars of all three open programs are now visible. Note that Cascade causes the windows to overlap.

Figure 7.7   **Task List**

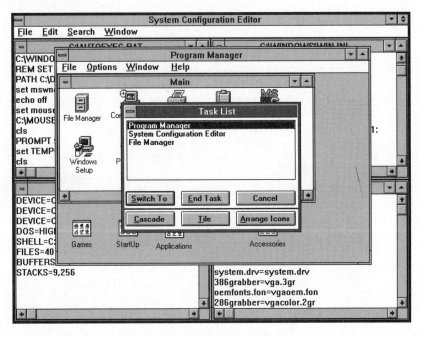

3. Double-click anywhere on the **Desktop** (that is, not inside an open window) to display the Task List.

4. This time, click on **Tile** to arrange all open program windows without overlapping them (see Figure 7.8).

5. Minimize the **System Configuration Editor** window. Note that the other windows maintain their size, shape, and position.

6. Display the **Task List** (press **Ctrl+Esc** or double-click on the **Desktop**). Click on **Tile**. Task List arranges only those programs running in windows, not those minimized to icons. Note the System Configuration Editor icon at the bottom of the screen (see Figure 7.9).

EXITING PROGRAMS WITH TASK LIST

Let's practice using the Task List to exit programs:

1. Display the **Task List**.

Figure 7.8   **Using Task List, Tile to keep open program windows from overlapping**

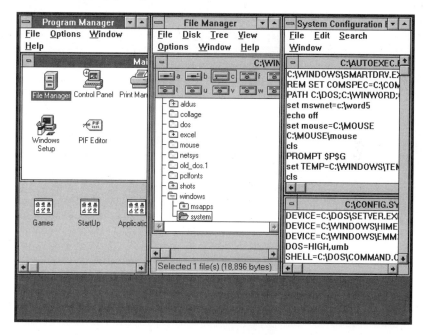

2. Click once on **System Configuration Editor** to select it.

3. Click on **End Task** to exit the System Configuration Editor program. Using the Task List in this manner is particularly useful for exiting programs that are not currently visible.

4. Use the Task List to exit **File Manager**.

ENLARGING THE PROGRAM MANAGER WINDOW

Finally, let's use the Task List to enlarge the Program Manager window:

1. Display the **Task List** and click on **Tile** to enlarge the Program Manager window to fill the entire screen. Program Manager is the only active program.

2. Drag the bottom border of the Program Manager window up about 1 inch (see Figure 7.10).

Figure 7.9   **System Configuration Editor as an icon**

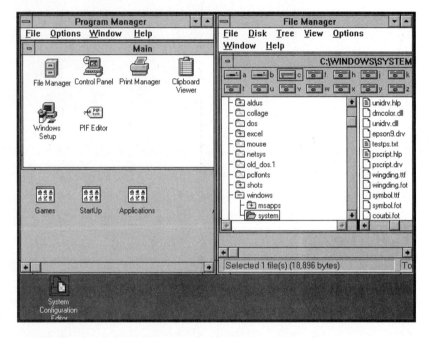

3. Select any one of the group icons that appear below the Main window.

4. Choose **Window, Arrange Icons** to arrange the group icons along the modified bottom of the Program Manager window.

CUSTOMIZING YOUR DESKTOP

The Desktop option in Control Panel enables you to customize the appearance and arrangement of your Desktop. The customization options include

- *Patterns* and *Wallpapers* are designs that appear on the Desktop behind open windows and icons. You tried out several different wallpapers in Chapter 6.

- *Screen Savers* are animated displays that automatically appear on your screen when there is no user activity (keystrokes, mouse movement) for a given time. They are used to prolong the life of your screen and, optionally, to provide security (you can use the Password Options box to set a password for a

screen saver). You tried out several different screen savers in
Chapter 6.

Figure 7.10   **Program Manager, after tiling and dragging**

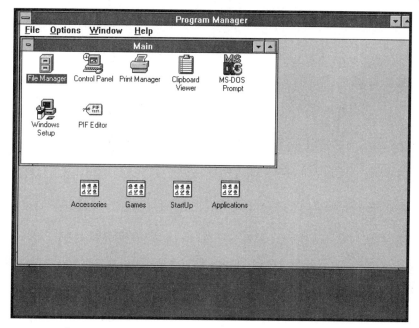

- The *Spacing* option in the *Icons* box determines the amount of
  space between on-screen icons. After setting the Spacing
  option, you must choose *Window, Arrange Icons* to rearrange
  your group or program-item icons according to your modified
  spacing.

- The *Wrap Title* option in the *Icons* box, when checked, causes
  long icon titles to wrap onto two or more lines, rather than
  allow the titles to occupy long, single lines that may overlap
  with neighboring icon titles.

- The *Granularity* option in the *Sizing Grid* box determines the
  on-screen position of program-item icons and program windows. When Granularity is set to a number greater than zero,
  an invisible grid is turned on, causing these icons and windows

to "snap" to the nearest grid line whenever you move them. When Granularity is set to zero, the grid is turned off.

- The *Border Width* option in the *Sizing Grid* box determines the width of all open window borders, except for those that have a fixed size (such as most dialog boxes). Some users find it easier to resize windows with wide borders.

Let's change a few of your current Desktop settings:

1. Run **Control Panel** (located in the Main group), and then choose (double-click on) the **Desktop** option.

2. Observe the Spacing setting in the Icons box. As mentioned, this number determines the amount of space between icons. Note that the Wrap Title option is checked, causing long icon titles to wrap onto additional lines.

3. Double the current icon spacing. (For example, if the current number is 75, change it to 150.) This will double the distance between your icons within their respective windows.

4. Observe the Border Width setting in the Sizing Grid box. Double the current border width.

5. Observe that Fast "Alt+Tab" Switching is checked in the Applications box. When this box is unchecked, Alt+Tab functions like Alt+Esc. Since we found Alt+Tab to be a highly desirable feature, we'll leave it checked.

6. Click on **OK**. Note that the window border width increases, but the space between icons does not. As mentioned, to enact the change that you made to the icon spacing, you must first issue an Arrange Icons command.

7. Activate the **Program Manager** window by clicking on its title bar.

8. Select any one of the group icons in Program Manager.

9. Choose **Window, Arrange Icons** to rearrange the icons in the Program Manager window according to your new icon spacing (see Figure 7.11). Remember that the Arrange Icons command affects only the window that contains the selected icon.

10. Activate the **Main** window, and then choose **Window, Arrange Icons** to rearrange its icons.

Figure 7.11   **Changing the icon spacing and window border width**

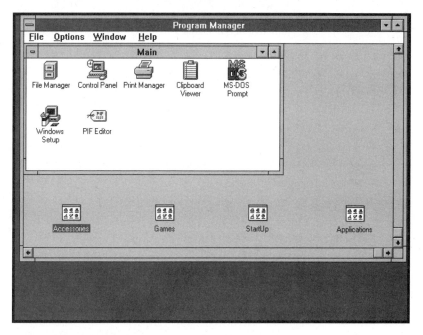

PRACTICE YOUR SKILLS

1. Switch to **Control Panel** (use Alt+Tab) and choose **Desktop**.

2. Change the icon spacing to **75** and the border width to **3**. Click on **OK** and close the **Control Panel** window.

3. Rearrange the group icons in the Program Manager window.

4. Rearrange the program-item icons in the Main window.

5. Close the Main window.

 SAVING SETTINGS IN PROGRAM MANAGER

As you learned in Chapter 1, by enabling the *Save Settings on Exit* option in the Program Manager menu, you can save your current Windows settings so that they will be restored when you next start Windows. Here we'll learn how to use this feature to save a particular arrangement of group icons and to save the size and position of the Program Manager window. To do this:

- Switch to *Program Manager*, if necessary.

- Arrange your group icons as desired.

- Size and move the *Program Manager* window as desired.

- Click on *Options* to display the drop-down Options menu. Observe the *Save Settings on Exit* option. If it is already enabled (preceded by a check), skip the rest of this step. If it is disabled (not preceded by a check), click on *Save Settings on Exit* to enable the save-settings feature.

- Exit Windows.

- Start Windows. Windows retains your modified icon arrangement and Program Manager window size/position.

- Choose *Options, Save Settings on Exit* to disable (uncheck) the save-settings feature.

Let's change the window size/position and icon arrangement in Program Manager and then save these changes:

1. Move and size the Program Manager window to resemble as closely as possible the window shown in Figure 7.12. (Ignore the misarrangement of program-item icons in your modified window; we'll fix this in the next step.)

2. Choose **Window, Arrange Icons** to arrange your group icons to fit the modified Program Manager window. Your screen should now match Figure 7.12.

3. Move the **Main** and **Accessories** icons into the upper-right corner of the window (see Figure 7.13). Many users find it helpful to place logically related icons in the same part of a group window, to visually underscore their relatedness and make it easier to locate them.

4. Click on **Options** and observe the Save Settings on Exit option. If it is already enabled (preceded by a check), skip to step 5. If it is disabled (not preceded by a check), click on **Save Settings on Exit** to enable the save-settings feature.

5. Exit Windows to save your modified Program Manager settings.

Figure 7.12   **Program Manager, after moving and sizing the window, and arranging icons**

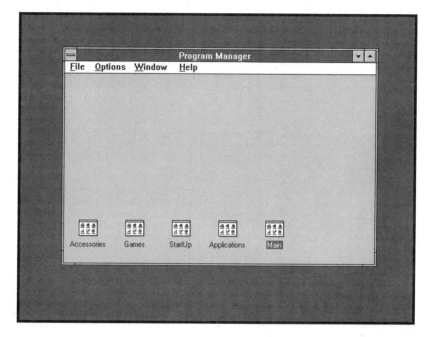

6. Start Windows. Note that the Program Manager window and group icons retain your modifications.

PRACTICE YOUR SKILLS

1. Return the group icons to their original positions. (Hint: Choose **Window, Arrange Icons.**)

2. Save this icon arrangement. (Hint: With *Save Settings on Exit* still enabled, exit Windows.)

3. Start Windows.

4. Disable (uncheck) the **Save Settings on Exit** option. As mentioned in Chapter 1, we recommend that you leave this option unchecked, except for those instances when you wish to change the appearance of your Desktop.

Figure 7.13   **Program Manager, after repositioning icons**

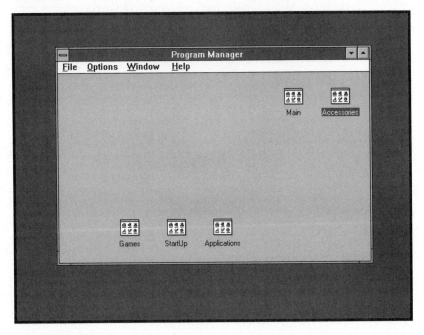

SUMMARY

With this chapter, you've completed our two-chapter introduction to Windows customization You learned how to use different Windows start-up options, how to examine your four major configuration files using the System Configuration Editor, how to manage multiple open programs, and how to customize your Desktop.

Here's a quick reference for the techniques you learned in this chapter:

Desired Result	How to Do It
Automatically run a program when you start Windows	Add the program file name to the WIN command line (for example, *win write*)
Automatically open a file when you start Windows	Add to the WIN command line the name of the program in which the file is to be opened, followed by the name of the file (for example, *win c:\windwork\memo.txt*)

Desired Result	How to Do It
Run Windows in Standard mode	Add an **/s** switch to the end of your WIN command line (for example, *win /s* or *win write /s*)
Run Windows in 386 Enhanced mode	Add a **/3** switch to the end of your WIN command line (for example, *win /3* or *win c:\windword\myfile.txt /3*)
Find out what mode Windows is running in	Choose **Help, About Program Manager** from the Program Manager menu
Switch to an open program	If the program's window is visible, click on its title bar
	Press **Ctrl+Esc** or double-click anywhere on the Desktop to display the Task List; double-click on the desired open program
	Press **Alt+Esc** to switch back to the most recently used program, or press and hold **Alt** and then press **Esc** repeatedly to cycle through all open programs
	Alt+Tab works the same way as Alt+Esc, but it is faster
Exit an open program	Display the **Task List**, select the desired program, click on **End Task**
Arrange all open program windows	Display the **Task List**, click on **Cascade** or **Tile**
Save an arrangement of group icons and/or the size and position of the Program Manager window	Switch to Program Manager, arrange your group icons as desired, size and move the Program Manager window as desired, enable the **Save Settings on Exit** option, exit Windows, start Windows, disable **Save Settings on Exit**

In the next chapter, you'll learn how to dynamically share data among your Windows programs, how to use the Clipboard Viewer to view and change the format of the Clipboard contents, and how to manage your Windows printers.

If you need to break off here, please exit Windows. If you want to proceed directly to the next chapter, please do so now.

CHAPTER 8: ADVANCED WINDOWS TOPICS

Object Linking and
Embedding (OLE)

The Clipboard
Viewer

Printer
Management

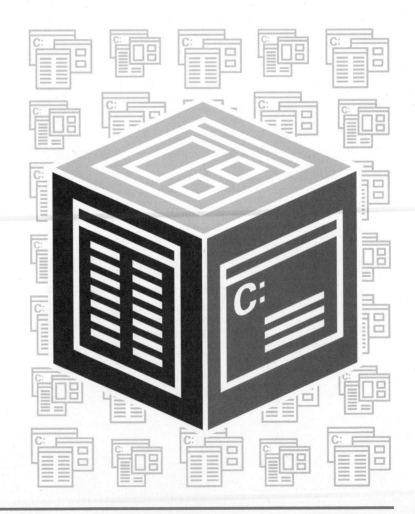

This chapter introduces a selection of advanced Windows topics that will increase your repertoire of useful Windows techniques while providing you with further insight into what makes Windows tick. We'll begin by exploring *object linking and embedding*, a powerful feature that enables you to share data (text or graphics) among various Windows programs. Then we'll take another look at the Clipboard and learn how its contents are stored in different formats and how you can choose the most appropriate format for the program to which you are pasting. We'll end the chapter with an in-depth look at printer management. You'll learn about printer drivers and fonts and how to install, select, and change your system printers.

When you're done working through this chapter, you will know

- How to use object linking and embedding to share data among Windows programs

- How to use the Clipboard Viewer to view and change the format of the Clipboard contents

- How to manage your Windows printers

OBJECT LINKING AND EMBEDDING (OLE)

As you learned in Chapter 4, the Windows Clipboard enables you to share data between documents by copying the data from one document to the other. When you do this, however, there is no dynamic connection between the original data and the copied data. If you revise the original data, and want these same revisions to be applied to the copied data, you must manually recopy the revised data. This two-step process of revision and recopying can grow quite tiresome, particularly if you go through several rounds of revision.

Windows 3.1 provides an ingenious solution to this problem: a procedure called *object linking and embedding*, or *OLE* (pronounced o-LAY). OLE enables you to use the Clipboard not merely to copy, but to *dynamically connect* objects in documents from different programs. (Remember that an *object* is simply an element of data, such as a Write paragraph or a Paintbrush picture.)

When you create a *link* to an object, changing the original object automatically changes the linked object. When you *embed* an object in a document, double-clicking on the embedded object runs the program the original object was created in and then places the embedded object into the program's workspace, enabling you to easily revise it. The terms *source program* and *source document* refer to the program and document in which the *source* (original) *object* resides; *destination program* and *destination document* refer to the program and document in which the object is linked or embedded. See Figure 8.1 for an illustration of the differences between copying, linking, and embedding.

OLE capability is not fully supported by all Windows programs. Some programs are *servers* (Paintbrush, for example); they can provide data to be linked or embedded, but cannot accept such data. Other programs are *clients* (Write, for example); they can accept linked or embedded data, but cannot provide such data. Still other programs, such as Microsoft Word for Windows, are clients *and* servers; they can both provide and accept linked or embedded data.

Figure 8.1   **Copying vs. linking vs. embedding**

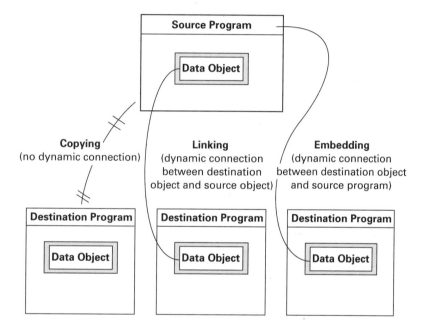

OBJECT LINKING

When you create a *link* in one document to an object in another document, you are not actually copying any data between the two documents. Instead, you are creating a dynamic reference from one object to another. The linked object refers to and is entirely dependent on the source object (the original object in the source document). Whatever changes you make to the source object will automatically be reflected in the linked object.

Those of you who have used spreadsheet programs (such as Excel or Lotus 1-2-3) may have had experience with linked spreadsheets, where the calculations in one spreadsheet (projected profits, for example) automatically reflect changes made to the numeric data in another spreadsheet (product markups, for example). OLE linking is very similar to spreadsheet linking.

The OLE linking feature is particularly useful when an object included in many documents is subject to continual revision, and this revision must be reflected in each document. For example, let's say you created a company logo in Paintbrush and needed to include this logo in a large variety of Write documents (letters, reports, proposals, memos, and so on). Rather than copy the logo to all these documents, you could create links in the documents to the original logo. Then if you needed to touch up the logo, you would revise the original and—Voilà!—all the linked logos in your various documents would automatically reflect your revision. Consider the ugly alternative: manually recopying the revised logo to each of your hundreds (or thousands!) of documents, and then repeating this entire procedure for every new logo revision.

To create a link in a document to an object in another document:

- Select the source object.

- Choose *Edit, Copy* to place a copy of the object on the Clipboard.

- Open the document in which you want to create a link to this object, and select the location where you want the link to appear.

- Choose *Paste, Link* to create the link.

Note: For this procedure to work, the source object must reside in an OLE server (or server/client) document, and the link must be created in an OLE client (or server/client) document.

To revise (edit) a linked object:

- Revise the source object; all of its linked objects will automatically reflect this revision.

- Save the revised source document. If you do not do this, the linked objects will all revert to their pre-revised states.

 OBJECT EMBEDDING

When you *embed* an object in a document, you are, in fact, copying the source object into your new document (unlike when you create a link, where no data is actually copied). But along with copying the source object, you are creating a dynamic connection to the source program (the program in which the source object was created). Double-clicking on an embedded object runs this program and places the embedded object in the program's workspace, enabling you to make revisions to the object.

The OLE embedding feature is particularly useful when an object included in many documents must be revised separately for each document. For example, let's say you wrote memos to your company's seven managers, and needed to include in each memo the portion of the company's overall organization chart that pertained to that manager. Rather than create seven separate partial organization charts in Paintbrush and then copy them, one by one, to your Write memos, you could create a single chart for your entire organization, embed this chart in each of your seven memos, and then double-click on the embedded chart from within each memo to run Paintbrush and erase the portion of the chart that did not pertain to the given manager.

To embed an object in a document:

- Select the source object.

- Choose *Edit, Copy* to place a copy of the object on the Clipboard.

- Open the document in which you want to embed this object, and select the desired embedding location.

- Choose *Paste*.

Note: For this procedure to work, the source object must reside in an OLE server (or server/client) document, and the embedded object must reside in an OLE client (or server/client) document.

To revise (edit) an embedded object:

- Double-click on the embedded object to run the source program and open the embedded object into its workspace.

- Revise the embedded object as desired.

- Choose *File, Update* (from the source program's menu) to save your revision.

- Close the source program, if desired.

PRACTICING LINKING AND EMBEDDING

If you are not running Windows, please start it now. Program Manager should be the only open window; if any other windows are open, please close them.

Let's begin by using the File, Run command to run Write and Paintbrush, the two programs we'll use for our OLE linking and embedding activities:

1. Choose **File**, **Run** (from the Program Manager menu) to open the Run dialog box.

2. Type **write** in the Command Line text box to specify the Write program file, WRITE.EXE (you do not have to include the .EXE extension). Check (click on) the **Run Minimized** option to tell Windows to run Write as an icon, rather than in a window. Click on **OK**; Write runs as an icon.

3. Choose **File**, **Run** to reopen the Run dialog box.

4. Type **c:\windwork\pictures\logo.bmp** in the Command Line text box, and then click on **OK**. Since .BMP files are associated with the Paintbrush program, issuing this command runs Paintbrush and automatically opens the file LOGO.BMP, which is stored in the directory C:\WINDWORK\PICTURES (see Figure 8.2).

Figure 8.2   **Opening LOGO.BMP in Paintbrush**

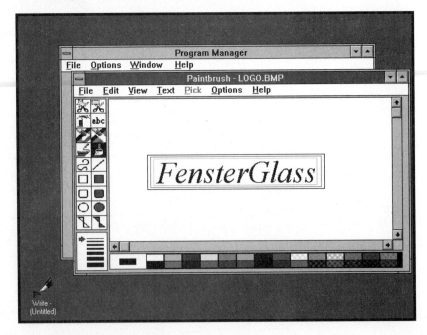

5. Choose **File, Save As**. In the File Name text box, type **c:\wind-work\mysource**. The data object in this file (that is, the logo) will be *linked* to a Write document. The name of the source document is an important part of the link. Click on **OK**.

Now let's create a link to our Paintbrush data object, and then embed this same object:

1. Use the Pick tool to select the *FensterGlass* logo. (For help using the Pick tool, see Chapter 4.)

2. Choose **Edit, Copy** to place a copy of the logo on the Clipboard.

3. Double-click on the **Write** icon to restore it to a window.

4. Type **Linking:** and then press **Enter** to insert a blank line. This heading will remind us later that the subsequent object is linked, not embedded.

5. Choose **Edit, Paste Link** to link the Paintbrush logo with the Write document (see Figure 8.3). Press **Enter** twice to insert two blank trailing lines.

Figure 8.3   **Linking a Paintbrush object with a Write document**

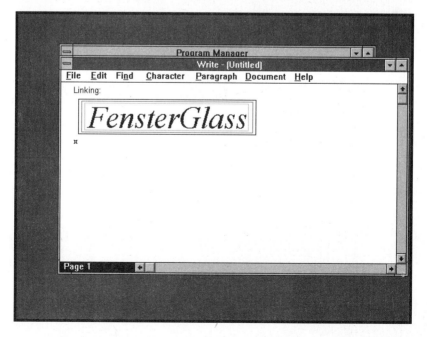

6. Type **Embedding**: and then press **Enter** to insert a blank line.

7. Choose **Edit**, **Paste** to embed the Paintbrush logo into the Write document (see Figure 8.4). Note that the linked and embedded objects look exactly alike. We'll explore their differences in the next activity.

Figure 8.4   **Embedding a Paintbrush object into a Write document**

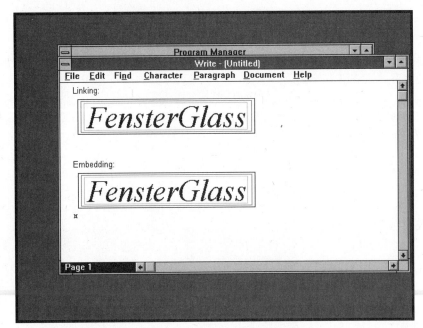

8. Choose **File**, **Save As**. In the File Name text box, type **c:\windwork\myole**, and then click on **OK** to save the Write document as MYOLE.WRI.

Now let's revise the Paintbrush source object and see how it affects our linked and embedded Write objects:

1. Press **Ctrl+PgUp** to move to the top of the Write document.

2. Switch to Program Manager and minimize it.

3. Tile the Write and Paintbrush program windows. (Double-click on the Desktop to display the Task List, and then click on **Tile**.)

4. Select the **Paintbrush** window. Use the Airbrush tool to spray some black paint onto the left half of the logo. (Remember, to change a linked object, you must change the source object.)

5. Observe the linked and embedded Paintbrush pictures in your Write document (see Figure 8.5). The linked picture reflects the changes you just made to the Paintbrush source object, whereas the embedded picture does not.

Figure 8.5   **Revising a linked object**

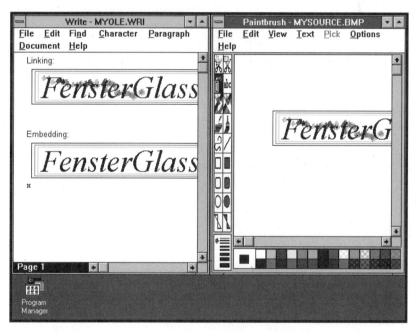

6. Select the **Paintbrush** window, if necessary. Choose **File, Save** to save your revised picture under the name MYSOURCE.BMP. Exit Paintbrush. Remember to save the source document to preserve the changes in the destination document.

Let's take a moment to examine our linked object in greater detail:

1. Maximize the **Write** window.

2. Choose **Edit**, **Links**. The Links dialog box lists all the links in the current document (see Figure 8.6). In this case, only one link is present: your Paintbrush picture, MYSOURCE.BMP.

Figure 8.6   **Links dialog box**

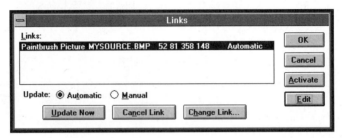

3. Observe the Activate and Edit buttons. These enable you to run the source program and to revise the source object of the selected link, much like double-clicking on an embedded object.

4. Observe the Update options, Automatic and Manual. *Automatic* processes each change to the source object automatically; *Manual* processes these changes only when you choose to update. Because the processing may take a fair amount of time, the Manual option runs faster.

5. Observe the Update Now button. Clicking on this button updates all selected links.

6. Observe the Cancel Link button. Clicking on this button breaks the link with the source document.

7. Observe the Change Link button. If the location of the linked data or the name of the source document has changed, clicking on this button allows you to specify the revised link information.

8. Click on **Cancel** (*not* on Cancel Link).

Let's finish our OLE activities by learning how to revise an embedded object:

1. Compare the linked and embedded objects in your Write document. Note, once again, that the embedded object does not

reflect the changes you made to the source object (the Paint-brush logo).

2. Double-click on the embedded object. Paintbrush runs from within Write and automatically places a copy of the embedded object in its workspace (see Figure 8.7), ready for revision. Remember that this is not the source Paintbrush object, MYSOURCE.BMP, but rather a copy of the object embedded in the Write document, MYOLE.WRI. To verify this, observe the Paintbrush title bar: *Paintbrush - Paintbrush Picture in MYOLE.WRI.*

Figure 8.7 **Double-clicking on the embedded object**

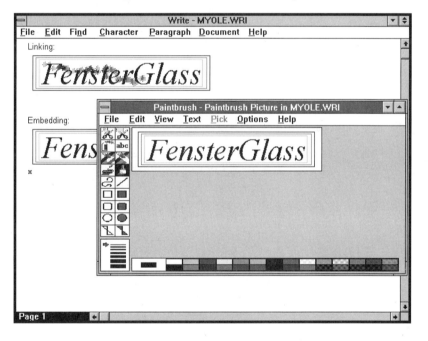

3. This time use the Roller tool to fill in the logo background with dark gray (see Figure 8.8).

4. Choose **File**, **Update** to save these changes to the embedded object in your Write document. Close the Paintbrush window, and then press **Up Arrow** to deselect the embedded object and verify that it has changed (see Figure 8.9).

Figure 8.8   **Revising the logo with the Roller tool**

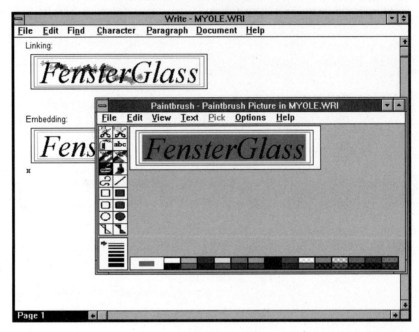

5. Now observe the linked picture. Note that it hasn't changed. Why not? Because you didn't change the source document (MYSOURCE.BMP) upon which this linked object depends. As mentioned earlier, a linked object is dynamically connected to the source *object*, and an embedded object is dynamically connected to the source *program*.

6. Choose **File**, **Save** to save the changes to MYOLE.WRI. Choose **File**, **New** to remove MYOLE.WRI from the workspace.

7. Minimize **Write**.

THE CLIPBOARD VIEWER

The Clipboard Viewer has two primary uses. The first, as you learned in Chapter 4, is to allow you to view the current contents of the Clipboard; that is, the last selection that you copied or cut from a Windows program. The second use, which is the one we'll discuss here, is to allow you to view and change the format of the Clipboard's current contents.

Figure 8.9   **Embedded object, after revising**

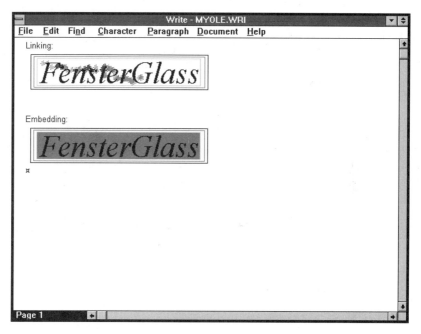

 CLIPBOARD DATA FORMATS

When you use the Copy or Cut command to store selected data on the Clipboard, the source program (the program you copy or cut *from*) automatically stores this data in several different formats. Then, when you use the Paste command to insert the contents of the Clipboard into a new document, you can choose the format most appropriate for the destination program (the program you paste *to*). In most cases, as you'll see in an upcoming activity, the Clipboard Viewer automatically selects the correct data format. Table 8.1 lists some common Clipboard data formats.

The Clipboard provides additional data formats that are specific to certain programs. For example, Excel can store data in BIFF (Binary Interchange File Format), SYLK (SYmbolic Link Format), DIF (Data Interchange Format), and several other formats. These formats are used for exchanging data with specific programs. For information on the data formats a program uses, consult its user documentation.

Table 8.1 **Common Clipboard Data Formats**

Data Format	Result
Display Text	Shows the size and origin of the selection
Paintbrush Picture Object	Shows the selection as a Paintbrush picture
Bitmap	Shows the selection as a bitmapped graphic
Link	Data for OLE
Native	Data for OLE
OwnerLink	Data for OLE
ObjectLink	Data for OLE
Rich Text Format (RTF)	A file format used by some word processors
Text	Uses the Windows screen-text font
OEM Text	Uses the DOS screen-text font
Owner Display	Shows the font used when the data were created

VIEWING AND CHANGING THE FORMAT OF THE CLIPBOARD'S CONTENTS

To view and change the format of the Clipboard's contents:

- Run the *Clipboard Viewer* (in the Main group).

- Choose *Display* to see a list of all the data formats that the current Clipboard selection is stored in. Data formats that cannot be displayed on-screen are dimmed.

- Click on the desired data format, if it is not already selected (checked). Or, click on *Auto* to allow the Clipboard Viewer to automatically determine the most appropriate data format for the current selection.

To save the current Clipboard contents in a file that you can later retrieve:

- Choose *File, Save As* (or *File, Save*) from the Clipboard Viewer menu.

- Specify the file name. (Do not include an extension; Clipboard files are automatically given the extension .CLP.)

- Specify the drive and directory, if necessary.

- Click on *OK*.

To open a .CLP file in the Clipboard (that is, to make this file the current Clipboard selection):

- Choose *File, Open* from the Clipboard Viewer menu.

- Specify the file name (without the .CLP extension).

- Specify the drive and directory, if necessary.

- Click on *OK*.

The Clipboard Viewer can open only Clipboard (.CLP) files. Opening a Clipboard file clears the current contents of the Clipboard.

The multiple data formats stored on the Clipboard occupy system memory. To clear the Clipboard and release this memory:

- Choose *Edit, Delete* from the Clipboard Viewer menu.

Let's examine some Clipboard Viewer display options:

1. Double-click on the **Program Manager** icon to restore it to a window.

2. Open the **Main** group and run the **Clipboard Viewer**. Note that the Clipboard contains a copy of the FensterGlass logo. It is the last thing that you copied to the Clipboard.

3. Switch to **Program Manager**. Choose **File, Run**, type **c:\windwork\pictures\ghia.bmp**, and then press **Enter** to run Paintbrush and open the file GHIA.BMP.

4. Use the Pick tool to select the picture of the car. (You may have to scroll to fit the entire car in the document window.) Choose **Edit, Copy** to place a copy of this selection on the Clipboard.

5. Switch to the **Clipboard Viewer** and maximize its window. Note that it shows a blown-up, coarse version of the Paintbrush car you just copied (see Figure 8.10).

Figure 8.10   **Viewing a Paintbrush picture in the Clipboard**

6. Choose **Display**. The drop-down Display menu lists the various data formats that Paintbrush used when it copied the selected car to the Clipboard. As mentioned earlier, the source program (Paintbrush, in this case) determines which formats are used. If you had copied selected text from Write, the Picture and Bitmap formats would not have been used, since these formats are associated with pictures rather than text. Note that some format types are dimmed and cannot be viewed. Note also that the Auto option is checked, indicating that the Clipboard Viewer automatically determines the data format of the current selection.

7. Choose **Bitmap** to display your selection in a bitmapped graphic format, the same format Paintbrush uses to create its .BMP picture files.

8. Choose **Display, Picture**. This is the default Clipboard format for graphics.

9. Choose **Auto** to return the Clipboard Viewer to Auto data formatting.

Now let's practice saving and opening a Clipboard file:

1. Choose **File, Save As**. As mentioned earlier, Clipboard data can be saved in files for later retrieval. Type **c:\windwork\ghia.clp** in the File Name text box and click on **OK** to save the Clipboard contents to GHIA.CLP. (Remember, you do not need to include the .CLP extension in your file name.)

2. Choose **Edit, Delete** and click on **Yes** to clear the Clipboard. The memory that was taken up storing your GHIA.BMP Clipboard selection is now free for use by other programs.

3. Choose **File, Open**. Type **c:\windwork\ghia** in the File Name text box and click on **OK** to open GHIA.CLP.

4. Choose **Display**. Note that the same format options are available as when you copied GHIA.BMP to the Clipboard in the previous activity.

5. Close **Clipboard Viewer**.

6. Double-click on the **Write** icon to restore it to a window.

7. Choose **Edit, Paste Special**. The Paste Special dialog box shows the original source of the data (GHIA.BMP) and lists the different Clipboard data formats that Write can accept (see Figure 8.11). Paintbrush Picture Object is the default format.

Figure 8.11   **Paste Special dialog box**

8. Click on **Paste** to embed the Paintbrush picture in the Write document.

9. Choose **File, New**. Click on **No** to close the current file without saving the changes.

10. Minimize **Write**.

PRINTER MANAGEMENT

In Chapter 3 you learned the basics of printing in Windows. In this chapter we'll delve deeper into the topic of Windows printer management. Over the next several sections, you'll learn

- How to install and select printer drivers

- How to change your Windows default printer

- How to use the Print Manager or Control Panel to change your printer setup options

- How to change the selection of fonts that Windows makes available for your text processing programs

- How to pause (and resume) the operation of a printer

- How to manage a print queue

 ### PRINTER DRIVERS

A *printer driver* is a file that contains instructions enabling Windows to successfully print text and graphics on a specific printer. For example, to print on an Epson FX-80 dot-matrix printer, the *Epson FX-80* printer driver must be installed *and* selected. (You'll practice installing and selecting drivers in an upcoming activity.)

Many printer drivers can be installed on your system, but only one driver can be selected at a time. Therefore, when you print, you must make sure that the currently selected printer driver matches the actual printer that you are using. Normally, you install printer drivers at the same time that you install Windows on your computer. You can, however, use the Control Panel to install additional drivers after completing your original Windows installation. To do this:

- Get your Windows Setup disks. To install a new driver, Windows requires printer data from these disks.

- Run *Control Panel*.

- Choose (double-click on) the *Printers* option to open the Printers dialog box.

- Click on *Add* >>. A list of available printer drivers is displayed.

- Select the desired driver from the list.

- Click on *Install*. Follow the on-screen prompts to insert one or more Setup disks.

- Click on *Close* to close the Printers dialog box.

Windows provides many different printer drivers. If none of these drivers supports your printer, you can contact Microsoft or the manufacturer of your printer to inquire what drivers are available.

THE DEFAULT PRINTER

Out of all your installed printer drivers, one—and only one—is designated as the *default printer*. This is the printer Windows will use whenever you submit a document (text or graphics) to be printed, unless you specifically tell Windows to use a non-default printer for that particular print job.

Only one printer at a time can be designated as the default; you can, however, change the default printer. Be aware that when you do this, you establish this new default for *all* your Windows programs.

To change the default printer, use any of these methods:

- Run *Print Manager*, choose *Options, Printer Setup*, and follow the dialog box prompts.

- Run *Control Panel*, choose the *Printers* option, and follow the dialog box prompts.

- Choose *File, Print Setup* from within a program, and follow the dialog box prompts.

This last method will work with most Windows programs. Some programs, however, such as Write and Paintbrush, allow you to change the printer for a specific print job, but do not allow you to change the default printer.

BEFORE YOU PROCEED

To complete the following printer activities, you must have at least two Windows printer drivers installed. Proceed as follows to ensure that your system meets this requirement:

1. Run **Control Panel** (in the Main group) and choose (double-click on) the **Printers** option.

2. Observe the Installed Printers list box. Note how many printer drivers are listed there. (The term *printer* is often used interchangeably with *printer driver*.)

3. Click on **Cancel** to close the Printers dialog box.

4. Close the **Control Panel**.

If two or more printers were listed in the Installed Printers list box, the printer requirement has been met; please skip the rest of this section and continue with "Changing the Default Printer."

If only one printer (or no printer) was listed, the printer requirement has not been met. Perform the following steps to remedy the situation. (To proceed, you'll need your Windows 3.1 Setup disks. If you do not have these disks—either originals or copies—skip the following activity and continue with "Changing the Default Printer." You'll have to work through the activities in this chapter using your current printer setup.)

1. Run **Control Panel** and choose the **Printers** option.

2. Click on **Add >>**. A list of printers appears at the bottom of the dialog box.

3. Select (click once on) the **Generic/Text Only** entry. Or, if this printer driver has already been installed—that is, if *Generic/Text Only* appears in the Installed Printers list box—select **AST Turbolaser/PS** (you'll have to scroll).

4. Click on **Install**. Follow the on-screen prompts to copy the necessary printer data from the Windows Setup disks to your hard disk. When the copying is finished, the printer should appear in the Installed Printers list box.

5. If you began this activity with no installed printers and now have just one installed printer, repeat steps 2 through 4 to install a second printer. Unless you have a specific preference, choose **AST Turbolaser/PS**.

6. Click on **Close** to close the Printers dialog box.

7. Close the **Control Panel**.

CHANGING THE DEFAULT PRINTER

Now that there are at least two printers installed on your system, we can begin the chapter's printing activities. Let's start by using Print Manager to change your Windows default printer:

1. Run **Print Manager** (in the Main group). All your currently installed printers are listed (see Figure 8.12; your list will be different).

Figure 8.12   **Running Print Manager**

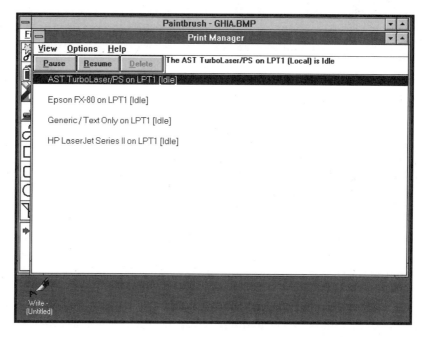

2. Choose **Options**, **Printer Setup** to open the Printer Setup dialog box.

3. In the Installed Printers list box, select (click once on) any currently unselected printer. For example, if Generic/Text Only is selected, select AST Turbolaser/PS (or whatever other printer is available).

4. Click on **Set As Default Printer** to designate your newly selected printer as the default printer.

5. Click on **Close** to remove the Printers dialog box, and then close **Print Manager.**

6. Switch to **Paintbrush.**

7. Choose **File, Print Setup**. Note that the default printer is the one you selected in step 3.

8. Click on **Cancel** to close the Print Setup dialog box, and then exit **Paintbrush.**

9. Double-click on the **Write** icon to restore it to a window.

10. Choose **File, Print Setup**. Note, once again, that the default printer is the one you selected in step 3. Since there can only be one default printer at a time, it is the same in every Windows program.

11. Click on **Cancel** to close the Print Setup dialog box.

 PRINTER SETUP

Most Windows programs provide a *Print Setup* option in their drop-down File menu. If you have more than one installed printer, you can use this option to select which printer to use for a particular print job. Once you've selected a printer, you can click on *Setup* or *Options* to change the setup data for that printer: paper orientation, paper size and type, number of copies, and so on.

Bear in mind that changing the setup of your default printer affects the way this printer functions with all your Windows programs, which might not be desirable. For example, let's say you needed to print a document in *landscape* orientation (sideways, across the length of a page) and you changed the default printer orientation setting to landscape. Every time you then used the default printer from any other Windows program, it would still be set to print in landscape (until you changed it back to portrait orientation). To avoid this kind of problem, many Windows programs provide their own setup options that override the default printer settings without permanently changing them.

PRINTERS AND FONTS

Some printers can print many different *fonts* (typefaces); others can print only a few. Depending on your currently selected printer, a certain set of fonts is made available to all your Windows programs that support text formatting (Write, Word for Windows, PageMaker, and so on). For example, if a PostScript printer (such as AST Turbolaser/PS) is selected, a large set of fonts will be available in your Windows text-formatting programs. If, on the other hand, the Generic/Text Only printer is selected, only a few fonts will be available.

Due to Windows's widely varying printer/font availability, you must exercise caution when formatting your documents, particularly if you use more than one printer in your daily work. For example, if you create and format a document when a PostScript printer is selected, and then decide to print this document to a Generic/Text Only printer, you will lose most of your PostScript fonts, because the Generic/Text Only printer cannot print them.

To avoid this problem, you should always select the printer that you will use to print a document *before* you begin formatting this document. If you use one computer to create your documents and another computer to print them, you should select the same printer on both computers.

TRUETYPE FONTS

TrueType fonts, a special category of fonts new to Windows 3.1, were created to ensure that the screen display of a document matches the actual document when printed. Non-TrueType fonts are normally stored in two separate files: a screen file containing instructions on how to display the font on-screen, and a printer file containing instructions on how to print the font on the selected printer. Due to this dual-file approach, discrepancies often arise between the screen display of a page and the actual printed page.

A TrueType font, on the other hand, is stored in one file; the same instructions are used both to display the font on-screen and to print it out. This, in turn, ensures that the font looks the same on your screen as it does on the printed page.

Another advantage of TrueType fonts is printer compatibility: They look the same on all printers that can print in the same size and resolution. By selecting a TrueType font, you make your documents easy to transfer from printer to printer.

Let's take a few moments to examine the relationship between fonts and printers:

1. Choose **Character**, **Fonts** from the Write menu to open the Font dialog box and display a list of currently available fonts. (The list in Figure 8.13 shows the fonts available for the AST Turbolaser/PS printer; your list may differ, depending on your current default printer.)

Figure 8.13   **Font list for the AST Turbolaser/PS printer**

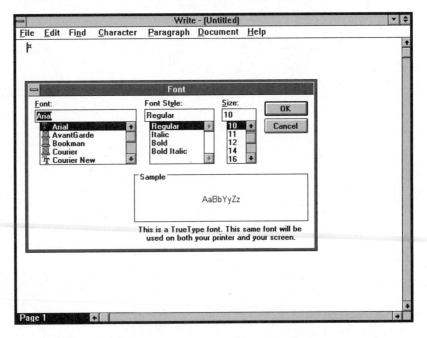

2. Click on **Cancel** to remove the Font dialog box. Now let's specify a new printer for your Write print jobs without changing the default printer.

3. Choose **File**, **Print Setup**. Select the **Specific Printer** option, click on the **down** arrow to the right of the list box, and select a currently unselected printer from the list. Click on **OK**.

4. Choose **Character, Fonts**. Note that the list of available fonts has changed to match your newly selected printer. (The list in Figure 8.14 shows the fonts available for the Generic/Text Only printer; your list may differ, depending on the printer you selected in step 3.)

Figure 8.14   **Font list for the Generic/Text Only printer**

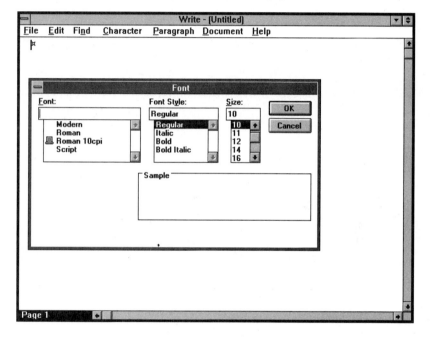

5. Click on **Cancel** to close the Font dialog box.

THE CONTROL PANEL

You can use the Printers and Fonts options in the Control Panel to manage your Windows printers and fonts, as follows. To change the default printer, or to change the printer setup options, or to install/remove printers:

• Run *Control Panel*.

• Choose the *Printers* option.

- Change the desired dialog box settings.
- Click on *OK*.

To install or to remove fonts, or to set options for using TrueType fonts:

- Run *Control Panel*.
- Choose the *Fonts* option.
- Change the desired dialog box settings.
- Click on *OK*.

Earlier, we used Print Manager to change the default printer. Now let's use the Printers option in the Control Panel to do the same thing:

1. Run **Control Panel** and choose the **Printers** option.

2. Observe the default printer. If the Use Print Manager option is not checked, please check it (click once on the check box). This option causes Windows to send all its print jobs to Print Manager.

3. Select a currently unselected printer and click on **Set As Default Printer**. Click on **Close**.

4. Close the Control **Panel** and switch to **Write**.

5. Choose **File**, **Print Setup**. Note that the default printer is the one you just selected from the Control Panel.

6. Click on **Cancel** to close the dialog box.

 PRINT MANAGER

When you print a text or graphic document from a Windows program, Windows sends the *print job* (the set of instructions that enables the currently selected printer to produce a printout of the document) to Print Manager, which can process these instructions much more quickly than most printers. As soon as Print Manager has received the entire print job, it begins to work in the background, feeding the job to the selected printer without disturbing your ongoing foreground computer work.

When you submit, in close succession, two or more documents to be printed, Print Manager creates a *print queue:* a lineup of print jobs waiting to be printed. The jobs in the print queue are stored in temporary files on the hard disk. You can use the options in Print Manager to delete or reorder the jobs in the queue. You can also *pause* (temporarily suspend) the operation of a printer and then later resume this operation.

Because the Print Manager queue is managed by your own computer, it is called a *local queue*. If you access a printer through a network server, then the network might have its own printer queues, managed by the network server. These queues are called *network queues*. You can use Print Manager to view network queues; however, you cannot manage (reorder, delete, and so on) a network queue from Print Manager.

To view the current Print Manager queue:

• Run *Print Manager*.

To change the order of print jobs in the queue:

• Run *Print Manager*.

• Drag the desired print job to a new location in the queue. You cannot change the order of the first job in a queue.

To delete a print job from the queue:

• Run *Print Manager*.

• Select the desired print job.

• Click on the *Delete* button.

To pause or resume the operation of a printer:

• Run *Print Manager*.

• Select the desired printer.

• Click on *Pause* to pause the printer. Or, click on *Resume* to resume the operation of a paused printer.

Let's create a multijob print queue, so we can practice viewing, reordering, and deleting jobs in the queue. First we'll pause the default printer, so that our print jobs remain in the queue without actually printing out:

1. Run **Print Manager**. All your installed printer drivers are listed.

2. Select (click on) the printer that you designated as the default printer in the last activity. (If you need to refresh your memory, choose Options, Printer Setup to view the current default.)

3. Click on the **Pause** button to temporarily suspend printing for the selected (default) printer. All Windows print jobs that you send to this printer will now be added to the print queue instead of actually being printed. Clicking on the Resume button will cause them to print.

4. Minimize **Print Manager**.

5. Switch to **Write**. Open the file **INVOICE1.WRI**, which is stored in your WINDWORK directory. Choose **File**, **Print** and click on **OK** to print this file. Although a message indicates that Write is printing, nothing is actually printed out. The print job is sent to Print Manager and placed in the queue.

6. Choose **File**, **Print** and click on **OK** to send a second copy of INVOICE1.WRI to Print Manager.

7. Open the file **INVOICE2.WRI** from your WINDWORK directory (without saving the changes to INVOICE1.WRI). Choose **File**, **Print** and click on **OK** to print this file. Choose **File**, **Print** and click on **OK** again to send a second copy of INVOICE2.WRI to Print Manager.

8. Exit **Write** without saving the changes.

9. Double-click on **Print Manager** to restore it to a window (see Figure 8.15). Note that all four print jobs have been sent to Print Manager and are waiting in the print queue for the paused printer to resume operation.

 THE HELP SYSTEM

We'll interrupt our print-queue activities for a moment to revisit an important Windows feature, the Help system. Program Manager, File Manager, Print Manager, and many other Windows programs offer their own on-line help.

To obtain help in such a program:

- Click on *Help* in the program's menu bar to display the drop-down Help menu.

- Click on the desired Help option.

Figure 8.15   **Print Manager, with four print jobs on the queue**

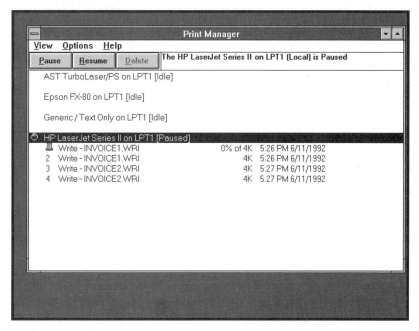

Let's use the on-line Help system to learn about the Print Manager print queue:

1. Choose **Help**, **Contents** to see the available Help topics for Print Manager.

2. Click on **What is Print Manager?** to display a brief description of Print Manager. Click on **Back** to return to the previous Help screen (the Contents).

3. Click on **Search** and type **c** to search for ways to cancel a print job. Click on **Show Topics** and then click on **Go To** to see the Help topic on Canceling Printing.

4. Click on **Pausing and Resuming Printing** to see a related Help topic.

5. Click on **Search** and type **print q** to search for ways to change the order of the print queue. Click on **Show topics**, and then click on **Go To**.

6. Click on **local printer** to see a definition of the term *local printer*. Click the mouse button again to close the definition.

7. Click on **History**. The History window lists all the Help topics that you viewed in the current Windows session. Double-clicking on a topic name in this list moves you directly to that Help screen. Close the History window.

8. Exit Help by choosing **File**, **Exit** from the Help window menu.

 MANAGING THE PRINT QUEUE

Let's end this chapter's activities by performing some typical print-queue management tasks:

1. Click on the print queue job **3 Write - INVOICE2.WRI** to select it.

2. Drag this job on top of *2 Write - INVOICE1.WRI* to change the order of these two jobs in the queue. The INVOICE2.WRI print job now precedes the INVOICE1.WRI print job.

3. Attempt to drag the first print job, **1 Write - INVOICE1.WRI**, on top of the second job to change the order again. It does not work. As mentioned earlier in this section, you cannot move the first job in a print queue.

4. Click on **3 Write - INVOICE1.WRI** to select it. Click on **Delete** and then click on **OK** to remove this job from the print queue.

5. Double-click on Print Manager's **Control** menu box to close Print Manager. An alert box appears, informing you that closing Print Manager will cancel all pending print jobs—that is, all jobs currently on the queue (see Figure 8.16).

6. Click on **OK**. You can use this technique—closing Print Manager—to quickly delete all your pending print jobs.

7. Run **Print Manager**. The print queue is empty and the default printer is no longer paused.

8. Choose **Options**, **Printer Setup**. Select the printer you will use for your daily print jobs, and then click on **Set As Default Printer** to set it as your system default. Click on **Close** to close the Printers dialog box.

9. Close **Print Manager**.

10. Close the **Main** group.

Figure 8.16   **Closing Print Manager to cancel all print jobs**

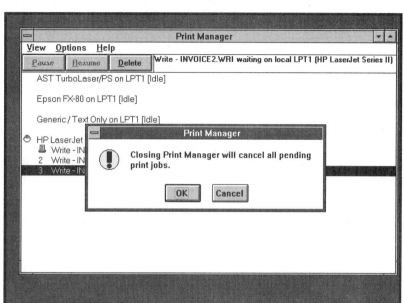

SUMMARY

In this chapter, you learned how to use object linking and embedding (OLE) to dynamically share data among your Windows programs, how to use the Clipboard Viewer to view and change the format of the Clipboard contents, and how to manage your Windows printers. Here's a quick reference for the techniques you learned in this chapter:

Desired Result

How to Do It

Create a link in a document to an object in another document

Select the source object; choose **Edit, Copy**; open the document in which you want to create a link; select the location where you want the link to appear; choose **Paste, Link**. (Note: For this procedure to work, the source object must reside in an OLE server or server/client document, and the link must be created in an OLE client or server/client document.)

Desired Result	How to Do It
Revise (edit) a linked object	Revise the source object; save the revised source document
Embed an object in a document	Select the source object; choose **Edit**, **Copy**; open the document in which you want to embed this object; select the desired embedding location; choose **Paste** (Note: For this procedure to work, the source object must reside in an OLE server or server/client document, and the link must be created in an OLE client or server/client document.)
Revise (edit) an embedded object	Double-click on the embedded object to run the source program and open the embedded object into its workspace; revise the embedded object as desired; choose **File**, **Update** (from the source program) to save your revision; close the source program, if desired
Display and change the format of the Clipboard's current contents	Run the **Clipboard Viewer** (in the Main group); choose **Display** to see a list of all the data formats that the current Clipboard selection is stored in; click on the desired data format, or click on **Auto** to allow the Clipboard Viewer to automatically determine the data format
Clear the Clipboard	Choose **Edit**, **Delete** from the Clipboard Viewer menu
Save the current Clipboard selection for use at a later time	Choose **File**, **Save As** (or **File**, **Save**) from the Clipboard Viewer menu; specify the file name; specify the drive and directory, if necessary; click on **OK**
Open a .CLP file in the Clipboard	Choose **File**, **Open** from the Clipboard Viewer menu; specify the file name; specify the drive and directory, if necessary; click on **OK**

Desired Result	How to Do It
Install additional printer drivers	Get your Windows Setup disks; run **Control Panel**; choose the **Printers** option; click on **Add >>** to display a list of available printer drivers; select the desired driver; click on **Install**; follow the on-screen prompts to insert one or more Setup disks; click on **Close**
Change the default printer	Run **Print Manager** and follow the dialog box prompts
	Run **Control Panel**; choose the **Printers** option; and follow the dialog box prompts
	Choose **File**, **Printer Setup** from within a program, and follow the dialog box prompts
Change the printer setup options, or install/remove printer drivers	Run **Control Panel**; choose the **Printers** option; change the desired dialog box settings; click on **OK**
Install or remove fonts, or set options for using TrueType fonts	Run **Control Panel**; choose the **Fonts** option; change the desired dialog box settings; click on **OK**
View the Print Manager queue	Run **Print Manager**
Change the order of print jobs in the queue	Run **Print Manager**; drag the desired print job to a new location in the queue
Delete a print job from the queue	Run **Print Manager**; select the desired print job; click on the **Delete** button
Pause or resume the operation of a printer	Run **Print Manager**; select the desired printer; click on **Pause** to pause the printer; or, click on **Resume** to resume the operation of a paused printer

Desired Result	How to Do It
Obtain on-line help from a program	Click on **Help** in the program's menu bar; click on the desired Help option

In the next chapter, you'll learn the basics of working with non-Windows programs. You'll find out how to run non-Windows programs from Windows, how to switch between Windows and non-Windows programs, and how to exchange data between Windows and non-Windows programs.

If you need to break off here, please exit Windows. If you want to proceed directly to the next chapter, please do so now.

CHAPTER 9: WORKING WITH NON-WINDOWS PROGRAMS

Running Non-Windows Programs from Windows

Switching between Windows and Non-Windows Programs

Exchanging Data between Windows Programs and Non-Windows Programs

Programs that are designed to run with DOS, but not specifically with Windows are called *non-Windows programs*. Popular
non-Windows programs include Word, WordPerfect, Lotus 1-2-3,
dBASE, Harvard Graphics, Norton Utilities, and Ventura. (Many of
these programs also come in Windows versions.) In this chapter
you'll learn how to run your non-Windows programs from within
Windows. This will enable you to take advantage of Windows's
many special features, such as its graphical user interface (GUI),
and its ability to switch between multiple programs, exchange data
between programs, and use extended memory (memory that lies
beyond the first megabyte of system RAM).

When you're done working through this chapter, you will know

- How to run non-Windows programs from Windows

- How to switch between Windows and non-Windows programs

- How to exchange data between Windows and non-Windows programs

RUNNING NON-WINDOWS PROGRAMS FROM WINDOWS

The next several sections introduce you to the theory and practice of running your non-Windows programs from Windows.

PROGRAM INFORMATION FILES (PIFS)

Windows uses a special set of instructions called a *program information file* (*PIF*) to run a non-Windows program. The PIF generally has the same file name as the executable program file and always has a .PIF extension. For example, the PIF for Microsoft Word is called WORD.PIF, and the PIF for Norton Utilities is called NORTON.PIF. Windows provides PIFs for many, but not all, non-Windows programs. If Windows cannot find a specific PIF for a non-Windows program, it will use its general PIF, called DEFAULT.PIF. (We'll take a look at a PIF in the first activity of this chapter.)

SWITCHING TO THE DOS SYSTEM PROMPT

The most important non-Windows program on your computer is DOS, the Disk Operating System. DOS is the foundation upon which all Windows and non-Windows programs run. As you learned in Chapter 7, Windows itself runs on top of DOS. (For more on DOS, see "The DOS Operating System" in Chapter 7.)

Typical DOS tasks, such as managing files, running programs, and setting the system date and time, can be performed from within Windows using File Manager and Control Panel. At times, however, you may want to issue DOS commands to perform these tasks. Users who feel comfortable entering standard DOS commands (such as DIR, DEL, COPY, DATE, TIME, and so on) may prefer these commands to their Windows equivalents. For this reason, Windows allows you to switch to the DOS system prompt, issue your desired commands, and then return to Windows. To do this:

- Run *MS-DOS Prompt* (in the Main group). The DOS system prompt appears.

- Issue your desired DOS command(s).

- Type *exit* and press *Enter* to exit MS-DOS Prompt and return to Windows.

Note: While it is running, Windows creates and stores various *temporary files* that are automatically deleted from your hard disk when you exit Windows. These files contain data critical to Windows's operation and must remain intact while Windows is running. For this reason, if you use MS-DOS Prompt to switch from Windows to the DOS system prompt, do not issue any commands that might change the configuration of your hard disk. These include the DOS commands CHKDSK /F (Check Disk) and CHCP (Change Codepage) and any disk-optimization utilities (such as Norton's SD or SPEEDISK). After you exit Windows, you are free once again to issue these commands.

If you are not running Windows, please start it now. Program Manager should be the only open window; if any other windows are open, please close them. Let's begin by running MS-DOS Prompt and issuing a few DOS commands. But first let's take a quick look at the MS-DOS Prompt program-item icon:

1. Open the **Main** group and select (click once on) the **MS-DOS Prompt** icon.

2. Choose **File, Properties** from the Program Manager Group to display the Program Item Properties dialog box. The Command Line text box shows the executable file for MS-DOS Prompt, DOSPRMPT.PIF. As mentioned earlier, a PIF (program information file) is a special set of instructions that Windows uses to run a non-Windows program, such as MS-DOS Prompt. Click on **Cancel** to remove the Program Item Properties dialog box.

3. Run **MS-DOS Prompt**. The DOS system prompt appears (see Figure 9.1).

4. Read the message at the top of the screen. It lets you know that Windows is still running in the background. As the first two bulleted items explain, to return from the system prompt to Windows, you must exit MS-DOS Prompt or switch from MS-DOS Prompt to Windows.

Figure 9.1 **Running MS-DOS Prompt**

```
┌─────────────────────────────────────────────────────────────┐
│  ▌ Type EXIT and press ENTER to quit this MS-DOS prompt and   │
│    return to Windows.                                         │
│  ▌ Press ALT+TAB to switch to Windows or another application. │
│  ▌ Press ALT+ENTER to switch this MS-DOS Prompt between a     │
│    window and full screen.                                    │
└─────────────────────────────────────────────────────────────┘

Microsoft(R) MS-DOS(R) Version 5.00
         (C)Copyright Microsoft Corp 1981-1991.

C:\WINDOWS>
```

5. Type **path** and press **Enter** to view the current DOS search path. PATH is one of the few DOS commands for which there is no direct Windows equivalent.

6. Type **dir** and press **Enter** to list the files in the current directory. Note that the message box scrolls beyond the top of the screen. From here on, you will not be able to tell that Windows is running simply by looking at the screen. Let's say that you forgot that Windows was running and attempted to restart it.

7. Type **win** and press **Enter**. A message appears, informing you that you are already running Windows. You cannot run two copies of Windows simultaneously.

8. Type **cls** and press **Enter**. Note again that you cannot tell that Windows is running simply by looking at the DOS system prompt. In the next activity, we'll show you how to modify this prompt to display a reminder that Windows is running.

9. Type **exit** and press **Enter** to return to Windows.

 USING BATCH FILES FOR DOS COMMAND SEQUENCES

A *batch file* is a text file that contains a sequence of DOS commands. When you run a batch file—from the DOS system prompt or from within Windows—these commands are automatically executed in the order they appear. For example, a batch file named WORK.BAT might, when executed, change the current directory to C:\NOVEL, run Microsoft Word, and load the document CHAPTER1.DOC into Word's workspace. All batch files use the extension .BAT. Because batch files are standard (unformatted) text files, you can use Notepad to create and edit them.

Let's use Notepad to examine the file PROMPT.BAT, and then let's run this batch file:

1. Run **Notepad** (in the Accessories group).

2. Open the file **PROMPT.BAT** from your **WINDWORK** directory (see Figure 9.2). This batch file contains two commands, one on each line. The first command modifies the system prompt to display a reminder that Windows is currently running. The second command switches from Windows to the DOS system prompt; it does this by loading COMMAND.COM, the DOS command interpreter. (Batch-file commands are beyond the scope of this book; if you are interested in learning more, please refer to your DOS reference manuals.)

Figure 9.2   **PROMPT.BAT in Notepad**

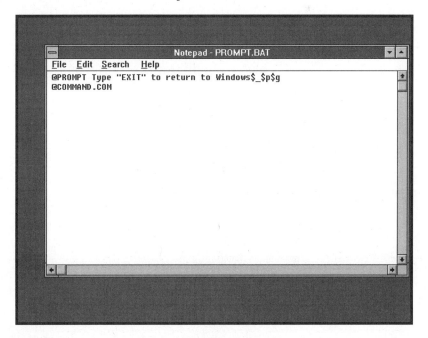

3. Exit **Notepad** and close the **Accessories** window.

4. Choose **File, Run**, type **c:\windwork\prompt.bat**, and click on **OK**. The modified DOS system prompt appears (see Figure 9.3). The message *Type "EXIT" to return to Windows* is now part of the system prompt and serves to remind you that Windows is running.

Figure 9.3   **Modified DOS system prompt**

```
Microsoft(R) MS-DOS(R) Version 5.00
        (C)Copyright Microsoft Corp 1981-1991.

Type "EXIT" to return to Windows
C:\WINDWORK>_
```

5. Type **dir** and press **Enter**. The *Type "EXIT"* message returns.

6. Type **cls** and press **Enter**. The *Type "EXIT"* message appears once again.

7. Type **exit** and press **Enter** to return to Windows.

RUNNING A NON-WINDOWS PROGRAM IN A FULL SCREEN OR IN A WINDOW

If Windows is running in 386 Enhanced mode, you can run a non-Windows program in a *full screen* or in a *window*. A full-screen non-Windows program takes up the entire screen, exactly as it would if you were running the program from DOS. A windowed non-Windows program is enclosed by a window that you can maximize, minimize, move, and size, exactly like a standard program window. If Windows is running in Standard mode, you can only run a non-Windows program in a full screen, not in a window.

When you run a non-Windows program from Windows, the program starts in a full screen (unless the program's PIF contains an instruction to run in a window). To run a full-screen non-Windows program in a window:

- Make sure that Windows is running in 386 Enhanced mode.

- Switch to the non-Windows program.

- Press *Alt+Enter*.

To run a windowed non-Windows program in a full screen:

- Repeat the above procedure. Alt+Enter toggles between window and full-screen modes.

Let's run the non-Windows program MS-DOS Prompt in a window. Perform this activity only if you are running Windows in 386 Enhanced mode. (To check, choose *Help, About Program Manager* from the Program Manager menu.) If you are running in Standard mode, you cannot run MS-DOS Prompt—or any other non-Windows program—in a window; please skip directly to "Different Methods for Running a Non-Windows Program."

1. Double-click on **MS-DOS Prompt** to run the program in a full screen. Read the third bulleted item at the top of the screen. MS-DOS Prompt can also run in a window.

2. Press **Alt+Enter** to run MS-DOS Prompt in a window (see Figure 9.4).

3. Click on this window's **Control** menu box. Note that the Close option is dimmed (unavailable). To close the MS-DOS Prompt window and return to Windows, you must type *exit* and press *Enter* at the DOS system prompt. (Don't do this now.) Click on the **Control** menu box again to close the Control menu.

4. Press **Alt+Enter** again to run MS-DOS Prompt in a full screen.

5. Type **exit** and press **Enter** to exit MS-DOS prompt and return to Windows.

PRACTICE YOUR SKILLS

You do not need to run MS-DOS Prompt in a full screen before exiting to Windows. Let's verify this:

1. Run **MS-DOS Prompt** in a window.

Figure 9.4   **MS-DOS Prompt, running in a window**

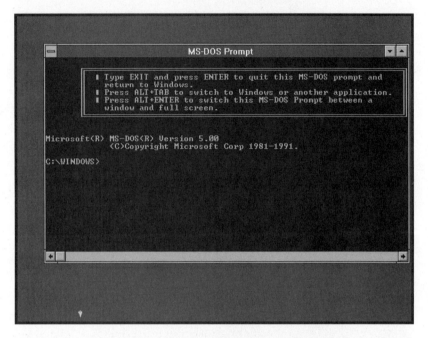

2. From within this window, type **exit** and press **Enter** to close the MS-DOS Prompt window and return to Windows.

 DIFFERENT METHODS FOR RUNNING A NON-WINDOWS PROGRAM

So far in this chapter, we've shown you two methods for running a non-Windows program: double-clicking on the program-item icon (this will only work, of course, if the program-item icon exists); and using the File, Run command. Here you'll learn a third method: double-clicking on the program-file icon within File Manager. Before proceeding, let's summarize.

Use any of the following methods to run a non-Windows program from Windows:

- In Program Manager, double-click on the program-item icon.

- In Program Manager or File Manager, use the *File, Run* command to run the program or PIF.

- In File Manager, double-click on the program-file icon.

Using this last method, let's run a non-Windows program called Alphabet:

1. Run **File Manager**.

2. Select the **windwork** directory.

3. Select the **alpha** subdirectory.

4. Double-click on the **alphabet.exe** program-file icon to run the Alphabet program (see Figure 9.5). Alphabet is a simple non-Windows text editor, developed solely for use with this book. It does not contain any standard Windows features, such as a menu bar or a Control menu box; it does not support use of the mouse. Note the current directory, C:\WINDWORK\ALPHA, which is displayed at the top left of the screen. Note also the blinking (active) prompt at the bottom of the screen, FILE\DIRECTORY NAME:, asking you for the name of the file you would like to open or the directory you would like to change to.

Figure 9.5   **Alphabet program**

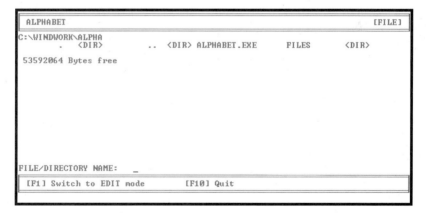

```
ALPHABET                                                          [FILE]
C:\WINDWORK\ALPHA
      .    <DIR>           ..  <DIR> ALPHABET.EXE     FILES    <DIR>
  53592064 Bytes free




FILE/DIRECTORY NAME:    _
    [F1] Switch to EDIT mode          [F10] Quit
```

5. Type **files** and press **Enter** to change the current directory to C:\WINDWORK\ALPHA\FILES, as indicated on the top left of the screen. This is the directory that Alphabet's files are stored in.

6. Type **memo.abc** and press **Enter** to open the file MEMO.ABC into Alphabet's workspace.

7. Press **F10** to exit Alphabet and return to Windows.

Now let's run Alphabet by double-clicking on its program-item icon. Since no program-item currently exists, we'll just have to create one:

1. Exit **File Manager**. We'll create our icon in Applications, an appropriate group for a program such as Alphabet.

2. Open the **Applications** group.

3. Choose **File, New**, verify that Program Item is selected, and then click on **OK**.

4. In the Command Line text box, type

   ```
   c:\windwork\alpha\alphabet.exe
   ```

   The full path is necessary because the C:\WINDWORK\ALPHA directory is not in your DOS search path.

5. In the Working Directory text box, type

   ```
   c:\windwork\alpha\files
   ```

   to specify Alphabet's default work directory (the directory that its files will be automatically opened from and saved to).

6. Click on **OK**. Your newly created Alphabet program-item icon appears in the Applications window. (See Figure 9.6; the contents of your Applications group will be different.) Note that Windows automatically chose a generic MS DOS picture for the Alphabet icon, indicating that this is a DOS (non-Windows) program. Note also that Windows chose the icon name *Alphabet*, which it took from the program name (ALPHABET.EXE).

7. Double-click on the **Alphabet** icon to run Alphabet. Note that the current directory is C:\WINDWORK\ALPHA\FILES, the one we specified in the Working Directory text box.

8. Type **budget.abc** and press **Enter** to open the Alphabet file, BUDGET.ABC (see Figure 9.7).

Figure 9.6 **Newly created Alphabet icon**

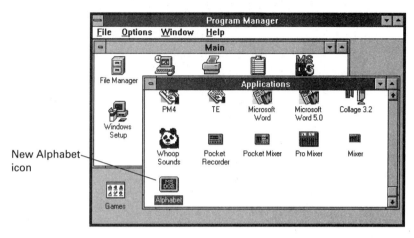

New Alphabet icon

Figure 9.7 **BUDGET.ABC in Alphabet**

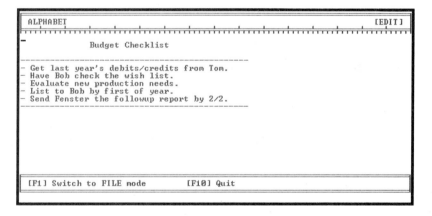

SWITCHING BETWEEN WINDOWS AND NON-WINDOWS PROGRAMS

In Chapter 7, you learned several techniques for switching between multiple open Windows programs. You can use two of these techniques to switch between Windows and Non-Windows programs, as follows:

• Press *Ctrl+Esc* (or double-click on the Desktop) to display the Task List, and then double-click on the desired program to switch to it.

- Or, hold down *Alt* and press *Tab* repeatedly to cycle through the names of all open programs, and then release *Alt* to switch to the currently displayed program.

Let's practice using both of these techniques to switch between Windows and non-Windows programs:

1. Use **Alt+Tab** to switch from Alphabet to **Program Manager**. Note that Alphabet is now running as an icon (see Figure 9.8).

Figure 9.8   **Alphabet running as an icon**

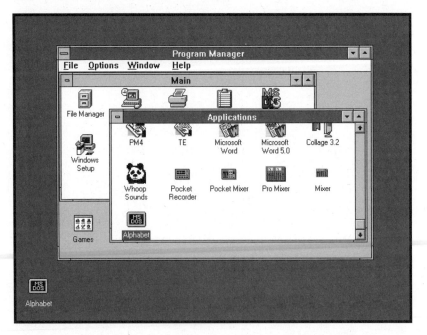

2. Close the **Applications** group.

3. Run **Write** (in the Accessories group). Now we have one open non-Windows program (Alphabet) and two open Windows programs (Write and Program Manager).

4. Press and hold **Alt**, and then press **Tab** repeatedly to cycle through these programs without actually switching to any of them. (Do not release Alt until the next step.) Note that the

Write program appears as *Write - (Untitled)*, because the Write workspace is currently empty.

5. When *Alphabet* is displayed, release **Alt** to switch to the Alphabet program.

6. Press **Ctrl+Esc** to display the Task List (see Figure 9.9). The currently open programs are listed: Alphabet, Write - (Untitled), and Program Manager. Note that the Task List display does not differentiate between Windows and non-Windows programs.

Figure 9.9 **Task List**

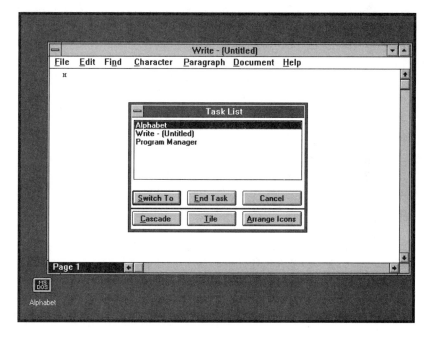

7. Double-click on **Program Manager** to switch to this program.

8. Switch to **Alphabet**. (Use whichever method you prefer, Alt+-Tab or the Task List.)

EXCHANGING DATA BETWEEN WINDOWS PROGRAMS AND NON-WINDOWS PROGRAMS

One major advantage of running your non-Windows programs from Windows (instead of from DOS) is that you can use the Clipboard to exchange data between these programs and your Windows programs. The exact procedure you must use to do this depends on whether the non-Windows program is running in a full screen or in a window, as explained in the following sections.

 ### COPYING DATA FROM A WINDOWS PROGRAM TO A NON-WINDOWS PROGRAM RUNNING IN A FULL SCREEN

To copy data from a Windows program to a full-screen non-Windows program:

- Run the Windows and non-Windows programs, if they are not already running.

- Switch to the Windows program. The non-Windows program will run as an icon.

- Select the data to copy.

- Choose *Edit, Copy* to copy the selection to the Clipboard.

- Click once on the icon of the non-Windows program to open its Control menu.

- Choose *Paste* (if you are running Windows in Standard mode), or choose *Edit, Paste* (if you are running in 386 Enhanced mode).

To copy data from a full-screen non-Windows program to a Windows program:

- Run the non-Windows and Windows programs, if they are not already running.

- Switch to the non-Windows program and display the desired data on the screen. (You can only copy one screen's worth of data at a time from a full-screen non-Windows program to a Windows program. To copy additional data, you must repeat this entire procedure.)

- Press *Print Screen* to copy the contents of the screen to the Clipboard. (The Print Screen key may appear on your keyboard as *Print Screen, Print Scrn, PrtScrn, PrtSc,* or some other variant.)

- Switch to the Windows program.

- Choose *Edit, Paste*.

- To copy additional data, repeat this procedure as needed.

Let's use this latter procedure to copy data from Alphabet, which is running in a full screen, to Write:

1. Switch to **Alphabet**, if necessary. The file BUDGET.ABC should be loaded in the workspace.

2. Press **Print Screen** (or *PrtScrn*, or *PrtSc*, and so on) to copy the contents of the current screen—in this case, the entire contents of BUDGET.ABC—to the Clipboard.

3. Switch to **Write**. Note that Alphabet is now running as an icon. Maximize the Write window.

4. Choose **Edit, Paste** to paste the contents of the Clipboard (BUDGET.ABC) into your Write document (see Figure 9.10). Note that the pasted data does not look exactly like the original Alphabet data (compare Figures 9.7 and 9.10). Some of Alphabet's special DOS characters—for example, the vertical tick marks on the ruler at the top of Figure 9.7—were lost when you copied the Alphabet screen to the Clipboard.

5. Choose **File, New** and click on **No** to open a blank Write document without saving the changes.

COPYING DATA FROM A WINDOWS PROGRAM TO A NON-WINDOWS PROGRAM RUNNING IN A WINDOW

To copy data from a Windows Program to a non-Windows program running in a window:

- Run the non-Windows and Windows programs, if they are not already running.

- Switch to the Windows program.

- Select the data to be copied.

- Choose *Edit, Copy*.

- Switch to the non-Windows program.

- Choose *Edit, Paste* from the program's Control menu.

Figure 9.10   **Copying from Alphabet to Write**

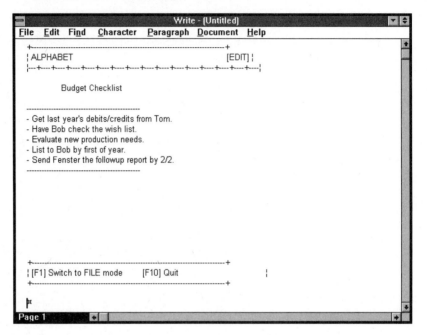

To copy data from a non-Windows program running in a window to a Windows program:

- Run the non-Windows and Windows programs, if they are not already running.

- Switch to the non-Windows program running in a window.

- Choose *Edit, Mark* from the program's Control menu.

- Drag (or hold down *Shift* and press the arrow keys) to select the data to be copied.

- Choose *Edit, Copy* from the Control menu.

- Switch to the Windows program.

- Choose *Edit, Paste.*

Let's run Alphabet in a window, select some text in BUDGET.ABC, and then copy this selection to Write. (As you learned earlier in this chapter, a non-Windows program can be run in a window only if Windows is running in 386 Enhanced mode. If you are running in

386 Enhanced mode, please continue with this activity. If you are running in Standard mode, skip directly to "Exchanging Data between Non-Windows Programs.")

1. Use **Alt+Tab** to switch to **Alphabet**.

2. Press **Alt+Enter** to run Alphabet in a window, and then maximize this window.

3. Click on Alphabet's **Control** menu box and choose **Edit, Mark**. A marker appears in the upper-left corner of the Alphabet window, and the Alphabet title bar changes to *Mark Alphabet* (see Figure 9.11).

Figure 9.11   **Choosing Edit, Mark from the Control menu box**

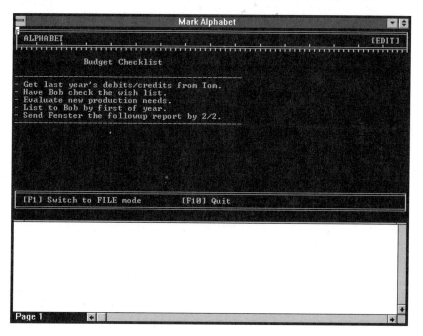

4. Drag to select (highlight) the first two items in the checklist (see Figure 9.12).

5. Click on the **Control** menu box and choose **Edit, Copy** to copy this selected text to the Clipboard. Note that the text is deselected (the highlighting is removed).

Figure 9.12   **Selecting text in Alphabet**

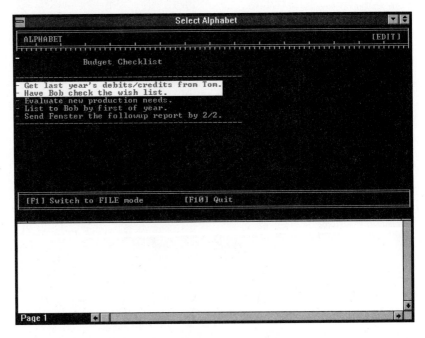

6. Switch to **Write**.

7. Choose **Edit, Paste** to paste your selected text to the Write document.

8. Choose **File, New** and click on **No** to open a blank document without saving the changes.

9. Minimize **Write**.

EXCHANGING DATA BETWEEN NON-WINDOWS PROGRAMS

To copy data from a full-screen non-Windows program to another non-Windows program:

• Run both non-Windows programs, if they are not already running.

• Switch to the non-Windows program you want to copy from.

• Press *Print Screen* to copy the contents of the screen to the Clipboard.

- If the non-Windows program you want to copy to is running in a full screen, click once on the program's icon to open its Control menu, and then choose *Paste* (if you are running in Standard mode) or *Edit, Paste* (if you are running in 386 Enhanced mode).

- If the non-Windows program you want to copy to is running in a window, switch to this program and choose *Edit, Paste* from its Control menu.

- To copy additional data, repeat this procedure as needed.

To copy data from a non-Windows program running in a window to another non-Windows program:

- Run both non-Windows programs, if they are not already running.

- Switch to the non-Windows program you want to copy from.

- Choose *Edit, Mark* from the program's Control menu.

- Drag (or hold down *Shift* and press the arrow keys) to select the data to be copied.

- Choose *Edit, Copy* from the Control menu.

- If the non-Windows program you want to copy to is running in a full screen, click once on the program's icon to open its Control menu, and then choose *Paste* (if you are running in Standard mode) or *Edit, Paste* (if you are running in 386 Enhanced mode).

- If the non-Windows program you want to copy to is running in a window, switch to this program and choose *Edit, Paste* from its Control menu.

PRACTICE YOUR SKILLS

In this Practice Your Skills activity, you'll copy data from a windowed non-Windows program to a full-screen non-Windows program.

1. Switch to Program Manager, and use **File, Run** to run the Alphabet program (C:\WINDWORK\ALPHA\ALPHABET.EXE). Press **F1** to switch to Edit mode.

2. Two copies of Alphabet are now running on your Desktop—one in a window and one in a full screen. The windowed Alphabet workspace contains the text shown in Figure 9.11; the full-screen Alphabet workspace is empty. Use **Alt+Tab** to verify this.

3. Use the procedure outlined above to copy the first two checklist items (the same items as in Figure 9.12) from the windowed Alphabet program to the full-screen Alphabet program.

4. Exit the full-screen Alphabet program. (Hint: Press **F10**; don't save the file.)

 COPYING THE SCREEN AS A BITMAPPED GRAPHIC OBJECT

When any program, Windows or non-Windows, is running in a window, you can copy the contents of the screen to the Clipboard as a bitmapped graphic object. You can then paste this object into a document in any program capable of importing standard bitmapped graphics (for example, Paintbrush or Write).

To copy the current windowed screen as a bitmapped graphic object:

• Press *Print Screen* to copy the entire screen to the Clipboard.

• Or, press *Alt+Print Screen* to copy only the active window to the Clipboard.

Let's use the first of these procedures to copy a windowed Alphabet screen to the Clipboard as a bitmapped graphic object. (Once again, you can perform this activity only if you are running Windows in 386 Enhanced mode. If you are running in Standard mode, skip directly to "Summary.")

1. Switch to **Alphabet**, if necessary. Alphabet should still be running in a maximized window.

2. Press **Print Screen**. As mentioned previously, when a program is running in a window, pressing Print Screen copies the entire screen to the Clipboard in bitmapped graphic format.

3. Press **Alt+Enter** to run Alphabet in a full screen.

4. Switch to **Write** and, if necessary, maximize the Write window.

5. Choose **Edit, Paste** to paste the Clipboard contents as a bit-mapped graphic object. Press **Left Arrow** once to reorient the object in the Write workspace (see Figure 9.13).

Figure 9.13   **Pasting the Alphabet graphic object into Write**

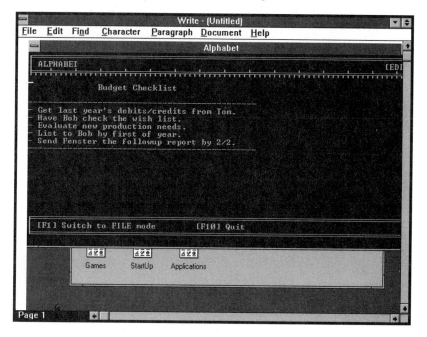

6. Click on the **down scroll** arrow to examine the document. Note that all the screen elements were captured when you pressed Print Screen in step 2, including icons, open windows, and the Desktop.

7. Exit **Write** without saving the changes.

8. Exit **Alphabet**.

9. Close the **Accessories** and **Main** windows.

SUMMARY

In this chapter you learned the basics of working with non-Windows programs. You now know how to run non-Windows programs from

Windows, how to switch between Windows and non-Windows programs, and how to exchange data between Windows and non-Windows programs.

Here's a quick reference for the techniques you learned in this chapter:

Desired Result	How to Do It
Switch to the DOS system prompt	Run **MS-DOS Prompt** (in the Main group)
Exit from the DOS system prompt to Windows	At the system prompt, type **exit** and press **Enter**
Run a full-screen non-Windows program in a window	Make sure Windows is running in 386 Enhanced mode; switch to the non-Windows program; press **Alt+Enter**
Run a windowed non-Windows program in a full screen	Repeat the above procedure (Alt+Enter toggles between window and full-screen modes)
Run a non-Windows program from Windows	In Program Manager, double-click on the program-item icon
	In Program Manager or File Manager, use the *File, Run* command to run the program or PIF
	In File Manager, double-click on the program-file icon
Switch between Windows and Non-Windows programs	Press **Ctrl+Esc** (or double-click on the Desktop) to display the Task List; double-click on the desired program
	Hold down **Alt** and press **Tab** repeatedly to cycle through the names of all open programs; release **Alt** to switch to the currently displayed program

Desired Result	How to Do It
Copy data from a Windows program to a full-screen non-Windows program	Run the Windows and non-Windows programs, if they are not already running; switch to the Windows program; select the data to copy; choose **Edit, Copy**; click once on the icon of the non-Windows program to open its Control menu; choose **Paste** (if you are running Windows in Standard mode) or choose **Edit, Paste** (if you are running in 386 Enhanced mode)
Copy data from a full-screen non-Windows program to a Windows program	Run the non-Windows and Windows programs, if they are not already running; switch to the non-Windows program and display the desired data on the screen; press **Print Screen**; switch to the Windows program; choose **Edit, Paste**; to copy additional data, repeat this procedure as needed
Copy data from a Windows Program to a non-Windows program running in a window	Run the non-Windows and Windows programs, if they are not already running; switch to the Windows program; select the data to be copied; choose **Edit, Copy**; switch to the non-Windows program; choose **Edit, Paste** from the program's Control menu
Copy data from a non-Windows program running in a window to a Windows program	Run the non-Windows and Windows programs, if they are not already running; switch to the non-Windows program running in a window; choose **Edit, Mark** from the program's Control menu; drag (or hold down Shift and press the arrow keys) to select the data to be copied; choose **Edit, Copy** from the Control menu; switch to the Windows program; choose **Edit, Paste**

Desired Result	How to Do It
Copy data from a full-screen non-Windows program to another non-Windows program	Run both non-Windows programs, if they are not already running; switch to the non-Windows program you want to copy from; press **Print Screen**; if the non-Windows program you want to copy to is running in a full screen, click once on the program's icon to open its Control menu, and then choose **Paste** (if you are running in Standard mode) or **Edit, Paste** (if you are running in 386 Enhanced mode); if the non-Windows program you want to copy to is running in a window, switch to this program and choose **Edit, Paste** from its Control menu; to copy additional data, repeat this procedure as needed
Copy data from a non-Windows program running in a window to another non-Windows program	Run both non-Windows programs, if they are not already running; switch to the non-Windows program you want to copy from; choose **Edit, Mark** from the program's Control menu; drag (or hold down Shift and press the arrow keys) to select the data to be copied; choose **Edit, Copy** from the Control menu; if the non-Windows program you want to copy to is running in a full screen, click once on the program's icon to open its Control menu, and then choose **Paste** (if you are running in Standard mode) or **Edit, Paste** (if you are running in 386 Enhanced mode); if the non-Windows program you want to copy to is running in a window, switch to this program and choose **Edit, Paste** from its Control menu
Copy the current screen to the Clipboard as a bit-mapped graphic object	Press **Print Screen** to copy the entire screen; or press **Alt+Print Screen** to copy only the active window

In the next chapter we'll show you several new file-management techniques. You'll learn how to open multiple File Manager directory windows, how to customize a directory window display, how to use wildcards to manage groups of files, how to print files from within File Manager, and how to use File Manager to create program-item icons.

If you need to break off here, please exit Windows. If you want to proceed directly to the next chapter, please do so now.

CHAPTER 10: ADVANCED FILE-MANAGEMENT TECHNIQUES

Opening Multiple
Directory Windows
in File Manager

Customizing a
Directory Window
Display

Using Wildcards to
Manage Groups of
Files

Selecting a Group
of Files

Printing Files from
Within File
Manager

Using File Manager
to Create Program-
Item Icons

F ile Manager is one of Windows's most powerful and versatile programs. In Chapters 3 and 5, you learned its basic file-management capabilities. In this chapter, you'll expand your File Manager skills by learning several advanced techniques for viewing, copying, moving, and deleting groups of files. You'll also find out how to open multiple File Manager directory windows and how to customize the display of these windows. Finally, you'll learn how File Manager can be used to print files and create program-item icons.

When you're done working through this chapter, you will know

- How to open multiple File Manager directory windows

- How to customize a directory window display

- How to use wildcards to manage groups of files

- How to print files from within File Manager

- How to use File Manager to create program-item icons

OPENING MULTIPLE DIRECTORY WINDOWS IN FILE MANAGER

File Manager allows you to open multiple directory windows at the same time. This simplifies the tasks of copying and moving files among different directories and drives. It can also provide you with a clear visual overview of the contents of several directories and the tree structure of several drives.

To open a new directory window:

- Double-click on the icon of the drive containing the desired directory.

A newly opened directory window inherits the characteristics of the directory window that was active (selected) when you opened the new window. For example, let's say you set the active directory window to display the directory tree only, rather than the tree *and* file contents (you'll find out how to do this in the upcoming section, "Changing the Main View"). If you open a new directory window, it will also display the directory tree only. The inheritance feature does not, however, work in reverse; changes you make to the active window do *not* affect any previously opened windows.

If you are not running Windows, please start it now. Program Manager should be the only open window; if any other windows are open, please close them.

Let's begin by running File Manager and opening two directory windows:

1. Run **File Manager** (in the Main group).

2. Maximize the File Manager application window, if necessary.

3. In File Manager, click once on the **windwork** directory icon to view the contents of your WINDWORK directory.

4. Double-click on the **C** drive icon to open a second directory window of your C drive.

5. Choose **Window, Tile** to tile the two directory windows (see Figure 10.1). Observe the two title bars C:\WINDWORK*.*:1 and C:\WINDWORK*.*:2. Multiple windows depicting the same drive and directory are numbered sequentially to prevent confusion.

Figure 10.1   **Tiling two directory windows**

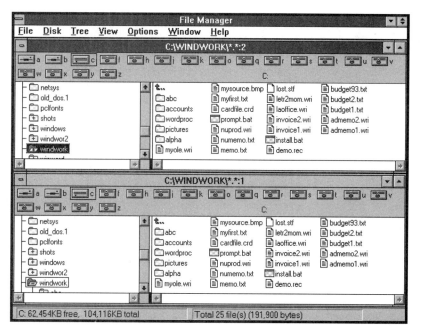

6. In the C:\WINDWORK*.*:2 window, double-click on the **windwork** directory icon to reveal its subdirectories. Click once on the **alpha** subdirectory icon to select it.

7. Activate the **C:\WINDWORK*.*:1** window by clicking on its title bar. Double-click on the **windwork** directory icon to reveal its subdirectories. Click once on the **wordproc** subdirectory icon to select it.

8. Observe the title bars; the numbers (1 and 2) are gone. File Manager only numbers multiple windows when they depict the same drive and directory. To verify this, select the **c:** directory

in the lower window, and then select **c:** in the upper window. The numbering scheme is reinstated.

CUSTOMIZING A DIRECTORY WINDOW DISPLAY

As you know from the many File Manager tasks you've performed in this book, the default File Manager directory window displays both the directory tree of the selected drive (on the left side of the window) and the contents of the selected directory (on the right side). Figure 10.2 depicts a default directory window display of the WINDWORK directory.

Figure 10.2   **Default File Manager directory window display**

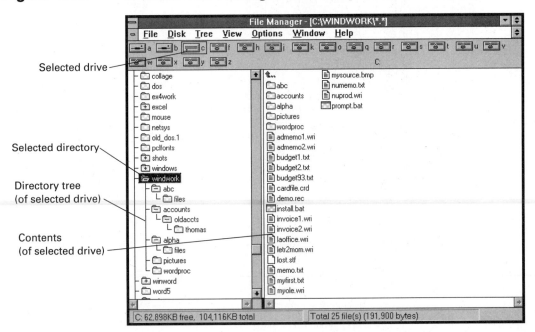

In keeping with Windows's open approach to user customization, File Manager enables you to change various key elements in a directory window display. You can display the directory tree and directory contents (this is the default setting), the directory tree only, or the directory contents only. You can sort files by any of the following criteria: name (default), type, size, or last modification date.

You can display any combination of the following file details along with the file names: file size, date and time of last modification, and file attributes.

 CHANGING THE MAIN VIEW

To change the main view of a directory window:

- Select the directory window.
- Click on *View* to display the drop-down View menu.
- Click on the desired view:
  - *Tree and Directory* displays both the tree and contents (this is File Manager's default view).
  - *Tree Only* displays the directory tree only.
  - *Directory Only* displays the directory contents only.

 CHANGING THE FILE SORT ORDER

To change the order in which files are sorted in a directory window:

- Select the directory window.
- Click on *View* to display the drop-down View menu.
- Click on the desired Sort By option:
  - *Sort by Name* sorts files alphabetically by name.
  - *Sort by Type* sorts files alphabetically by extension.
  - *Sort by Size* sorts files by size, largest to smallest.
  - *Sort by Date* sorts files by date, latest to earliest.

 CHANGING THE FILE DETAILS

To display all file details in a directory window:

- Select the directory window.
- Choose *View, All File Details*.

To display selected file details in a directory window:

- Select the directory window.
- Choose *View, Partial Details*.

- Check the file detail options you would like to display (size, last modification date, last modification time, file attributes).

- Click on *OK*.

Let's practice changing the main view of one of our directory windows:

1. Activate the **C:*.*:1** window.

2. Choose **View, Tree Only** to display only the tree structure of the selected directory, C:\ (see Figure 10.3; your tree structure will be different).

Figure 10.3   **Tree Only view**

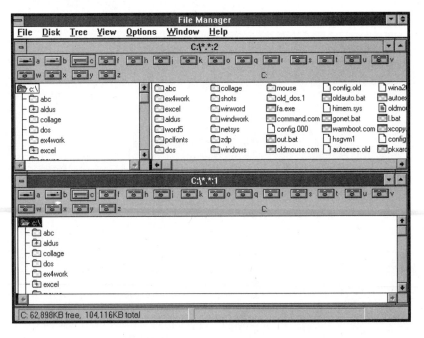

3. Compare the C:*.*:1 window with the C:*.*:2 window. Note that View changes affect only the active window.

4. In the C:*.*:1 window, choose **View, Directory Only** to display only the contents (the files and subdirectories) of the selected directory, C:\.

5. Maximize the **C:*.*:1** window to expand your view (see Figure 10.4).

Figure 10.4   **Directory Only view, maximized**

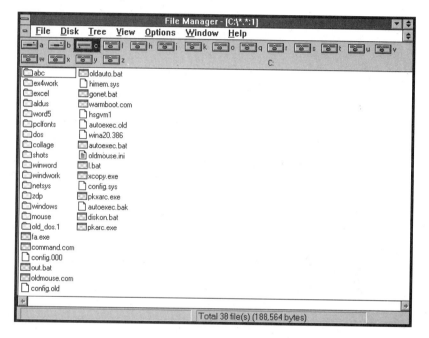

6. Choose **View, All File Details** to display file size, date and time of last modification, and file attributes.

7. Choose **View, Name** to return the file display to names only.

8. Choose **View, Tree and Directory** to return to the default display of both the directory tree and contents.

9. Click on the double-arrowed **Restore** button to shrink the **C:*.*:1** window back to its original (tiled) size and position.

10. Choose **View, Split**. Use your mouse to move the split bar so that it lines up with the split bar in the other directory window (C:*.*:2). Click once to fix the bar's new position.

Now let's change the sort order of the files stored in WINDWORK:

1. Maximize the **C:*.*:2** directory window.

2. Select the **windwork** directory. Note that WINDWORK's files are sorted alphabetically by file name.

3. Choose **View, Sort by Type** to resort these files alphabetically by type (file extension): .BAT, .BMP, .CLP, .CRD, and so on (see Figure 10.5).

Figure 10.5   **Contents of WINDWORK, sorted by type**

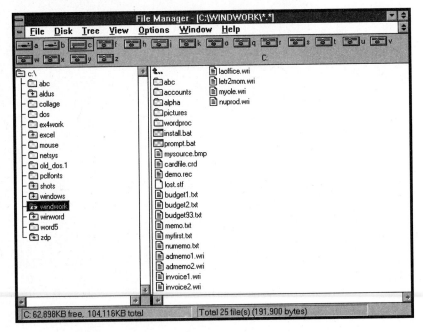

4. Choose **View, Sort by Size** to sort files by size, largest to smallest.

5. Choose **View, Sort by Date** to sort files by the date of last modification, latest to earliest.

6. Choose **View, Sort by Name** to sort files alphabetically by file name. This is the default sorting order.

CHANGING THE FILE ATTRIBUTES

File attributes are used by Windows and DOS to identify different types of files and, in doing so, to control the tasks that you can perform with these files. For example, a file with a read-only attribute can be viewed (read from), but cannot be modified (written to). There are four file attributes: read only (abbreviated as *r*), archive (*a*), system (*s*), and hidden (*h*). Table 10.1 lists these attributes and provides brief descriptions.

Table 10.1   **File Attributes** *

Attribute	Description
r (read only)	A read-only file can be viewed, but cannot be modified or deleted. The read-only attribute is generally given to critical program or document files, so that they cannot be inadvertently modified.
a (archive)	An archive file is a newly created or modified file that has not been backed up for safekeeping. Disk-backup utilities often refer to this attribute to know which files need to be backed up.
s (system)	A system file is a special file used by the DOS operating system. It cannot be viewed (see note below), modified, or deleted.
h (hidden)	The hidden attribute is generally given to a file that one wishes to hide for the sake of security or privacy. Like a system file, a hidden file cannot be viewed (see note below), modified, or deleted.

*   Note: Both system and hidden files cannot normally be viewed in a File Manager directory window. You can, however, override this feature by choosing *View, By File Type* and then checking the option *Show Hidden/System Files*

To display file attributes in a directory window:

- Select the directory window.

- Choose *View, All File Details*. Or, choose *View, Partial Details* and then check *File Attributes*.

- Click on *OK*. The attributes (r, a, s, or h) are displayed in the four rightmost columns from the file name. If a file has no attributes, these columns are left blank.

To change a file's attributes:

- Select the file.

- Choose *File, Properties*.

- Check or uncheck the desired attributes.

- Click on *OK.*

Let's view the attributes of the files stored in WINDWORK:

1. Choose **View, Partial Details** to open the Partial Details dialog box.

2. Check the **File Attributes** option. If necessary, uncheck **Size, Last Modification Date**, and **Last Modification Time**.

3. Click on **OK** to view file names and attributes. Scroll down through the file list. Note that several files have the *a* (archive) attribute. These are the files that you created or modified, but have not yet backed up.

Now let's change the attribute of a file in the WORDPROC directory:

1. Open the **wordproc** directory by double-clicking on its icon in the contents list.

2. Select (click once on) **template.wri**.

3. Choose **File, Properties**. Observe the Properties for the TEM-PLATE.WRI dialog box. Note the four file attributes: Read Only, Archive, Hidden, and System. Archive is checked, because you did not back up TEMPLATE.WRI since modifying it in Chapter 9.

4. Check **Read Only** to add the read-only attribute to TEM-PLATE.WRI.

5. Click on **OK**. Observe the contents list. The *ra* to the right of the file name indicates that this is a read-only and archive file (see Figure 10.6). TEMPLATE.WRI can now be read, but not modified or deleted.

Let's see what happens when we try to modify a read-only file:

1. Double-click on **template.wri** to run the Write program and open the document TEMPLATE.WRI.

Figure 10.6 **TEMPLATE.WRI as a read-only file**

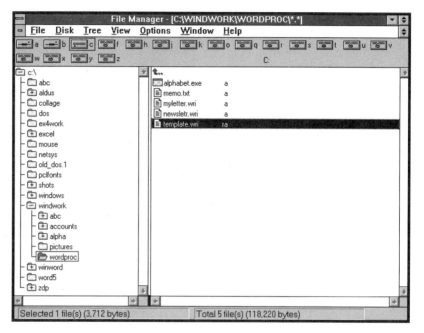

2. Maximize the **Write** window.

3. Type today's date.

4. Place the insertion point above the Fenster logo and type your name.

5. Choose **File, Save** to attempt to update the file. Write prompts

`The file is read-only. Use a different filename.`

TEMPLATE.WRI cannot be updated because it is now a read-only file and cannot be modified or deleted. (Updating a file deletes the original file and saves the revised file in its place.) Making a file read-only can be useful for creating template or boilerplate documents (such as a standard memo format) that you do not want accidentally modified or deleted.

6. Click on **OK**. The Save As dialog box appears, allowing you to save the revised file under a different name.

7. Type **mynumemo** and click on **OK** to save the file as MYNUMEMO.WRI.

8. Exit **Write**.

9. Observe the directory window. Note that MYNUMEMO.WRI is an archive file (a)—meaning it has not been backed up—but it is not a read-only file.

PRACTICE YOUR SKILLS

1. Remove the read-only attribute from TEMPLATE.WRI. (Hint: Use the **File, Properties** command.)

2. View files by name only, not by name and attribute. (Hint: Choose **View, Name**.)

THE SAVE SETTINGS ON EXIT FEATURE

You can use the Save Settings on Exit feature to save your File Manager directory-window setup. When you select Save Settings on Exit from the Options menu, Windows saves the size, shape, location, view, and drive/directory of each directory window that is open when you exit File Manager and restores this setup the next time you run File Manager.

To save your File Manager directory-window setup:

- Click on *Options* to display the drop-down Options menu.

- If the Save Settings on Exit option is not preceded by a check, click on it to select it. If it is preceded by a check, it is already selected; click on *Options* again to remove the drop-down menu.

- Exiting File Manager will now save the current directory-window setup. Running File Manager will restore this setup.

Note: The Save Settings on Exit option is selected (checked) by default when you first install Windows. As you'll recall, we turned it off in Chapter 5 to prevent you from accidentally saving an undesired File Manager setup.

USING WILDCARDS TO MANAGE GROUPS OF FILES

In Chapter 5, you learned how to copy, move, and delete a group of files, rather than a single file. Here you'll learn how to use *wildcards* to simplify your group-file tasks. A wildcard is a special character that stands for one or more arbitrary file-name characters (a–z, A–Z, 0–9, and all valid file-name punctuation marks). Windows provides two different wildcards:

*	Stands for any number of arbitrary characters
?	Stands for a single arbitrary character

To use wildcards to manage (view, select, copy, move, or delete) a group of files, you must first create a *wildcard statement* that combines wildcards and actual file-name characters to specify the desired group of files. Table 10.2 provides several examples of wildcard statements, files that match these statements, and files that do not match.

Table 10.2   **Wildcard Statement Examples**

Wildcard Statement	Matching Files	Non-Matching Files
*.DOC	FYE89.DOC, LETTER.DOC	FYE89.DO, LETTER
???92.TXT	FYE92.TXT, W1292.TXT	FY92.TXT, W1292.DOC
WILD*.*	WILDCRD.DOC, WILD.PAS	_WILDCRD.DOC, WIL.PAS
BR??N.??	BRAIN.NU, BROWN.NU	BRAN.NU, BROWN.NUT

 VIEWING A GROUP OF FILES

You can use wildcards to view a specific group of files—rather than all the files—from a selected directory. This is particularly useful when you are searching through a crowded directory for one type of file. For example, let's say you wanted to see all the batch (.BAT) files that were stored in a directory named UTILS that was filled with over 100 .COM, .EXE, .TXT, .DOC, and .BAT files. You could select the directory and scroll back and forth through its contents list, searching the screen for .BAT files. Or, you could use the wildcard statement *.BAT and let File Manager do all the work for you, displaying only .BAT files in the contents list.

To use wildcards to view a specific group of files:

- Select the directory window.

- Choose *View, By File Type*.

- Type a wildcard statement that specifies the group of files you want to display (for example, *.bat*).

- Click on *OK*.

Let's practice using wildcards to view specific groups of files:

1. Click on the **windwork** directory icon to display its contents.

2. Choose **View, By File Type** to open the By File Type dialog box. Observe the Name text box. The default file name is *.*, a wildcard statement specifying all files—any number of arbitrary characters for both the file name and the file extension.

3. Type **nu*.*** and press **Enter**. Only those files beginning with NU are listed (see Figure 10.7). Note that the title bar displays the wildcard statement used to generate the current file list (nu*.*). We recommend that you keep an eye on the title bar, so that you will know whether you are seeing a directory's full contents (indicated by *.*) or partial contents (indicated by a wildcard statement such as nu*.*).

4. Choose **View, By File Type**.

5. Type **??memo.*** and press **Enter**. NUMEMO.TXT is the only file in WINDWORK that matches this wildcard statement. Observe the wildcard statement displayed in the title bar (??memo.*).

6. Choose **View, By File Type**.

7. Type ***.wri** and press **Enter** to display only Write files.

8. Double-click on the **C** drive icon to open a new directory window. Note that the title bar displays the *.wri* wildcard statement, along with the number *2* to indicate that it is the second open directory window for C:\WINDWORK. As mentioned early on in this chapter, a new directory window inherits the setup of the window it was opened from.

Figure 10.7   **Files matching the wildcard statement *nu*.**

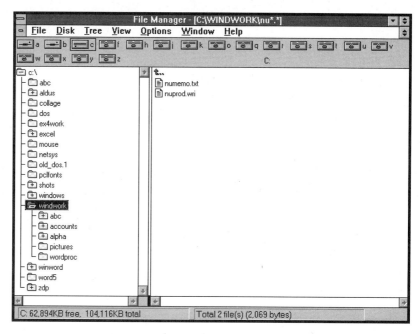

9. Close this new directory window. Make sure to use the lower Control menu box to do this; the upper Control menu box belongs to the File Manager program, not the directory window.

10. Choose **View, By File Type**. Type ***.*** and press **Enter** to return the contents list to show all files.

COPYING OR MOVING A GROUP OF FILES

You can use wildcards to copy or move a group of files from one directory to another. To do this:

● Choose *File, Copy* or *File, Move*.

● In the From text box, type a wildcard statement specifying the files you want to copy or move (for example, **.doc*). If these files are not in the current directory, include the full path name in your wildcard statement (for example, *c:\windwork\wordproc*.wri*).

- In the To text box, type the full path of the destination directory—the directory to which you are copying or moving the files (for example, *a:\docfiles*).

- Click on *OK*.

Let's use this procedure to copy a group of files:

1. Click on **Window**. All currently open directory windows can be viewed and selected from the Window drop-down menu.

2. Click on **1 C:*.*:1** to activate this directory window.

3. Select the **windwork** directory. Note that the title bar changes to C:\WINDWORK*.*:2, because the same drive (C) and directory (WINDWORK) are now selected in both open directory windows.

4. Choose **File, Copy** to open the Copy dialog box.

5. Press **Shift+Tab** to select the From text box, and then type the wildcard statement **budget*.*** to specify the group of files you want to copy. It is not necessary to enter the full path of these files (c:\windwork\budget*.*), because C:\WINDWORK is the current directory, as indicated in the dialog box.

6. Press **Tab** to select the To text box, and then type **c:\windwork\alpha** to specify the directory to which you want to copy. Your Copy dialog box should now match that shown in Figure 10.8.

7. Click on **OK** to copy all the files in C:\WINDWORK that match the wildcard statement *budget*.** to C:\WINDWORK\ALPHA.

8. Select the directory C:\WINDWORK\ALPHA by clicking on the **alpha** subdirectory icon. Note that BUDGET1.TXT, BUDGET2.TXT, and BUDGET93.TXT have been copied into this directory.

SELECTING A GROUP OF FILES

You can use wildcards with the Select Files command from the File menu to select (rather than just view) a group of files in the current directory. To do this:

- Select the desired directory.

- Choose *File, Select Files*.

- In the File(s) text box, type a wildcard statement specifying the group of files you want to select.

Figure 10.8   **Copy dialog box, ready to copy**

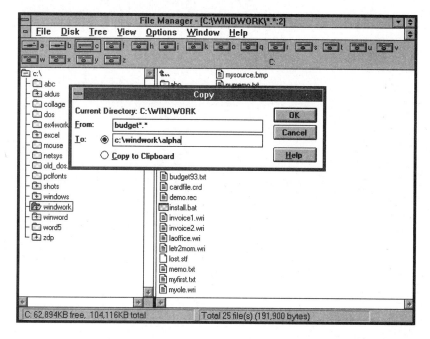

- Click on *Select*.

- To add files to the current selection, highlight the File(s) text box entry and repeat the previous two steps.

- To remove files from the current selection, highlight the File(s) text box entry, type a wildcard statement specifying the group of files you want to deselect, and then click on *Deselect*.

- When your selection is complete, click on *Close*.

Once you've used this procedure to select a group of files, you can move, copy, or delete them exactly as you would any other group of selected files.

Let's use the Select Files command to select all of WINDWORK's .TXT and .WRI files:

1. Select the **windwork** directory.

2. Choose **File, Select Files**.

3. Type ***.txt** and click on **Select**. Note that all of WINDWORK's .TXT files are selected (enclosed by a box). Note also that the

Select Files dialog box remains on screen, enabling you to add files to the current selection.

4. Double-click on your ***.txt** entry in the File(s) text box to highlight it. Type ***.wri** and click on **Select** to add all .WRI files to your selection.

5. Click on **Close** to close the dialog box. Your selected files are now highlighted (see Figure 10.9).

Figure 10.9   **Selecting files by using File, Select Files**

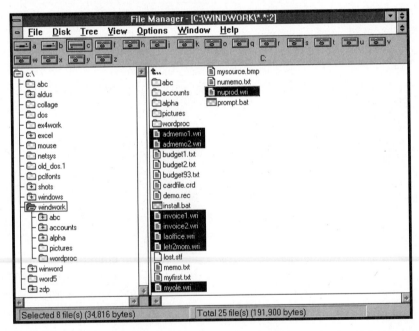

6. Hold down **Ctrl** and click on **nuprod.wri** to deselect this single file from the selected group.

Now let's copy our group of selected files to the C:\WINDWORK-\ALPHA directory:

1. Choose **File, Copy**. Note that the selected files are listed in the From text box, but that only the beginning of this list is visible.

2. Press **Shift+Tab** to select the From text box, and then use the **Left** and **Right Arrow** keys to scroll through the list of selected files.

3. Press **Tab** to select the To text box. Type **c:\windwork\alpha** and click on **OK**. A Confirm File Replace box appears, asking you if you'd like to replace C:\WINDWORK\ALPHA\BUDGET1.TXT with C:\WINDWORK\BUDGET1.TXT. (You already copied BUDGET1.TXT to WINDWORK\ALPHA in a previous activity.)

4. Click on **Yes to All** to copy all the selected files from C:\WIND-WORK to C:\WINDWORK\ALPHA, without having any intervening Confirm File Replace boxes.

5. Select **c:\windwork\alpha** to verify that the files were copied. Your file list should match that shown in Figure 10.10.

Figure 10.10   C:\WINDWORK\ALPHA, after group copying

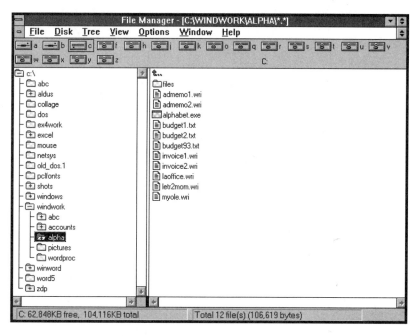

 SEARCHING FOR A GROUP OF FILES

File Manager provides a Search feature that you can use to find a single file or, if you enter a wildcard statement, a group of files. When you run Search, it creates a Search Results window in which it lists all the files that match your search criteria. You can use the

Search Results window in much the same way as you would use a normal directory window. For example, you can select files from the Search Results window and then move, copy, or delete them.

To search for one or more files:

- Choose File, Search.

- Type the name of the file you want to search for. To search for a group of files, type an appropriate wildcard statement (for example, *.bmp).

- To search the current directory only, uncheck Search All Subdirectories. To search the current directory and all its subdirectories, check Search All Subdirectories (this option is, by default, checked).

- Click on OK.

Let's use the Search feature:

1. Select the **windwork** directory.

2. Choose **File, Search** to open the Search dialog box.

3. Type ***.wri**. Verify that the Search All Subdirectories option is checked, and then click on **OK** to search for Write (.WRI) files in the current directory (WINDWORK) and all of its subdirectories. Examine the Search Results window; it should match the window shown in Figure 10.11.

4. Click on **File**. Note that all the File menu options are available (that is, they are printed in normal, undimmed letters). As mentioned earlier, you can perform the same operations on files in a Search Results window as on files in a directory window. Click on **File** to close the menu.

5. Click on **Window**. While it remains open, the Search Results window is listed as a Window menu choice. Click on **Window** to close the menu.

6. Close the **Search Results** window. Make sure you use the Control menu box for the Search Results window (the lower of the two Control menu boxes), not the one for File Manager.

Figure 10.11   **Search Results window, after searching for** **.wri*

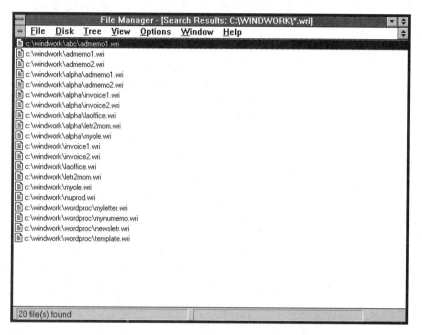

DELETING A GROUP OF FILES

You can use wildcards to delete a group of files from a directory. To do this:

- Choose *File, Delete*. Or, press *Del*.

- In the Delete text box, type a wildcard statement specifying the files you want to delete (for example, **.bak*). If these files are not in the current directory, include the full path name in your wildcard statement (for example, *c:\windwork*.bak*).

- Click on *OK*.

Earlier in this chapter, you copied several .TXT and .WRI files to the C:\WINDWORK\ALPHA directory. Let's use wildcards to delete these files:

1. Select the **c:\windwork\alpha** directory.

2. Choose **File, Delete** to open the Delete dialog box.

3. Type ***.txt** to instruct File Manager to delete all .TXT files from the ALPHA directory. Click on **OK**. The Confirm File Delete box appears, asking if you would like to delete BUDGET1.TXT, the first of ALPHA's .TXT files.

4. Click on **Yes to All** to delete all of ALPHA's .TXT files at once, without having File Manager ask you to confirm each deletion.

5. Press **Del** to open the Delete dialog box. As mentioned, pressing Del is equivalent to choosing File, Delete from the menu.

6. Type ***.wri** and click on **OK**. The Confirm File Delete box appears, asking if you would like to delete ADMEMO1.WRI, the first of ALPHA's .WRI files.

7. Click on **Yes to All** to delete all of ALPHA's .WRI files at once. Your contents list should now match that shown in Figure 10.12.

Figure 10.12   **C:\WINDWORK\ALPHA, after wildcard deletions**

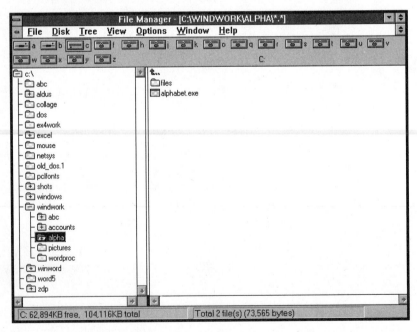

PRINTING FILES FROM WITHIN FILE MANAGER

Up to now, you've always printed a file by running a program, opening the file, and choosing the File, Print command. Here you'll learn how to print your files from within File Manager. You can use either of these methods:

- Choose File, Print from the File Manager menu.

- Drag file icons from File Manager to Print Manager.

File Manager and Print Manager must know the program that was used to create a file before they can print that file. For this reason, both of the above printing methods will work only with associated files. As discussed in Chapter 7, an *associated file* is a file that is associated with a specific program. For example, .TXT files are, by default, associated with the Notepad program. To find out if a file is associated, observe its File Manager icon. An associated file icon appears as a miniature page filled with lines of text; a non-associated file icon appears as a blank page.

Note: The associated program must be a Windows program. You cannot, for example, print a file associated with Microsoft Word for DOS or WordPerfect for DOS from within File Manager.

 ### PRINTING WITH FILE, PRINT

To print a file by using File, Print from the File Manager menu:

- In File Manager, select (click once on) the file you want to print. Remember that this file must be associated with its program of creation.

- Choose *File, Print* to open the Print dialog box.

- Click on *OK*.

- Respond to any additional print dialog boxes that may appear. These boxes are generated by the associated program.

Let's use the File, Print method to print from within File Manager. (If you do not have a printer, please read through the following steps without performing them.)

1. Select the **windwork** directory.

2. Select (click once on) **numemo.txt**. Note that this file is associated; its icon appears as a page filled with lines.

3. Choose **File, Print** to open the Print dialog box, and then click on **OK**. The following sequence of events occurs: Notepad (the associated program) runs; NUMEMO.TXT is opened; a dialog box appears briefly to indicate that NUMEMO.TXT is being sent to the printer; the Print Manager icon appears at the bottom of the screen; Notepad is closed; the Print Manager icon is closed.

4. Observe this sequence of events once again by choosing **File, Print** and clicking on **OK**.

Now let's see what happens when we try to print a non-associated file:

1. Select **lost.stf**. Note that this file is not associated; its icon appears as a blank page.

2. Choose **File, Print** and click on **OK**. A Cannot Print File box appears, displaying the message

   ```
   No application is associated with this file.
   Choose Associate from the File menu to create an association.
   ```

3. Click on **OK** to remove the message box.

PRINTING WITH PRINT MANAGER

To print a file by dragging the file icon from File Manager to Print Manager:

- In File Manager, choose *File, Run*.

- Type *printman* and click on *OK* to run Print Manager.

- Minimize Print Manager. The Print Manager icon must be visible at the bottom of your screen.

- Drag the desired file from File Manager to the Print Manager icon.

- Respond to any print dialog boxes that may appear. These boxes are generated by the associated program.

Let's use the file-icon dragging method to print from within File Manager:

1. Choose **File, Run** from the File Manager menu.

2. Type **printman** and click on **OK** to run Print Manager.

3. Minimize **Print Manager**. Verify that it is visible as an icon at the bottom of your screen.

4. Drag the file **numemo.txt** to the Print Manager icon. Observe the results. Notepad runs, NUMEMO.TXT is opened and printed, and then Notepad is automatically closed. Note that Print Manager remains running as an icon, enabling you to use the dragging technique to print more files. Let's do this now.

5. Drag **nuprod.wri** to the Print Manager icon. Write runs, NU-PROD.WRI is opened, and a Print dialog box appears (see Figure 10.13). This is the default dialog box that is always displayed when you print a file from Write.

Figure 10.13   The Print dialog box from Write

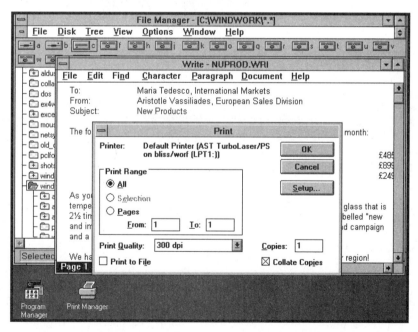

6. Click on **OK**. NUPROD.WRI is printed and Write is closed.

7. Close **Print Manager**.

USING FILE MANAGER TO CREATE PROGRAM-ITEM ICONS

In Chapter 6, you learned how to create program-item icons from within Program Manager, by using the File, New command. Windows also allows you to create program-item icons from within File Manager. To do this:

• Set up your screen so that both the File Manager window and the Program Manager window are displayed. (You can manually move and resize the windows, or you can use the Task List to tile the windows.) Both programs must be running in windows, not as icons.

• In the File Manager window, select the file for which you want to create a program-item icon. Drag this file to the appropriate Program Manager group.

Let's use this procedure to create a new program-item icon:

1. Use **Alt+Tab** to switch to Program Manager. Close the **Main** group, if necessary.

2. Press **Ctrl+Esc** to display the Task List, and then click on **Tile** to tile the Program Manager and File Manager windows. In Program Manager, choose **Window, Arrange Icons** to fit all group icons in the tiled window.

3. Open the **Accessories** group. This is the group in which we will create our new program-item icon.

4. Activate the **File Manager** window and open the directory **c:\windows\system**. Choose **View, Directory Only** to view the contents list of the SYSTEM directory.

5. Scroll the contents list window until the file SYSEDIT.EXE is visible.

6. Drag **sysedit.exe** to a blank area of the Accessories group window in Program Manager. Note that a Sysedit program-item icon is automatically created (see Figure 10.14).

7. Activate the **Accessories** group and double-click on the **Sysedit** icon to run the System Configuration Editor (SYSEDIT.EXE).

8. Close the **System Configuration Editor**. Now let's delete the Sysedit icon.

Figure 10.14   **Creating a Sysedit program-item icon by dragging**

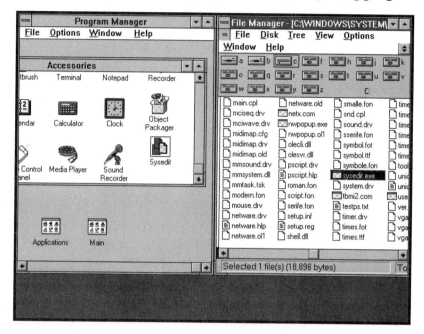

9. Verify that the Sysedit icon is still selected, and then press **Del**. Windows prompts

   ```
   Are you sure you want to delete the item 'Sysedit'?
   ```

10. Click on **Yes** to delete the Sysedit program-item icon.

    As mentioned earlier in this chapter, if the Save Settings on Exit option is selected (preceded by a check), Windows will save your current directory-window setup when you exit File Manager and restore this setup when you next run File Manager.

Since we do not want to save the current File Manager setup, let's verify that Save Settings on Exit is deselected:

1. Activate the **File Manager** window. Click on **Options** and observe the drop-down menu.

2. If the Save Settings on Exit option is selected (checked), click on it to deselect it. If it is already deselected, click on **Options** again to remove the Options menu. Now we can safely exit

File Manager without preserving our current labyrinthine directory-window setup.

3. Exit **File Manager**.

4. Close the **Accessories** group and return the Program Manager window to its original size and location, as depicted in Figure 10.15. Choose **Windows, Arrange Icons** to rearrange the group icons. (Your icons may be in a different order than those in Figure 10.15.)

Figure 10.15 **Program Manager window, after rearranging**

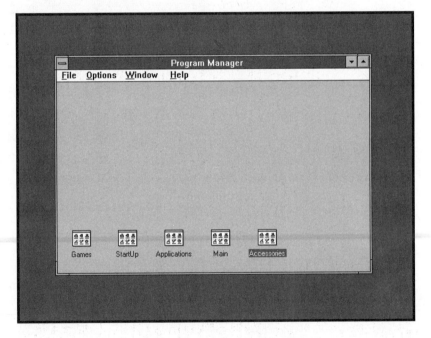

SUMMARY

In this chapter you learned how to open multiple File Manager directory windows, how to customize a directory window display, how to use wildcards to manage groups of files, how to print files from within File Manager, and how to use File Manager to create program-item icons.

Here's a quick reference for the techniques you learned in this chapter:

Desired Result	How to Do It
Open a new File Manager directory window	Double-click on the icon of the drive containing the desired directory
Change the main view of a directory window	Select the directory window; click on **View** to display the drop-down View menu; click on the desired view (Tree and Directory, Tree Only, or Directory Only)
Change the order in which files are sorted in a directory window	Select the directory window; click on **View** to display the drop-down View menu; click on the desired Sort By option (Sort by Name, Sort by Type, Sort by Size, or Sort by Date)
Display all file details in a directory window	Select the directory window; choose **View, All File Details**
Display selected file details in a directory window	Select the directory window; choose **View, Partial Details**; check the desired file detail options (Size, Last Modification Date, Last Modification Time, File Attributes); click on **OK**
Display file attributes in a directory window	Select the directory window; choose **View, All File Details** or choose **View, Partial Details** and check **File Attributes**; click on **OK**
Change a file's attributes	Select the file; choose **File, Properties**, check or uncheck the desired attributes; click on **OK**
Save your File Manager directory-window setup	Click on **Options** to display the drop-down Options menu; if the Save Settings on Exit option is not preceded by a check, click on it to select it; if Save Settings on Exit is preceded by a check, it is already selected—click on **Options** again to remove the drop-down menu

Desired Result	How to Do It
Use wildcards to view a specific group of files	Select the directory window; choose **View, By File Type**; type a wildcard statement that specifies the group of files you want to view; click on **OK**
Use wildcards to copy or move a group of files from one directory to another	Choose **File, Copy** or **File, Move**; in the From text box, type a wildcard statement specifying the files you want to copy or move; in the To text box, type the full path of the destination directory; click on **OK**
Use wildcards to select a group of files in the current directory	Select the desired directory; choose **File, Select Files**; in the File(s) text box, type a wildcard statement specifying the group of files you want to select; click on **Select**; to *add files* to the current selection, highlight the File(s) text box entry and repeat the above two steps; to *remove files* from the current selection, highlight the File(s) text box entry, type a wildcard statement specifying the group of files you want to deselect, and then click on **Deselect**; when your selection is complete, click on **Close**
Search for one or more files	Choose **File, Search**; type the name of the file you want to search for; to search for a group of files, type an appropriate wildcard statement; to search the current directory only, uncheck **Search All Subdirectories**; to search the current directory and all its subdirectories, check **Search All Subdirectories**; click on **OK**
Use wildcards to delete a group of files from a directory	Choose **File, Delete** or press **Del**; in the Delete text box, type a wildcard statement specifying the files you want to delete; click on **OK**

Desired Result	How to Do It
To create program-item icons from within File Manager	Set up your screen so that both the File Manager window and the Program Manager window are displayed; in the File Manager window, select the file for which you want to create a program-item icon; drag this file to the appropriate Program Manager group
Print an associated file from File Manager	In File Manager, select (click once on) the file you want to print (this file must be associated with its program of creation); choose **File, Print** to open the Print dialog box; click on **OK**; respond to any additional print dialog boxes that may appear
Print a file by dragging the file icon from File Manager to Print Manager	In File Manager, choose **File, Run**; type **printman** and click on **OK** to run Print Manager; minimize Print Manager (the Print Manager icon must be visible at the bottom of your screen); drag the desired file from File Manager to the Print Manager icon; respond to any print dialog boxes that may appear

In the next chapter, we'll introduce you to five new Windows accessory programs. You'll learn how to use Character Map (or the keyboard) to enter extended characters in a document; Calendar to manage your daily appointments; Cardfile to manage index-card type information; Object Packager to insert a packaged object into a document; and Recorder to create macros that automate repetitive tasks.

If you need to break off here, please exit Windows. If you want to proceed directly to the next chapter, please do so now.

CHAPTER 11: WINDOWS ACCESSORY PROGRAMS

Character Map

Calendar

Cardfile

Object Packager

Recorder

When you install Windows, Setup automatically creates an Accessories group in Program Manager and fills this group with a dozen or so special utilities, called *accessory programs*. You're already familiar with several of these programs: Write, Paintbrush, Notepad, and Clock. This chapter provides you with an overview of five new accessory programs—*Character Map*, *Calendar*, *Cardfile*, *Object Packager*, and *Recorder*—the skillful use of which will greatly increase your power and flexibility when working with Windows.

When you're done reading through this chapter, you will know

- How to use Character Map or the keyboard to enter extended characters in a document

- How to use Calendar to manage your daily appointments

- How to use Cardfile to manage index-card type information

- How to use Object Packager to insert an icon representing a data object into a document

- How to use Recorder to create macros that automate repetitive tasks

CHARACTER MAP

When you are creating or editing a document, you may sometimes need to insert a character that is not included on your keyboard—for example, the German letter *ü* or the British pound sterling sign *£*. Windows provides you with two methods for inserting these *extended characters* in your documents:

- Entering an extended-character code at the keyboard

- Using the Character Map accessory program

 ### USING THE KEYBOARD TO ENTER EXTENDED CHARACTERS

A unique four-digit code is assigned to each extended character in a font. For example, in the Courier font, the code for *ü* is 0252 and the code for *£* is 0163. To use the keyboard to enter an extended character in a Windows document (a document created in a Windows program):

- Run the Windows program, open the document, and position the cursor at the desired location.

- Press and hold down the *Alt* key.

- On the numeric keypad, enter the four-digit code that corresponds to the desired extended character. (Normally, you can only enter a number on the numeric keypad when Num Lock is turned on. However, when entering an extended-character code, it does not matter whether Num Lock is on or off.)

- Release the *Alt* key. The extended character will appear at the cursor in the active document.

Note: In the next section, "Using Character Map to Enter Extended Characters," we'll show you an easy way to find an extended character's numeric code.

If you are not running Windows, please start it now. Program Manager should be the only open window; if any other windows are open, please close them.

Let's begin by using the keyboard to enter extended characters:

1. Run and maximize **Write** (in the Accessories group).

2. Type **Arlene**, and press **Enter** twice, and then type **Fenster**.

3. Press and hold down the **Alt** key. Use the numeric keypad to type **0174**, and then release **Alt**. (As mentioned, it doesn't matter whether Num Lock is on or off.) The registered trademark symbol (®) appears at the cursor.

4. Press **Spacebar**. Type **brand storm window model 201 sells for** and then press **Spacebar** again.

5. Press and hold **Alt**, use the numeric keypad to type **0165**, and then release **Alt**. The Japanese yen sign (¥) appears.

6. Type **10,000 in the Pacific region.** and press **Enter** twice. Your screen should now match Figure 11.1.

 ## USING CHARACTER MAP TO ENTER EXTENDED CHARACTERS

The *Character Map* accessory program enables you to insert an extended character in a Windows document without entering the character's numeric code. To do this:

- Run the Windows program, open the document, and position the cursor at the desired location.

- Switch to Program Manager and run *Character Map* (in the Accessories group). Or, if Character Map is already running, switch to it.

- Select the desired font.

- Select the desired extended character. To enlarge the character display, point to the character and then press and hold the mouse button.

Figure 11.1   **Using the keyboard to enter extended characters**

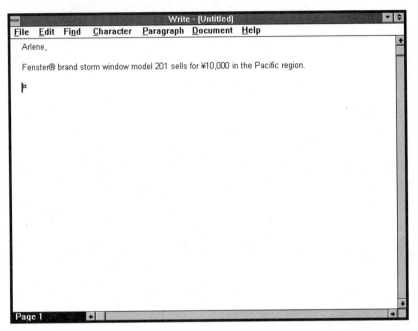

- Click on *Select* to place the character in the Characters to Copy box.

- Click on *Copy* to copy the selected character to the Clipboard.

- Click on *Close* to close Character Map. Or, if you intend to enter more extended characters, leave Character Map open.

- Switch to the Windows program, and choose *Edit, Paste* to copy the character into the document.

Note: Extended character sets vary according to font. For example, the fonts Courier and Symbol have very different extended character sets. (Figure 11.2 shows the complete character sets of these two fonts. Compare their respective extended-character sets—the last three rows of characters in the two windows.) For this reason, you may have to switch to a different font to enter a specific extended character.

Figure 11.2 **Courier and Symbol character sets**

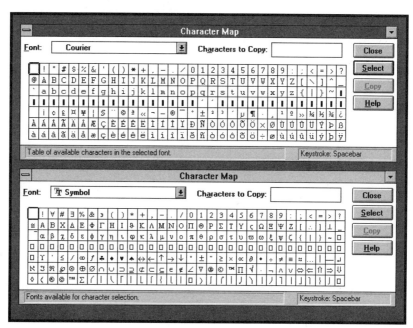

Now let's use Character Map to enter extended characters in our Write document:

1. Switch to **Program Manager** and run **Character Map** (in the Accessories group).

2. Spend a few moments selecting different fonts and comparing their extended character sets.

3. Select the **Courier** font.

4. Select (click once on) the registered trademark symbol (®). Press and hold the mouse button to enlarge the character display. Release the mouse button.

5. Observe the status bar. Note that the numeric code for the selected character is displayed (Keystroke: Alt+0174). Whenever you need to know the code for an extended character, simply run Character Map, select the font and character, and then look at the status bar.

6. Select the British pound sign (**£**). Observe the numeric code (Alt+0163). Press and hold the mouse button to enlarge the character display.

7. Release the mouse button, and then click on **Select**. The £ character appears in the Characters to Copy text box (see Figure 11.3).

Figure 11.3   **Selecting the extended character £ in Character Map**

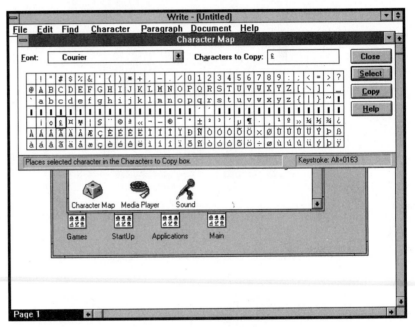

8. Click on **Copy** to copy the £ to the Clipboard.

9. Click on **Close** to close Character Map.

10. Switch to **Write**. Type **The same model sells for** and press **Spacebar**.

11. Choose **Edit**, **Paste** to paste the £ into your Write document. Type **50 in Great Britain.** and press **Enter** twice. Type your first name and press **Enter**.

12. Compare your screen with Figure 11.4.

Figure 11.4   **Completed memo to Arlene**

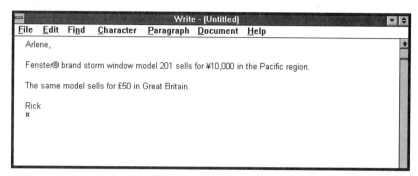

13. Save the file to your WINDWORK directory as **mychars.wri**.

14. Exit **Write**.

CALENDAR

The Windows *Calendar* accessory combines a daily appointment calendar with a monthly overview calendar. To use Calendar to manage your appointments:

• Run *Calendar*.

• To open a calendar file, choose *File*, *Open*.

• To display the daily calendar (default), choose *View*, *Day*; or double-click on the desired day in the monthly calendar.

• To display the monthly calendar, choose *View*, *Month*; or double-click on the day/date display to the right of the status-bar scroll arrows in the daily calendar.

• To enter a new appointment, display the daily calendar; select the day (by clicking on the right and left scroll arrows in the status bar); select the time (by clicking on the desired hour); and type the appointment information.

• To change the appointment interval (the number of minutes between displayed appointments), hour format (12- or 24-hour clock), or starting time (the earliest appointment of the day), choose *Options*, *Day Settings*; set the desired Interval, Hour Format, or Starting Time values; and then click on *OK*.

- To insert a special appointment time in the calendar (a time not currently shown), display the daily calendar; choose *Options, Special Time*; set the desired time; and then click on *OK*.

- To mark a day in the monthly calendar, select the desired day; choose *Options, Mark*; check the desired mark symbol (the symbol that will appear in the monthly calendar); and then click on *OK*.

- To sound an alarm at a specific appointment time, display the daily calendar; select the appointment time; and choose *Alarm, Set*.

- To print out a copy of your daily appointments, select the desired day; choose *File, Print*; and click on *OK*.

- To save a calendar file, choose *File, Save* As (for a new file) or *File, Save* (for an updated file).

- To create a new calendar file (and, in doing so, to close the current calendar file), choose *File, New*.

Let's explore the Calendar accessory:

1. Run **Calendar** (in the Accessories group). The default daily appointment calendar for today's date is displayed. Maximize the Calendar window (see Figure 11.5; your date and time will be different).

2. Click several times on the **right scroll** arrow in the status bar to move forward, one day per click. Click on the **left scroll** arrow as many times as needed to move backward to the current date.

3. Choose **Options, Day Settings** and observe the dialog box. Interval specifies the interval, in minutes, between appointment times; the default interval is 60 minutes, resulting in appointment times of 8:00, 9:00, 10:00, 11:00, and so on. Hour Format determines whether appointment times are displayed in 12- or 24-hour format; 2:00 p.m. appears as 2:00 PM in 12-hour format or 14:00 in 24-hour format. Starting Time specifies the calendar's earliest daily appointment time; the default is 7:00 AM.

4. Set the Interval to **30** minutes. Set the Hour Format to **12**. Set the Starting Time to **6:00 AM**. Click on **OK**.

5. Observe your revised Calendar format (see Figure 11.6). Compare it with the format in Figure 11.5.

Figure 11.5   **Calendar window, maximized**

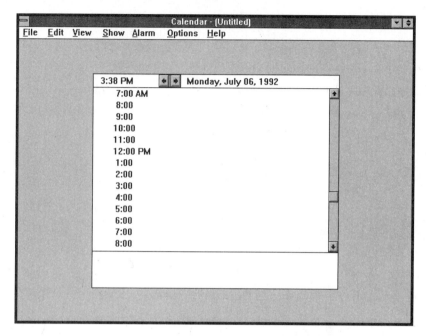

Figure 11.6   **Revised Calendar format**

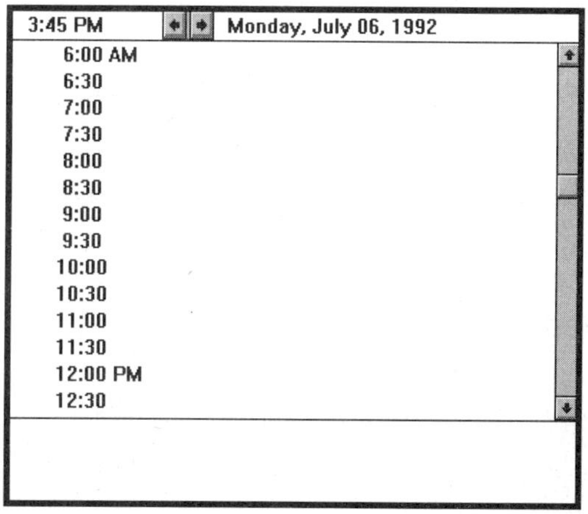

Now let's add an appointment for tomorrow to the calendar:

1. Choose **View, Month** to change the calendar to month view.

Note that today's date is selected (highlighted and flanked on either side by > and <).

2. Double-click on tomorrow's date to select it and return to day view. (If today's date is the last day of the month, click on the **right scroll** arrow to display the next month, and then double-click on the first day of this month.) Now let's say your appointment was for 11:20 AM, a time that does not appear in the calendar. (11:00 and 11:30 are shown, but not 11:20.)

3. Choose **Options, Special Time** to insert a special time in your calendar. Note that AM is the default selection. Type **11:20** and press **Enter**.

4. Type **Lunch with sales reps** to record your appointment (see Figure 11.7). Let's say that this was a particularly important meeting, and that you wanted to mark this day on your monthly calendar so you wouldn't forget.

Figure 11.7   **Adding an appointment at a special time**

4:00 PM	◄ ►	Tuesday, July 07, 1992	
11:20 AM	Lunch with sales reps		▲
11:30			
12:00 PM			
12:30			
1:00			
1:30			
2:00			
2:30			
3:00			
3:30			
4:00			
4:30			
5:00			
5:30			▼

5. Choose **Options, Mark**. Check **Symbol 1 - []** and click on **OK**. Note that your daily appointment calendar display does not change. Marked appointments only show up on the monthly calendar.

6. Double-click on the day/date display to the right of the scroll arrows in the status bar to switch to month view. Note that

tomorrow's date is now marked—its number is enclosed by a box as a result of your having selected the [] mark symbol (see Figure 11.8).

Figure 11.8   **Marking a day with the [] symbol**

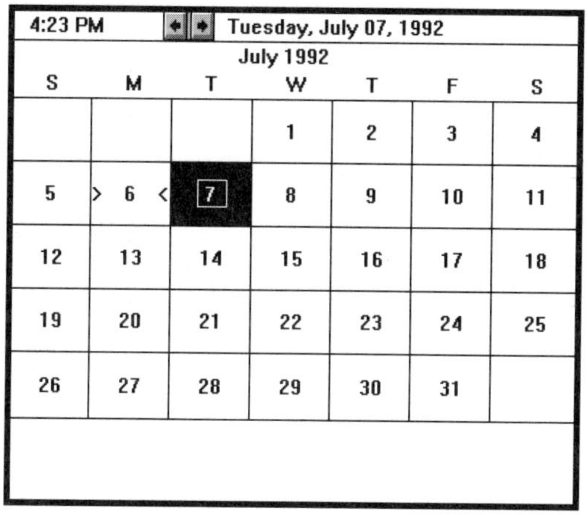

4:23 PM	◀ ▶	Tuesday, July 07, 1992

July 1992

S	M	T	W	T	F	S
			1	2	3	4
5	> 6 <	[7]	8	9	10	11
12	13	14	15	16	17	18
19	20	21	22	23	24	25
26	27	28	29	30	31	

7. Save the file to your WINDWORK directory as **mymonth.cal**.

8. Choose **File, Print**. Note that you can specify a single date or a range of dates to be printed. Click on **Cancel**.

9. Exit **Calendar**.

10. Run **Calendar**. Scroll forward to tomorrow's date. Note that your *Lunch with sales rep* appointment does not show up. Why? Because you did not open the file in which you stored this appointment, MYMONTH.CAL. To view your appointments, you must open the appropriate calendar file.

11. Open **mymonth.cal** from your WINDWORK directory and select tomorrow's date. Your lunch appointment appears as expected.

12. Exit **Calendar**.

CARDFILE

The Windows *Cardfile* accessory is an electronic version of an index-card filing system. You can use it to store information that you want to be able to retrieve quickly, such as names, addresses, phone numbers, directions, recipes, and so on. A cardfile can contain a single card or a multitude of cards; its maximum size is limited by the amount of free memory in your computer.

PARTS OF A CARDFILE CARD

A Cardfile card consists of a single *index line* at the top and an 11-line *information area* below (see the sample card in Figure 11.9). The index line, which may contain up to 39 characters, generally holds a name or brief description to help you identify the card. The information area, each line of which may contain up to 40 characters, holds the body of the card's information, which may consist of text or graphics (such as a Paintbrush .BMP picture).

Figure 11.9 **Sample index card**

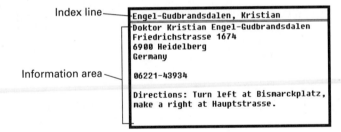

Index line —

Information area —

To use Cardfile to manage information:

- Run *Cardfile*.

- To open a cardfile, choose *File, Open*.

- To display entire cards, one at a time, choose *View, Card* (default). To display a list of index lines only, choose *View, List*.

- To add a card to a cardfile, choose *Card, Add*; type the index line; click on *OK*; and then fill in the card's information area.

- To delete a card from a cardfile, select the desired card; choose *Card*, *Delete*; click on *OK*.

- To search through a cardfile for a specific item of information (such as an area code), choose *Search*, *Find*; type the text you want to search for; set the Match Case and Direction options as desired; click on *Find Next* repeatedly to find successive occurrences of your search text; click on *Cancel* to close the Find dialog box.

- To print the top card in a cardfile, choose *File*, *Print*. To print all cards in a cardfile, choose *File*, *Print All*.

- To save a cardfile, choose *File*, *Save As* (for a new file) or *File*, *Save* (for an updated file).

- To create a new cardfile (and, in doing so, to close the current cardfile), choose *File*, *New*.

Let's take a look at the Cardfile program:

1. Run and maximize **Cardfile** (in the Accessories group).

2. Open **cardfile.crd** from your WINDWORK directory (see Figure 11.10). Note from the status line that there are four cards—one blank and three filled—in this cardfile. Note also that these cards are, by default, sorted alphabetically by index line (which is why last names are entered first on the index lines). The blank card sorts to the top; it serves to mark the beginning of the stack.

3. Click on the index line of the **Anderson, Claude** card to select it. Note that when you select a card, it moves to the top of the stack so you can view its information area.

4. Select the **Kennedy, Mike** card. Select the **Smith, Lisa** card. Select the blank card.

5. Click on the **right scroll** arrow in the Cardfile status line to select the next card (Anderson, Claude). Click on the **right scroll** arrow three more times to cycle forward through the remaining cards and return to the blank card.

6. Click on the **left scroll** arrow four times to cycle through the stack backward and return to the blank card.

7. Choose **View, List** to view a list of the index lines of all the cards in CARDFILE.CRD.

8. Choose **View, Card** to return to card view.

Figure 11.10   **CARDFILE.CRD cardfile**

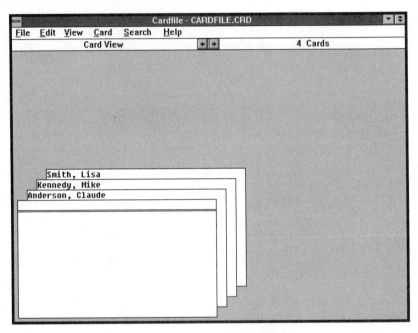

Now let's add a card to the cardfile:

1. Choose **Card, Add** to open the Add dialog box.

2. Type **Anderson, Samantha** to create the index line of your new card, and then click on **OK**. The new card appears at the top of the stack and is arranged alphabetically with respect to the other cards.

3. Type the following information onto the card, remembering to press **Enter** at the end of each line. (Hint: To type the *é* in *née*, hold down **Alt** and type **0233** on the numeric keypad.)

   ```
   Mrs. Samantha Anderson (née Huberle)
   54 Dayton Ave.
   Pittsburgh, PA 34453
   ```

4. Save the modified cardfile as **mycards1.crd**.

Now let's use the Search, Find command to search through the stack of cards for a specific item of information:

1. Select the blank card.

2. Choose **Search**, **Find** to open the Find dialog box. Verify that Match Case is unchecked, and that Direction is set to Down.

3. Type **pittsburgh**. Since the Match Case option is not selected, you can type *pittsburgh* to find the city *Pittsburgh*.

4. Click on **Find Next** to find the first occurrence of Pittsburgh, in Claude Anderson's card (see Figure 11.11). Click on **Find Next** again to find the next occurrence of Pittsburgh, in Samantha Anderson's card.

Figure 11.11 **Using Search, Find to find *pittsburgh***

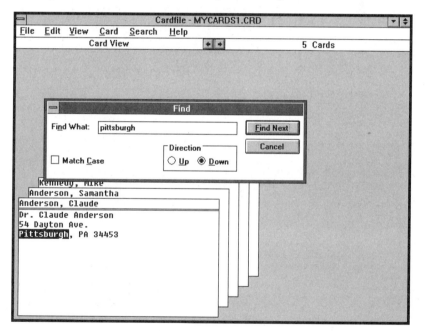

5. Click on **Find Next** again. The Pittsburgh entry in Claude Anderson's card is found for the second time. After it finds the final occurrence of your search text (in this case, the Samantha Anderson occurrence), Find Next cycles back through the previous occurrences. Click on **Find Next** again to verify this; the Pittsburgh entry in Samantha Anderson's card is found. Find will continue to cycle through these two Pittsburgh entries for as long as you click on Find Next.

6. Click on **Cancel** to remove the Find dialog box.

7. Click on **File** and observe the drop-down menu. Note the two print options, Print and Print All. As mentioned earlier, Print prints only the top card in the stack, whereas Print All prints all cards in the stack.

8. If you have a printer, click on **Print** to print the top card, Samantha Anderson. If you don't have a printer, click on **File** again to close the drop-down menu.

 MERGING CARDFILES

By using the File, Merge command, you can combine the contents of two or more cardfiles into a single cardfile. To do this:

• Run *Cardfile*.

• Open one of the cardfiles to be merged.

• Choose *File, Merge*.

• Select another of the cardfiles to be merged, and click on *OK*.

• If necessary, repeat the above two steps to merge additional cardfiles.

• Choose *File, Save As* to save the merged cardfile with a new name. Or, choose *File, Save* to save the merged cardfile with the same name as the first cardfile you opened.

PRACTICE YOUR SKILLS

1. Choose **File, New** to close MYCARDS1.CRD. A new, untitled cardfile appears, containing a single blank card.

2. Use **Card, Add** to create the following two cards. (In both cases, the first line is the index line.)

```
O'Flaherty, Joseph
Dr. Joseph O'Flaherty
172 Fairway Lane
Rochester, NY 14607
```

```
Scott, Eliza
Ms. Eliza Scott
272 Apesmouth Blvd.
Fremont, CA 94538
```

3. Save this cardfile to your WINDWORK directory as **mycards2.crd**.

4. Merge the contents of MYCARDS1.CRD with the contents of MYCARDS2.CRD. (Hint: Follow the procedure outlined above.) Your stack should now consist of eight cards, six filled and two blank, as shown in Figure 11.12.

Figure 11.12   Merging MYCARDS1.CRD with MYCARDS2.CRD

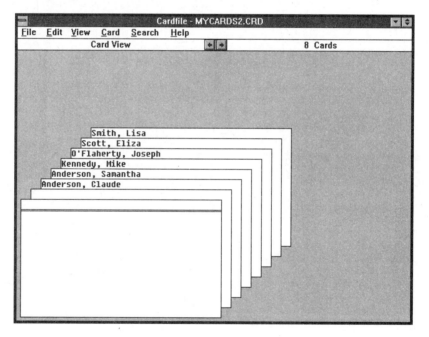

5. Delete the top blank card. (Hint: Use **Card, Delete**.)

6. If you have a printer, print out all seven cards.

7. Save the merged cardfile as **mymerge.crd**.

8. Exit **Cardfile**.

OBJECT PACKAGER

You can use the *Object Packager* accessory to create an icon that represents a data object (text and/or graphics) and then insert this icon into a Windows document. Instead of seeing the actual object in the document, you see the icon that represents the object. This enables you to apply the Windows icon-oriented approach to your documents and, in doing so, to make them tidier and more concise.

The icons you create by using Object Packager are called *packages*. Figures 11.13 and 11.14 will help you visualize the process of object packaging. We created a package of the Paintbrush data object depicted in Figure 11.13 (text and graphics) and then inserted this package into the Write document in Figure 11.14. To see the full Paintbrush picture, the Write user would merely have to double-click on the GHIA Ad icon.

Figure 11.13   Paintbrush object that was packaged

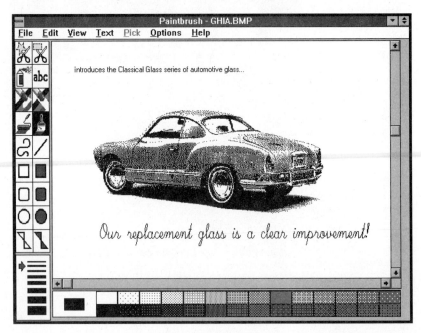

Figure 11.14 **Package inserted in a Write document**

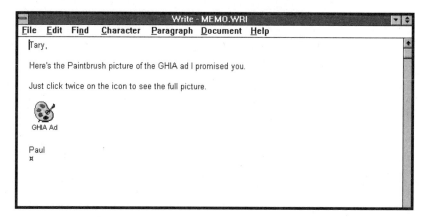

 OBJECT PACKAGER WINDOW

The Object Packager window is divided into two parts, the *Appearance* window and the *Content* window (see Figure 11.15). The Appearance window shows how the package will look when it is inserted into the destination document. The Content window shows either a description or a picture of the object to be packaged, depending on whether the Description or Picture option is selected.

Figure 11.15 **Object Packager window**

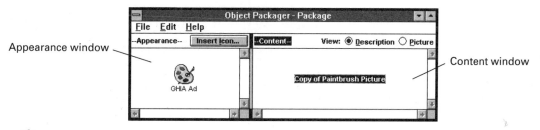

Appearance window

Content window

 CREATING AN OBJECT PACKAGE

You can use Object Packager to package a selection from a document (for example, one detail from a Paintbrush picture) or the entire document (the entire Paintbrush picture). Two caveats:

- You can package a selection only if it is from an OLE server document (a document which can provide linked and embedded objects). You can package an entire document whether it is an OLE server document or not.

- You can insert a package only into an OLE client document (a document that can accept linked and embedded objects).

To package a selection from a document:

- Run the source program and open the source document.

- Select the source object (the data to be packaged) and copy it to the Clipboard.

- Run *Object Packager*.

- Choose *Edit, Paste* to paste the Clipboard data object into Object Packager.

- If desired, edit the package to change the icon or the label.

- Choose *Edit, Copy Package* to copy the package back to the Clipboard.

- Run the destination program, open the destination document, and position the cursor where you want the package to be pasted.

- Choose *Edit, Paste* to paste the package into the destination document.

To package an entire document:

- Run *Object Packager*.

- Choose *File, Import*.

- Select the file to be packaged.

- Edit the package as needed to change the icon or the label.

- Choose *Edit, Copy Package* to copy the package to the Clipboard.

- Run the destination program, open the destination document, and position the cursor where you want the package to be pasted.

- Choose *Edit, Paste* to paste the package into the destination document.

Let's package a selected object from a Paintbrush document and then insert this package into a Write document:

1. Run **Paintbrush**.

2. Open the file **logo.bmp** from your C:\WINDWORK\PICTURES directory.

3. Use the Pick tool to select the **FensterGlass** logo.

4. Choose **Edit**, **Copy** to copy the logo to the Clipboard.

5. Exit **Paintbrush**.

6. Run **Object Packager**.

7. Observe the **Content** window. As mentioned earlier, this window describes or displays the object to be packaged. The Content window is blank, because you have not yet pasted an object into Object Packager.

8. Choose **Edit**, **Paste** to paste the logo from the Clipboard into Object Packager.

9. Observe the Content window status line. Note that the Description option is selected. Select the **Picture** option to display, rather than describe, your logo object.

10. Maximize the Object Packager window to view the entire logo (see Figure 11.16).

11. Activate the Appearance window by clicking on the word **Appearance**. As mentioned, this window shows how the package will look when it is pasted into the destination document.

12. Choose **Edit**, **Label** to change the name of the package. Type **Logo** and click on **OK**.

13. Choose **Edit**, **Copy Package** to copy the package to the Clipboard.

14. Exit **Object Packager**. Now we're ready to paste our package into a document.

15. Run **Write**.

16. Type the following, pressing **Enter** twice at the end of each line:

    ```
    Arlene,
    Here's the logo you asked for. What do you think?
    ```

17. Choose **Edit**, **Paste** to paste your Logo package from the Clipboard to the Write document.

Figure 11.16   **Object Packager, with the Picture option selected**

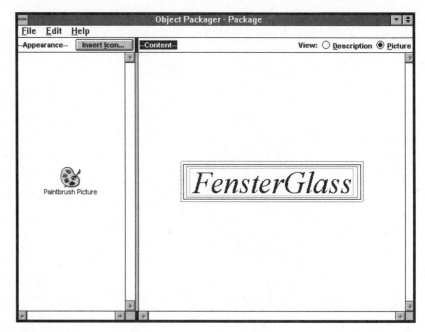

18. Press **Enter**, type your first name, and press **Enter** once more.

19. Save the file to your WINDWORK directory as **mypack.wri**.

Your document should now match that shown in Figure 11.17 (except for the name).

 EDITING A PACKAGE

Once you have pasted a package into a destination document, you can edit this package from inside the document, without having to run Object Packager or the program in which the packaged object was created. You can edit the package itself (the icon or label). Or, you can edit the object represented by the package (in our case, the FensterGlass logo).

To edit a package label or icon:

• In the destination document, select the package.

Figure 11.17 **Pasting the Logo package into a Write document**

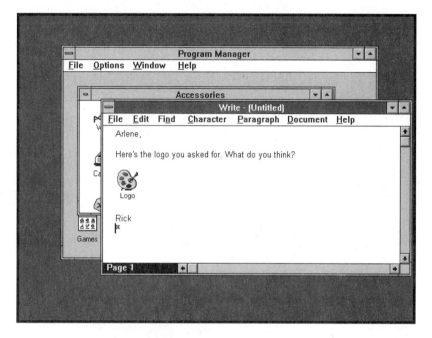

- Choose *Edit, Package Object, Edit Package*. This automatically runs Object Packager and loads the package into its workspace.

- Change the label and/or icon as desired.

- Choose *File, Update* to save these changes.

- Choose *File, Exit* to exit Object Packager and return to the destination document. The package will reflect the changes you made to it.

To edit the object represented by a package:

- In the destination document, double-click on the package. This runs the source program and opens the packaged object into the program's workspace.

- Edit the object as desired.

- Choose *File, Update* to save your editing changes.

- Choose *File, Exit & Return to ContentObject* to exit the source program and return to the destination document.

Let's edit the object represented by the Logo package in MYPACK.WRI:

1. Double-click on the **Logo** package to run Paintbrush and to open a copy of your packaged logo object (see Figure 11.18). Note the title bar—*Paintbrush - Paintbrush Picture in ContentObject*—indicating that the content of the Paintbrush workspace is a packaged object.

Figure 11.18   **Editing the packaged logo object**

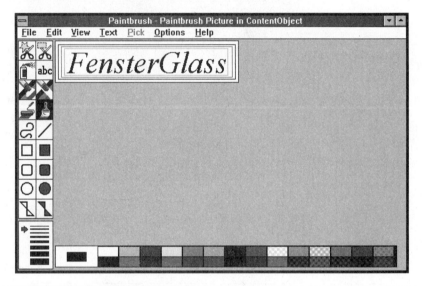

2. Use the Airbrush tool to spray some black paint over the logo.

3. Choose **File, Update** to save your modified object.

4. Choose **File, Exit & Return to ContentObject** to exit Paintbrush and return to the Write document. Note that the Logo package has not changed in appearance; you edited the packaged object (the logo), not the package label or icon.

5. Double-click on the **Logo** package to run Paintbrush and open a copy of the packaged object. Note that the airbrushed version of the logo has been saved.

6. In Paintbrush, open **logo.bmp** from your C:\WINDWORK\-PICTURES directory. After LOGO.BMP is opened, Windows

automatically switches to Write, because these two programs are connected in a package/object relationship.

7. Switch to **Paintbrush**. Note that the original source object, the
FensterGlass logo in LOGO.BMP, remains intact. Modifying a
packaged object that was pasted into a document changes the
packaged object only, not the source object from which the
package was created.

8. Exit **Paintbrush**.

9. Exit **Write** without saving the changes.

RECORDER

You can use the *Recorder* accessory to record (create), run, and edit
macros. A *macro* is a sequence of user actions (keystrokes and/or
mouse movements) that performs a specific task. For example, you
might create a macro named WORK that would initialize your Windows working environment by performing the following sequence
of actions:

• Run Write.

• Run Paintbrush.

• Run Cardfile.

• Run Character Map.

• Open the Task List and tile all of the above programs.

• Activate Write and select your desired font style and size in
preparation for creating a new document.

Macros enable you to automate tasks that always use the same keystrokes and/or mouse actions (as in the above example). Typical
macro tasks include running a set of programs, backing up files, au-
tomating screen displays for business presentations, demonstrat-
ing software products, creating keyboard shortcuts for menu
commands, and formatting documents.

You should use the keyboard as much as possible when recording
macros. A macro that uses the mouse to choose menu commands
or select dialog box options will be sensitive to the size and location
of the active windows and dialog boxes. If the size or location
should change, your mouse movements may no longer be valid.

Also, macros that use the mouse tend to run more slowly than those that use the keyboard.

To run a Recorder macro:

- Run *Recorder*.

- Choose *File*, *Open* to open the desired macro file.

- Select the desired macro and choose *Macro, Run*; or, press the macro's shortcut key.

To edit the properties of a Recorder macro:

- Select the desired macro.

- Choose *Macro, Properties*.

- Edit the properties, as desired.

- Click on *OK*.

Let's open a sample Recorder macro, examine its properties, and then run it:

1. Run **Recorder**.

2. Open the macro **demo.rec** from your WINDWORK directory. The macro name (Setup the desktop) is displayed in the Recorder window, along with the macro shortcut key (Ctrl+S), the key combination that, when pressed, will run the macro.

3. Choose **Macro, Properties** to view the properties assigned to DEMO.REC (see Figure 11.19). These include the macro name, the shortcut key, the playback speed (the speed at which the macro runs), and a description of the macro. Note that DEMO.REC's playback speed is set to *Recorded Speed*, meaning that it will play back at the speed with which it was originally recorded. Click on **Cancel** to close the Macro Properties dialog box.

4. Choose **Macro, Run** and observe your screen. DEMO.REC performs the following set of actions: minimizes Recorder; uses the File, Run command to run File Manager (minimized); runs Clock (minimized); runs Write (not minimized); types the beginning of a to-do list; and then stops, waiting for you to fill in this list (see Figure 11.20).

5. Exit **Write** (without saving the changes). Close **Clock** and **File Manager**.

Figure 11.19   Properties of the macro DEMO.REC

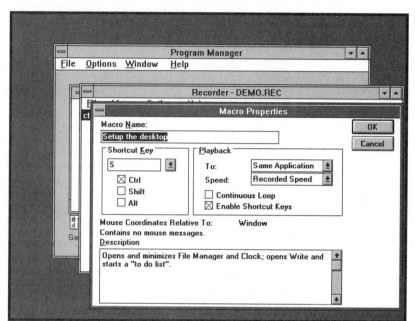

6. Restore the **Recorder** icon to a window.

PRACTICE YOUR SKILLS

DEMO.REC is set to run at Recorded Speed for instructional purposes, to enable you to easily follow the macro's progress on your screen. Normally, you would run this macro at Fast speed, to set up your Desktop as quickly as possible.

1. Change the playback speed of DEMO.REC to **Fast**. (Hint: Use the *Macro, Properties* command.) Rerun the macro. Note how much faster it now runs.

2. Exit **Write** (without saving the changes).

3. Close **Clock** and **File Manager**.

4. Restore the **Recorder** icon to a window.

Figure 11.20   **Desktop, after running DEMO.REC**

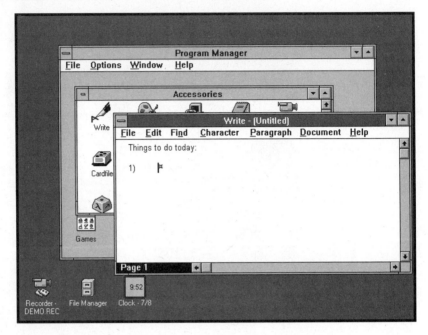

RECORDING A MACRO

You create a macro by recording it, much as you would record a TV program on your video recorder. You start recording, perform the desired macro actions, and then stop recording. After saving the macro, you can run it and sit back while Recorder automatically performs the actions you recorded.

To record (create) a macro:

- Run *Recorder* and minimize it to an icon.

- Set up the context in which your macro will run. For example, if you are creating a macro that applies a complex format to a Word for Windows document, you must run Word for Windows and open an appropriate document in its workspace before you begin to record the macro.

- Restore *Recorder* to a window.

- Choose *Macro, Record* to open the Record Macro dialog box.

- Fill in your desired macro properties. (These are the same properties that you can later view and edit by using the Macro, Properties command.) Macro properties include

  - *Record Macro Name* identifies a macro by name (up to 39 characters, including spaces).

  - *Shortcut Key* specifies a key combination for running a macro.

  - *Playback* designates the conditions under which a macro will be run.

  - *Record Mouse* determines how mouse actions will be recorded, if at all.

  - *Relative to* specifies how the mouse-pointer position will be recorded, relative to the upper-left corner of the screen or the upper-left corner of the active window.

  - *Description* describes what the macro does.

- Click on *Start* to start recording. Recorder shrinks to an icon and blinks to inform you that you are recording.

- Perform the actions that you want to record, using the keyboard as much as possible.

- When you are finished, stop the recording by pressing Ctrl+Break. A Recorder dialog box appears, prompting you to save, resume, or cancel your recording.

- Choose *Save Macro* and press *Enter*.

Let's record a macro that opens the Clock and Write programs:

1. Minimize **Recorder**.

2. Verify that Program Manager is running in a window, and that this window is activated (that the title bar is highlighted). Our macro will issue two File, Run commands from the Program Manager menu. To do this, Program Manager must be running in an activated window. As mentioned, you must set up the context in which a macro will run before beginning to record.

3. Restore **Recorder** to a window.

4. Choose **Macro, Record** to open the Record Macro dialog box.

5. In the Record Macro Name text box, type **My Setup**.

6. In the Shortcut Key text box, type **M**. Verify that Ctrl is checked and that Shift and Alt are unchecked. Ctrl+M is now set as the shortcut key for the macro.

7. In the Description text box, type **Opens Clock and Write**.

8. Click on **Start**. Recorder is minimized to an icon and begins to blink, indicating that you are recording.

9. Press **Alt+f** to display the Program Manager drop-down File menu, and then press **r** to choose the Run command. As mentioned earlier, you should use the keyboard to choose menu commands and select dialog box options when recording macros.

10. Type **clock** to specify the program to run (CLOCK.EXE). Press **Tab** to select the Run Minimized option, and then press **Spacebar** to check this option. Note that we, once again, used the keyboard rather than the mouse. Press **Enter** to run the Clock as an icon.

11. Press **Alt+f** and then press **r** to choose the Run command.

12. Type **write** and press **Enter** to run Write in a window.

13. Press **Ctrl+Break** to stop recording. The Recorder dialog box appears. Click on the **Save Macro** option (if it is not already selected), and then click on **OK** to save your macro. You can use the mouse now, since you are finished recording.

14. Close **Clock** and **Write**.

15. Restore the **Recorder** icon to a window. Note that your My Setup macro is now listed as the second macro in DEMO.REC.

16. Save the macro file to your WINDWORK directory as **mymacro.rec**.

Now let's test our new macro:

1. Press **Ctrl+m** to run My Setup. Your recorded sequence of actions is played back at fast speed (see Figure 11.21).

2. Close **Clock**, **Write**, and **Recorder**.

3. Press **Ctrl+m** to attempt to rerun the My Setup macro. Nothing happens. Why? Because to run a macro, you must first run Recorder and open the .REC file the macro is stored in.

Figure 11.21   After running the My Setup macro

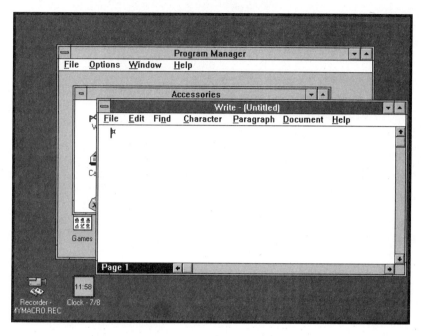

PRACTICE YOUR SKILLS

1. Run the My Setup macro.

2. Close **Write**, **Clock**, and **Recorder**.

3. Close the **Accessories** group.

4. Exit **Windows**.

SUMMARY

In this chapter we introduced you to five new Windows accessory programs. You now know how to use Character Map (or the keyboard) to enter extended characters in a document, how to use Calendar to manage your daily appointments, how to use Cardfile to manage index-card type information, how to use Object Packager to insert a packaged object into a document, and how to use Recorder to create macros that automate repetitive tasks.

With this chapter, you've completed your foundation of Windows 3.1 skills. Congratulations on becoming a bona-fide Windows user! May you manage your Desktop, your windows, your files, and your programs with great authority and skill.

Here's a quick reference for the techniques you learned in this chapter:

Desired Result	How to Do It
Use the keyboard to enter an extended character in a Windows document	Run the Windows program, open the document, and position the cursor at the desired location; press and hold down **Alt**; on the numeric keypad, enter the four-digit code that corresponds to the desired extended character; release **Alt**
Use Character Map to enter an extended character in a Windows document	Run the Windows program, open the document, and position the cursor at the desired location; switch to Program Manager and run **Character Map** (or, if Character Map is already running, switch to it); select the desired font; select the desired extended character; click on **Select** to place the character in the Characters to Copy box; click on **Copy** to copy the selected character to the Clipboard; click on **Close** to close Character Map (or if you intend to enter more extended characters, leave Char-acter Map open); switch to the Win-dows program, and choose **Edit**, **Paste** to copy the character into the document
Open a calendar file	Run **Calendar**; choose **File**, **Open**
Display the daily calendar (default)	Choose **View**, **Day** (or double-click on the desired day in the monthly calendar)
Display the monthly calendar	Choose **View**, **Month** (or double-click on the day/date display to the right of the status-bar scroll arrows in the daily calendar)
Enter a new appointment	Display the daily calendar; select the day (by clicking on the right and left scroll arrows in the status bar); select the time (by clicking on the desired hour); type the appointment information

Desired Result	How to Do It
Change the appointment interval, hour format, or starting time	Choose **Options, Day Settings**; set the desired Interval, Hour Format, or Starting Time values; click on **OK**
Insert a special appointment time in the calendar	Display the daily calendar; choose **Options, Special Time**; set the desired time; click on **OK**
Mark a day in the monthly calendar	Select the desired day; choose **Options, Mark**; check the desired mark symbol; click on **OK**
Sound an alarm at a specific appointment time	Display the daily calendar; select the appointment time; choose **Alarm, Set**
Print out a copy of your daily appointments	Select the desired day; choose **File, Print**; click on **OK**
Save a calendar file	Choose **File, Save As** (for a new file) or **File, Save** (for an updated file)
Open a cardfile	Run **Cardfile**; choose **File, Open**
Display entire cards (default)	Choose **View, Card**
Display a list of index lines only	Choose **View, List**
Add a card to a cardfile	Choose **Card, Add**; type the index line; click on **OK**; fill in the card's information area
Delete a card from a cardfile	Select the desired card; choose **Card, Delete**; click on **OK**
Search through a cardfile for an item of information	Choose **Search, Find**; type the text you want to search for; set the Match Case and Direction options as desired; click on **Find Next** repeatedly to find successive occurrences of your search text; click on **Cancel** to close the Find dialog box

Desired Result	How to Do It
Print the top card in a cardfile	Choose **File, Print**
Print all cards in a cardfile	Choose **File, Print All**
Save a cardfile	Choose **File, Save As** (for a new file) or **File, Save** (for an updated file)
Create a new cardfile (close the current cardfile)	Choose **File, New**
Merge two or more cardfiles into a single cardfile	Open one of the cardfiles to be merged; choose **File, Merge**; select another of the cardfiles to be merged, and click on **OK**; if necessary, repeat the above two steps to merge additional cardfiles; choose **File, Save As** to save the merged cardfile with a new name (or choose **File, Save** to save the merged cardfile with the same name as the first cardfile you opened)
Package a selection from a document	Run the source program and open the source document; select the source object (the data to be packaged) and copy it to the Clipboard; run **Object Packager**; choose **Edit, Paste** to paste the Clipboard data object into Object Packager; edit the package label and icon as needed; choose **Edit, Copy Package** to copy the package back to the Clipboard; run the destination program, open the destination docu-ment, and position the cursor where you want the package to be pasted; choose **Edit, Paste** to paste the package into the destination document
Package an entire document	Run **Object Packager**; choose **File, Import**; select the file to be packaged; edit the package label and icon as needed; choose **Edit, Copy Package** to copy the package to the Clipboard; run the destination program, open the destination docu-ment, and position the cursor where you want the package to be pasted; choose **Edit, Paste** to paste the package into the destination document

Desired Result	How to Do It
Edit a package label or icon	In the destination document, select the package; choose **Edit**, **Package Object**, **Edit Package**; change the label and/or icon as desired; choose **File**, **Update** to save these changes; choose **File**, **Exit** to exit Object Packager and return to the destination document
Edit the object represented by a package	In the destination document, double-click on the package; edit the object as desired; choose **File**, **Update** to save your editing changes; choose **File, Exit & Return to ContentObject** to exit the source program and return to the destination document
Run a Recorder macro	Run **Recorder**; choose **File**, **Open** to open the desired macro file; select the desired macro and choose **Macro, Run** (or press the macro's shortcut key)
Edit the properties of a Recorder macro	Select the desired macro; choose **Macro, Properties**; edit the properties as desired; click on **OK**
Record (create) a macro	Run **Recorder** and minimize it to an icon; set up the context in which your macro will run; restore **Recorder** to a window; choose **Macro, Record** to open the Record Macro dialog box; fill in your desired macro properties; click on **Start** to start recording; perform the actions that you want to record, using the keyboard as much as possible; when you are finished, stop the recording by pressing **Ctrl+Break**; choose **Save Macro** and press **Enter**

Following this chapter are three appendices for your reference.

Appendix A: Installing and Configuring Windows	Walks you through Windows 3.1 installation and configuration

Appendix B: Upgrading from Windows 3.0 to Windows 3.1	Lists the differences between Windows versions 3.0 and 3.1
Appendix C: Networking and Telecommunications	Provides basic information for using Windows 3.1 with a network

APPENDIX A: INSTALLING AND CONFIGURING WINDOWS

Before You Begin the Installation

Installing Windows

Program Information Files (PIFs)

Memory and Swap Files

This appendix contains instructions for installing Windows 3.1 on your computer. It also contains information about special files (PIFs) that enable non-Windows programs to run from the Windows environment. Lastly, this appendix discusses the different types of computer memory and how Windows uses them, in combination with special *swap files,* to run your programs efficiently.

BEFORE YOU BEGIN THE INSTALLATION

Please read through the following two sections before you begin the installation procedure.

PROTECTING YOUR ORIGINAL INSTALLATION DISKS

Windows 3.1 comes with several floppy disks, which you'll need to install the program on your computer. Before you begin, you should protect your original installation disks from accidental erasure. When a disk is protected, its data can be read, but not modified.

To protect a 5¼-inch disk, place a write-protect tab over the notch on the edge of the disk. To protect a 3½-inch disk, slide the plastic locking button in the corner of the disk to its uppermost position.

REQUIRED HARD-DISK SPACE

To install and run Windows, your computer's DOS should be version 3.1 or later. You can check your version by typing **ver** at the DOS prompt and pressing **Enter**.

How much memory and disk space is required depends on whether you run Windows in *386 Enhanced* mode or *Standard* mode. To run Windows in 386 Enhanced mode, you'll need

- An 80386 processor (or higher)
- 640k (kilobytes) of conventional memory
- 1,024k of extended memory
- At least 8Mb (megabytes) of free disk space (the more the better)
- At least one floppy-disk drive

To run Windows in Standard mode, you'll need

- An 80286 processor (or higher)
- 640k of conventional memory
- 256k of extended memory
- At least 6Mb of free disk space
- At least one floppy-disk drive

If you do not have enough free space on your hard disk, you must delete enough files from your hard disk to bring the total disk space to at least the required amount. For help doing this, please refer to your DOS or Windows manuals. *Remember to back up (copy to a floppy disk) any files that you wish to preserve before deleting them from your hard disk.*

INSTALLING WINDOWS

Windows offers two kinds of installation, the *Express Setup* and the *Custom Setup*. We strongly recommend using the Express Setup. When you use the Express Setup, the program will automatically identify your computer's components and create and/or update any necessary files. If you do not have enough free disk space at the time of installation, the program will automatically propose a partial setup, which will exclude optional Windows components.

Follow these steps to install Windows 3.1 by using the Express Setup:

1. Turn on your computer.

2. After the DOS prompt appears, insert installation **Disk 1** in your floppy-disk drive.

3. Type the letter of the drive containing Disk 1, followed by a colon (:); for example, if you're using drive A, type **a:**

4. Press **Enter**.

5. Type **setup** and press **Enter** to start the Windows installation program. Momentarily, the Windows Setup screen is displayed.

6. Press **Enter** to begin the installation. You are now prompted to choose Express Setup or Custom Setup.

7. Press **Enter** to choose Express Setup.

8. The suggested directory in which Windows will be installed, C:\WINDOWS, is displayed.

9. Press **Enter**.

10. If an earlier version of Windows is currently installed on your computer, it will be detected, and you will be prompted to press Enter if you wish to upgrade your current version of

Windows to version 3.1. If this message is displayed, press **Enter**. The message

```
Setup is copying files...
```

is displayed. After the copying is completed, you will be prompted to insert Disk 2.

11. Remove Disk 1 and insert **Disk 2** in its place.

12. Press **Enter**. Again, the message

```
Setup is copying files...
```

is displayed. After the files that run Windows have been copied, the installation program will automatically bring you into the Windows environment, within which you will finish the installation. The Windows Setup dialog box is displayed.

13. Type your name in the Name box.

14. If you want to enter your company name in the Company box, press the Tab key to move the insertion point (the flashing vertical line) to the Company box. Then type your company's name.

15. Press **Enter**; or place the mouse pointer on the Continue button, and click the leftmost mouse button. The Windows Setup dialog box now displays the information as you entered it.

16. If the information is correct, press **Enter** or click on **Continue**. If the information is incorrect, click on **Change**, make the necessary corrections, click on **Continue**, and click on **Continue** once again to accept the changes. Momentarily, you will be prompted to insert Disk 3.

17. Remove Disk 2 and insert **Disk 3**.

18. After you have inserted Disk 3, press **Enter** or click on **Continue**. The Windows Setup dialog box will display a horizontal bar graph, which indicates what percentage of the files has been copied. After all the files on Disk 3 have been copied, you will be prompted to insert Disk 4.

19. Remove Disk 3 and insert **Disk 4**.

20. Press **Enter** or click on **Continue**. After the files on Disk 4 have been copied, you will be prompted to insert Disk 5.

21. Remove Disk 4 and insert **Disk 5**.

22. Press **Enter** or click on **Continue**. After the files on Disk 5 have been copied, you will be prompted to insert Disk 6.

23. Remove Disk 5 and insert **Disk 6**.

24. Press **Enter** or click on **Continue**. After the files on Disk 6 have been copied, the Exit Windows Setup dialog box will be displayed. Windows is now set up.

25. Press **Enter** or click on **Restart Windows** to remain in Windows; or click on **Exit to DOS** to exit Windows. The installation is now completed.

PROGRAM INFORMATION FILES (PIFS)

Program Information Files (*PIFs*) are special files that contain information about non-Windows programs, such as how much memory the program requires and how it uses the components of your computer. Windows uses this information to run the program in the most efficient way.

All non-Windows programs use a PIF to run in the Windows environment. Upon installation, Windows automatically searches for a PIF, and then uses that information to perform tasks such as creating icons for these programs. If a PIF is not found during installation, then Windows searches for the information needed to create the PIF. If Windows finds the necessary information, then a dialog box displays to confirm that you want to use the information to create a PIF. If you choose Yes, then a PIF is set up for that application. If no information is found, then the default PIF is used. Many non-Windows applications can use the default PIF.

 ## MODIFYING A PIF

If a non-Windows application does not run properly in Windows, then you may need to modify its PIF. PIFs can be modified and saved just like any other file. You can use the *PIF Editor* to modify the PIF.

The PIF Editor dialog box features vary, depending on whether you are in Standard or Enhanced mode. A PIF is designed to run in the mode that you are in when you create it. You can change the mode by using the *Mode* menu command.

Here are some of the PIF features:

- *PIF Mode* displays options for the mode the program will run in. The options are different for Standard and Enhanced modes.

- The *Program Filename* is the name of the executable file.

- The *Window Title* is the description name that will be displayed in the Window Title Box.

- *Optional Parameters* are parameters such as those you might enter when starting the program from DOS, like a file name or a switch. Parameters are specific to the application.

- *Memory Requirements* are based on the requirements of the non-Windows program.

MEMORY AND SWAP FILES

Personal computers use three basic types of memory: *conventional*, *expanded*, and *extended*. Windows recognizes all three types of memory. When your computer runs in either Standard (286) mode or 386 Enhanced mode, it can use any combination of conventional, expanded, or extended memory.

CONVENTIONAL MEMORY

Conventional memory refers to the only type of memory that was available on early DOS-based computers (those with 8086 or 8088 processors). Because of the design of these computers and limitations imposed by the MS-DOS and PC-DOS operating systems (collectively called DOS), conventional memory can be no larger than 640k; that is, without employing special software tricks.

When you start your computer, DOS uses some of the conventional memory, as do the utilities and programs listed in your CONFIG.-SYS and AUTOEXEC.BAT files. Windows uses the remaining conventional memory to manage your system and run programs.

EXPANDED MEMORY

Some programs overcome the 640k limitation of conventional memory by using expanded memory. Although DOS provides direct access to only 640k of conventional memory, these programs manage to perform a kind of "juggling act" between expanded memory and conventional memory to go beyond DOS's memory limitations.

Data is swapped one "page" at a time from expanded memory into conventional memory as needed. When no longer needed for processing, the data are returned to expanded memory. In this way, more memory is available with conventional and expanded memory than with conventional memory alone.

Windows and Windows programs do not use expanded memory, but some non-Windows programs require it. To run those programs, Windows comes with an expanded memory *emulator*. This emulator makes the extended memory that Windows uses appear to the non-Windows application as expanded memory.

EXTENDED MEMORY

The 80286, 80386, and 80486 processors were designed to overcome the limitations of earlier processors. These machines can address at least 16,000k (16Mb) of conventional memory. Conventional memory that extends beyond the original 640k limit is called extended memory. Computers that use extended memory can use expanded memory as well.

Windows and Windows-based programs require extended memory. To recognize and manage the extended memory, Windows comes with an extended memory manager, the *HIMEM.SYS* file. The memory manager coordinates the use of the extended memory, to ensure that several applications do not try to use the memory at the same time.

Windows requires that your CONFIG.SYS file loads the HIMEM.SYS driver or an equivalent driver in order for your computer to recognize extended memory. Other drivers, such as *SMARTDRV.SYS*, can alter the way Windows optimizes its use of memory. Refer to your *Microsoft Windows User's Guide* for more information on drivers.

VIRTUAL MEMORY

Just as some applications swap expanded and conventional memory to make more memory available, computers running in 386 Enhanced mode can swap memory to special files, called *swap files,* on the hard disk, simulating more memory than the computer really has. Because the swap file on the hard disk has many of the virtues of real memory and enables you to run more programs and work with larger documents, this scheme is called *virtual memory*.

 SWAP FILES

As was defined in the previous section on virtual memory, a swap file is a hidden file that reserves space on the hard disk in order to simulate additional memory. Windows uses swap files in different ways, depending on whether you are using 386 Enhanced mode or Standard mode. Windows's 386 Enhanced mode uses a swap file for virtual memory. Standard mode uses application swap files only.

If you are using 386 Enhanced mode, then the Windows Setup program will create a permanent swap file, if possible, based on the type of memory and the amount of space available on the hard disk. If a permanent swap file is not set up, then Windows creates a temporary swap file whenever you start Windows in 386 Enhanced mode.

Program Swap Files

Standard mode does not use a swap file for virtual memory. However, when running non-Windows programs in Standard mode, Windows creates a temporary *program swap file* for that program. When you switch from the program to another program, Windows moves some or all of the program data from memory to the swap file. This makes the memory available for the other program. Windows deletes the application swap files when you exit the non-Windows program for which the swap file was created.

Note: Windows's 386 Enhanced mode does not use program swap files.

Now that you've installed Windows 3.1 on your computer, you're ready to learn about the exciting world of Windows. When you're ready to begin, please turn to Chapter 1 of this book.

APPENDIX B: UPGRADING FROM WINDOWS 3.0 TO WINDOWS 3.1

TrueType Fonts

Object Linking and Embedding

File Manager

Multimedia Support

Printing Enhancements

On-Line Tutorial

Installation Enhancements

Application Support

Desktop Enhancements

Performance Enhancements

Help System Enhancements

T his appendix discusses some of the features that are new to
Windows in version 3.1.

TRUETYPE FONTS

TrueType fonts are a new set of fully scalable fonts, meant to appear on your screen almost exactly as they will appear when printed, thus eliminating the need for matching screen fonts. Furthermore, TrueType fonts will print the same way on different printers if you are printing at the same size and resolution. A new accessory, the *Character Map,* gives you easier access to complete character sets.

OBJECT LINKING AND EMBEDDING

Object Linking and Embedding (*OLE*) supported by many Windows applications and accessories, offers new ways to share data between different documents.

Object linking allows you to use the same information in several different documents. When the original document is changed, all the documents containing the information are automatically updated.

Object embedding allows you to create an object—for example, a drawing—in one application and then insert it into a document, such as a report, created in another application. When you want to make changes to the embedded drawing, you can open the graphics program from within the word processor, make changes, and save them, without having to find and open a separate file.

FILE MANAGER

File Manager's new split window makes it easier to view directories and their contents at the same time. Additional File Manager enhancements include

- Improved commands for sorting and selecting groups of files
- More clearly labeled windows and paths
- A variety of fonts, allowing you to control the amount of information visible in File Manager windows
- More information about disk space

MULTIMEDIA SUPPORT

Two new accessories, *Media Player* and *Sound Recorder,* as well as some Control Panel enhancements, allow you to install device drivers and work with multimedia devices. Sound, graphics, animation, and video elements can be added to your Windows documents.

PRINTING ENHANCEMENTS

Windows printer drivers and the Print Manager have been improved to print more quickly and more easily. You can print files from File Manager by dragging their icons to the Print Manager.

ON-LINE TUTORIAL

A tutorial covering basic Windows concepts and the use of the mouse has been added to the Program Manager Help menu.

INSTALLATION ENHANCEMENTS

The Windows installation procedure has been greatly simplified. Most users can choose *Express Setup* for automatic installation and setup of Windows (the recommended method for this book). Also, you can now place icons for programs you wish to run automatically in the new Setup group in Program Manager. These programs will run automatically whenever you run Windows.

APPLICATION SUPPORT

Windows now provides more Program Information Files (PIF) for non-Windows applications as well as full mouse support for non-Windows programs running in a window (in 386 Enhanced mode only). Program Manager and the file MORICONS.DLL offer a new collection of icons for both Windows and non-Windows programs. Many dialog boxes now have a standard appearance in all Windows applications.

DESKTOP ENHANCEMENTS

Improvements to the *File Properties* dialog box give you more control over how your application icons run. There are now more color schemes to choose from, as well as screen savers that can be password protected. You can preserve the content and location of windows and icons from one Windows session to another.

PERFORMANCE ENHANCEMENTS

Windows 3.1 contains several important features that greatly enhance its performance:

- The Program Manager requires less system memory.

- File Manager screens update more quickly, and lengthy procedures can be interrupted before they are complete.

- Running non-Windows applications in a window (in Enhanced mode) and switching between applications is faster.

HELP SYSTEM ENHANCEMENTS

Improvements to the Windows *Help* system include more convenient access to glossary definitions and a *History* feature, which tracks all the Help topics you view in a particular session. *Context-sensitive* Help is available in many dialog boxes.

APPENDIX C: NETWORKING AND TELECOMMUNICATIONS

Attaching to and
Disconnecting
from a Network

Using Network
Printers

Orientation to the
Terminal Program

This appendix provides basic information for using Windows with a network. The *Terminal* program, a Windows accessory program that you can use to transfer data between your computer and another computer, is also introduced.

ATTACHING TO AND DISCONNECTING FROM A NETWORK

Windows 3.1 is fully compatible with many network systems. This means that Windows provides you with full access to file servers, printer servers, and special features, such as the ability to send messages through the network to other Windows users. Some network systems are not fully supported. NETWORKS.WRI, a text file that the Windows Setup program placed in your WINDOWS directory, lists all of the network systems that are compatible with Windows. You can use Write to read this text file.

If you are in a network that is fully Windows-compatible, then you can use Windows's Control Panel and the File Manager to disconnect from file servers and network drives. You can also quit Windows and use normal network commands to log out.

If you installed a network when setting up Windows, then the Control Panel includes a Network icon. Some of the tasks you might be able to perform from the Network icon are

- Signing on and off the network

- Changing a password or ID

- Sending network messages

RUNNING NETWORK SOFTWARE

Before you run Windows, you must first start your network. With a Novell network, for example, you do this by running IPX.COM and NET3.COM (or equivalent).

ATTACHING FILE SERVERS

You can attach to file servers before or after you run Windows. If your network system is not fully supported by Windows, then you might have to attach file servers before you start Windows.

When you work with a network drive, other users might also work with the same drive. Press F5 to ensure that you are seeing the most recent list of files in a directory. File Manager will update that directory window.

USING NETWORK PRINTERS

In addition to using your network system to share files, you can use it to share printers as well. Just as you must set up your printer drivers (from the Control Panel or from an application's Printer Setup menu) to print to your local printer, you must also set up printer drivers for network printers.

CONNECTING AND PRINTING TO A NETWORK PRINTER

If you attach to your file server after you run Windows, then you might also have to use the Control Panel to connect to network printers.

Once you have attached and set up your network printer, you use it the same way you use a local printer (one attached directly to your computer).

THE PRINT MANAGER AND NETWORK PRINT QUEUES

Because the network uses its own printer queueing system, it is redundant to use Print Manager, Windows's printer queue. Windows normally bypasses Print Manager when you print to a network printer. If you want to use the Print Manager queue, then run Print Manager and choose Options, Network Settings. Deselect Print Net Jobs Direct, and click on OK.

ORIENTATION TO THE TERMINAL PROGRAM

Terminal is a communications program. It enables you to transfer data between your computer and another computer. You can communicate with another computer via a modem that uses an ordinary telephone service. (A *modem* is a device that converts computer signals into a format that can be transmitted over the telephone lines.) Or you can connect your computer directly to another computer with a *null-modem cable,* which eliminates the need for a modem when the computers are near each other.

Terminal provides setup options that are available through menu commands. These setup options enable you to specify such things as the type of connection you are using, the protocol you want to use for transferring files, and the way you would like your computer to behave as a terminal. When you run Terminal and have established the setup options, you must connect to another computer before you can begin communication.

INDEX

boxes, types of, 4
Box tool, 96
British pound sign, entering, 274–279
Browse dialog box, 141
buttons
    Cancel, 4
    command, 4
    default, 50
    Maximize, 20
    OK, 4
    option, 4
    Restore, 20–21
bytes, 110

A

Accessories menu, 5
Accessories window, 6
accessory group of programs, 24–27, 273–308
activating windows, 29–31
alphabet program, 223–227, 230–235
applications
    associating files with, 136–137
    exiting, 11, 166–167
    managing multiple open, 163–168
    running, 10
    running from File Manager, 18–19
    selecting in the Task List, 31
    switching between, 164–165
    Version 3.1 support for, 323
application windows, 68–70
appointment calendar, 279–283
arranging the Desktop, 165–166
associated file, 263
Associate dialog box, 137
associating files with programs, 136–137
AST Turbolaser/PS printer font list, 202
attributes, file, 249–252
AUTOEXEC.BAT, 160–162

B

batch (.BAT) files, 218–220
bitmapped graphics object, 234–235

C

Calculator program, 25–26
Calendar program, 24, 279–283
Calendar window, 281
Cancel button, 4
CARDFILE.CRD, 286
Cardfile program, 24, 284–289
cardfiles
    merging, 288–289
    parts of, 284
    searching, 286–288
Character Map program, 25, 274–279, 322
Character menu, 54–55
characters, entering special, 274–279
check boxes, 4
clicking the mouse, 3
clients, 180–181
Clipboard
    and changing data formats, 192–195
    contents as bitmapped graphic object, 234–235
    data formats, 191–192
    examining contents of, 102
    and graphics in word processing documents, 102–106
    moving text or a graphic to, 98–99
    and non-Windows program data, 228–235

■ TO RECEIVE 3½-INCH DISK(S)

The Ziff-Davis Press software contained on the $5\frac{1}{4}$-inch disk(s) included with this book is also available in $3\frac{1}{2}$-inch (720k) format. If you would like to receive the software in the $3\frac{1}{2}$-inch format, please return the $5\frac{1}{4}$-inch disk(s) with your name and address to:

Disk Exchange
Ziff-Davis Press
5903 Christie Avenue
Emeryville, CA 94608